FEARLESS DAVE ALLISON

BORDER LAWMAN

FEARLESS DAVE ALLISON

BORDER LAWMAN

A *TRANSITIONAL* LAWMAN ON A *TRANSITIONAL* FRONTIER

BY BOB ALEXANDER

High-Lonesome Books
Silver City, New Mexico

ISBN #0-944383-63-7 softcover
ISBN #0-944383-62-9 hardcover

Library of Congress Control Number: 2002114291

First Edition February 2003
Hardcover Edition Limited to 500 Copies

High-Lonesome Books
P.O. Box 878
Silver City, New Mexico 88062

DEDICATED IN MEMORY OF

THOMAS M. "MITTY" PHILLIPS

LIKE HIS UNCLE DAVE ALLISON, A *"COWBOY OF THE OLD SCHOOL"*

TABLE OF CONTENTS

PREFACE & ACKNOWLEDGMENTS

Surely it is tempting to simply say, "this book needed writin' and I wrote it." For indeed it is a historic fact, Dave Allison had a compelling story to tell but, for whatever reason, he opted to remain silent about bold participation in a stirring string of highly publicized Western frontier events. Allison's conscious decision to refrain from blabbermouth boasting speaks volumes about the man. Dave Allison was a doer, not a self-promoter. So his story would have to be told sans his personal and purposeful input, if it was to be reported at all. Neither was Dave Allison an idealistic statesman type or a romantic proponent of theoretic deliberations. Someone else could formulate policy and ponder weighty questions, tasks Dave Allison had no time for. Others were allowed the pleasure of safely passing judgment from afar, and then haranguing about what Allison had done, or just how he had done it. In truth though, Dave wasn't bothered at all. Dave Allison was comfortable knowing he did what he had to do, when he had to do it. He was the sort of man who would matter-of-factly mention deeds he had accomplished yesterday, but was not in the least inclined to tell about something he was *gonna* do tomorrow. Dave Allison was keen on results. At an early age Dave Allison pinned on a badge, and years later, well-past his sixtieth birthday, he was still toting a six-shooter and wearing a tin-star the day he died. This book is about those in-between years.

Over the course of those years Dave Allison developed a hard-fought, but legitimately earned Southwestern reputation as a fearless frontier lawman. All who knew him attested to his unbridled courage. And, without doubt, if mama's ageless advice was true, and one really was judged by the company he was keeping, well, Dave Allison had no reason to be socially embarrassed. Many of his personal friends and admirers themselves provided exhilarating fodder for later-day biographers and/or Western writers, such as: "Border Boss" John R. Hughes, the legendary Texas Ranger Captain; Frank Augustus Hamer, the celebrated Lone Star lawman who much later orchestrated the past due killings of America's top-flight public enemies, Bonnie and Clyde; Burt Mossman and Thomas Rynning, well-recognized Arizona Ranger Captains; Oklahoma Adjutant General and occasionally notorious peace officer, Frank M. Canton;

Colonel William C. "Bill" Greene, the flamboyant Mexico mining mogul; former legit cowboy, and a Pinkerton detective, turned author, Charles A. Siringo; and George S. Patton, Jr., who would later earn battlefield fame, but in 1915 he wrote with awe about Dave Allison, succinctly commenting he was "the most noted gunman here in Texas."

There were of course many more, mainly prominent powerhouse ranchers. For apart from law enforcement talents, Dave Allison, an ex-cowboy, was a disciple of the West Texas cow business. From time to time Dave Allison rubbed shoulders and agreeably hobnobbed with: Christopher Columbus Slaughter, who for awhile was the largest individual taxpayer in the Lone Star State; Elisha "Lish" Estes, an extensive livestock operator, whose **7Z7** brand was recognized throughout Texas; John Scharbauer, the man who first brought Hereford cattle to the Midland area; W. E. Connell, stockman and banking tycoon; E. B. "Berk" Spiller, long-time Secretary for the politically potent Texas and Southwestern Cattle Raisers Association; and an assemblage of other big-time cattle barons, fastidious ranch foremen, and everyday working cowboys. Dave Allison was their kind of man, through and through.

And too—just to name a few—longtime lawman Dave Allison was personally acquainted with a whole horde of the Southwest's most notable scalawags and shady scoundrels. Characters like the dangerously volatile John Wesley "Little Arkansas" Hardin; the iniquitous New Mexican owl-hoot and fugitive, Martin Mroz; a cowboy turned bad, Bob Brown, the abortive Fairbank, Arizona, train robber; an incorrigible killer of the informant Con Gibson, John M. "Green" Denson; the continually conspiring and conniving West Texas misfit, Manning Clements, Jr.; an imported riotous firebrand, "Three-Fingered Jack" Laustenneau; sometime revolutionist and sometime bandit, Pascual Orozco Jr.; rodeo roper turned rustler, Milton Good; and, the icily-nerved and treacherously poisonous cowman gone wrong, Hillary U. Loftis, better known throughout the annals of Old West history by a barefaced alias, the ever uncompromising, Tom Ross. An incomplete but, nevertheless, sinister sampling to be sure!

Just as surely, although it hasn't been ironclad proved with paper documentation, at least as of yet, it is not unreasonable to presume Dave Allison was also in varying degrees acquainted with such notable players as: the now legendary "good man with a gun," Jeff Milton; an always audacious borderland law officer, George Scarborough; the thoroughly corruptible, yet, viperously dangerous sometimes lawman and bounty hunter, Charles C. Perry; two of El Paso's more dubious lawmen, "Uncle" John and "Little" John Selman; the impressively credentialed veteran of the celebrated Round Rock shoot-out and a career peace officer, Dick Ware; and a rightly tough Thomas Decatur Love, the Borden County sheriff who dogged the trail of an escaping baby-faced gangster from Oklahoma, Bill Cook, and after the grueling chase parked the little hellion on a four-legged pine bench, squarely before the judicial bench of Judge Isaac Parker at Fort Smith. Irrefutably, they, and William Davis "Dave" Allison too, were all roaming about on that same colossal chunk of West Texas real estate—at the same time.

Somehow, since Dave Allison wasn't puffing up his exploits to the cadre of early day twentieth-century Western writers, his rousing true story was overshadowed. As one year blended with the next—several decades later—the emphasis of some capable scholars and knowledgeable grass-root historians focused on debunking the myths which had previously been inflicted on a sometimes gullible and misinformed generation. All the same, the battle of Earpville splendidly rages even today, as do thoughtful arguments regarding whether a bona fide "Wild West" ever actually existed in the first place. Somewhere along the way Dave Allison got lost in the shuffle. This then is Dave Allison's story.

Tackling a biographic project handicaps the writer, corralling him/her into the realm of reality, collecting, scrutinizing, analyzing and repeating facts, a process wholly, but pleasantly dependent on people. The chronicle of Dave Allison's thrilling life could not have been written without the affable assistance of so many, and they rightfully merit mention.

Two at the top of the list are Pat Phillips Treadwell at Tahoka, Texas and Linda Stockley Weiler at Roswell, New Mexico. This pair of biographical collaborators proved indispensable. Pat, a family member from the Dave Allison side, and Linda, a relative of Dave's wife, Lena, made the story round. For it was in their living rooms and around their kitchen tables, that the frayed-edged shoe boxes and photo albums were opened for enthusiastic perusal. Actual inspection of old letters, family pictures, personal and public documents, and even a set of Dave Allison's inlaid spurs was akin to, at last, finding the buried treasure. Graciously they have shared with the author, and the reader, much of this historic material.

A hand of thanks must appreciably be extended to well-known Western writers, Leon Metz and Bill O'Neal. Leon candidly shared his thoughts regarding the Mexican Revolution and Pascual Orozco, Jr., as well as making available unpublished manuscript material from a forthcoming book. At his home base in Carthage, Texas, Bill graciously made accessible a tremendous amount of research material he had collected during his writing of *The Arizona Rangers*. Additionally, educator and writer James Irving Fenton of Lubbock, Texas amiably provided invaluable historic information on one of the major collateral players contributing to the rousing Dave Allison saga, Tom Ross. I am pleasantly in debt to all three.

During the course of my several research trips, I was indeed fortunate to have met, visited, or talked with numerous people, several of whom were related to mentioned characters other than Dave and Lena Allison. Particularly helpful were the following: Nancy McKinley, Midland; Carol Marlin and Sarah Hindman, Albia, Iowa; Penny and Ryn Rains, Post, Texas; Marvin Garlick, Gazelle, California; Button Garlick, Van Horn, Texas; and Bill Love at Sierra Blanca, Texas. Additionally a special thanks is extended to Hudspeth County rancher Mart Tidwell for giving me a personally guided tour of that richly historic and pleasingly addictive mountain and desert country situated between the circuitous Rio Grande and Sierra Blanca, Texas.

Equally as important were the thoroughly resourceful and proficient efforts of those professionals cited below:

Susan Wagner, Managing Editor, and Sherrie Caraway, *The Cattleman*, Fort Worth; Cheri Wolfe, Director, and Cynthia Zwadzke, Texas & Southwestern Cattle Raisers Association Museum, Fort Worth; Peggy Fox, Director, Harold B. Simpson Research Center, Hillsboro, Texas; Christina Stopka, Director, and Librarian Judy Shofner, Texas Ranger Research Center, Texas Ranger Hall of Fame & Museum, Waco; Vicki Jones, Southwest Collection, Texas Tech University, Lubbock; Jim Bradshaw, Nita Stewart Haley Memorial Library & J. Evetts Haley History Center, Midland; Donaly Brice, Texas State Library and Archives Commission, Austin; Betty Bustos, Panhandle-Plains Historical Museum, Canyon, Texas. Stephanie Malmarous, The Center for American History, University of Texas, Austin; Nancy McKinley, Midland County Historical Society, Midland; Todd Houck, Director of Archives, Permian Basin Petroleum Museum Library and Hall of Fame, Midland; Mandy York, Archivist, Southwestern Writers Collection, Albert B. Alkek Library, Southwest Texas State University, San Marcos; Linda Puckett, Director, and Jackie Gonzales, Garza County Historical Museum, Post, Texas; Mary Thornberry, Heritage Center Museum, Seminole, Texas; Helen Hall, Central Museum, McKinney, Texas; Julia Jenkins and Ellen Tidwell, Hudspeth County Museum, Sierra Blanca, Texas; Robert Stuckey, Culberson County Historical Museum, Van Horn, Texas; Maxine Chance, Culberson County Historical Commission, Van Horn, Texas; Elvis E.

Fleming, Historical Center for Southeast New Mexico, Roswell; Linda Offeney, Yuma Territorial Prison State Historic Park, Yuma; Nancy Sawyer, Arizona Department of Library, Archives and Public Records, Phoenix; Rose Byrne, Arizona Historical Society, Tucson; Darla Bushman, Midland County Public Library, Midland; Penny Trosper, McKinney Memorial Public Library, McKinney, Texas; Brenda Perkins, Brownwood Public Library, Brownwood, Texas; Gaylan Corbin and Melleta Bell, Bryan Wildenthal Memorial Library, Sul Ross University, Alpine, Texas; Michael Pilgrim, National Archives, Washington, D. C.; Milton Gustafson, National Archives, College Park, Maryland; Dick Staley, El Paso Public Library, El Paso; Terri Grant, Border Heritage Center, El Paso; Janis Test, Abilene Public Library, Abilene, Texas; Kim Scroggins, Gaines County Public Library, Seminole, Texas; Mary Beth Wright, Roswell Public Library, Roswell; Jamie Greco, Glacier County Library, Cut Bank, Montana; Linda McDonald, Culberson County District Clerk, Van Horn, Texas; Patricia Bramblett, Hudspeth County District Clerk, Sierra Blanca, Texas; Virginia Stewart, Gaines County District Clerk, Seminole, Texas. Sylvia Berkram, Glacier County Clerk and Recorder, and Gail Davis, Cut Bank, Montana; Jon Key, Sheriff, Gaines County, Seminole, Texas; Gary Painter, Sheriff, Midland County, Midland; Marla White, Records Supervisor, Midland County Sheriff's Office, Midland. Clayton McKinney, Chief Deputy, Midland County Sheriff's Office, Midland. Richard Lucero, Roswell Police Department, Roswell; Joseph A. Hamilton, Hudspeth County Sheriff's Office, Sierra Blanca, Texas. Imelda Powell, and Border Patrol Agent John Sullivan, Sierra Blanca, Texas; Margie Garlick, and Border Patrol Agent W. W. Crowe III, Van Horn, Texas; Paul D. Males, South Park Cemetery, Roswell, and a researcher extraordinaire and reliably devoted Western aficionado, Dennis McCown, Austin, Texas.

INTRODUCTION

Non-fiction writer Bob Alexander has done it again. This release, a biography of frontier lawman William D. "Dave" Allison, is an illustrious paradigm for Old West aficionados.

With *Dangerous Dan Tucker*, author Alexander exhumed for public inspection the life of an authentic New Mexico gunfighter and regional peacekeeper—a journalistic coup long overdue. And in the writing of *John H. Behan, Sacrificed Sheriff*, the true story of Tombstone's often maligned and mischaracterized sheriff, Alexander adroitly laid bare the myth about Wyatt Earp's arch-rival, and exposed stark reality. Again, a historical debt in arrears.

Now, with *Fearless Dave Allison,* an examination of yet another *bona fide* Southwest lawman, Bob Alexander, with characteristic detailed research and full-of-life writing, once more has followed the dim trail of a heretofore overlooked six-shooter stalwart. During the time he lived in the American Southwest, nearly everyone, at least by reputation, was acquainted with fearless Dave Allison. Later, with overemphasis and exaggeration, other less capable lawmen rode the crest of popularity to lasting fame while Allison's good name and deeds were submerged. Dave Allison's gripping narrative has now found a voice.

And I will venture a bet that author Bob Alexander is by now cutting for fresh sign in the Old West record and already at work on another first rate story. Let's hope so.

Leon C. Metz, author of
The Encyclopedia of Lawmen, Outlaws, and Gunfighters

William Davis "Dave" Allison, "a very quiet looking old man with a sweet face and white hair," almost angelically mild-mannered, but wholly fearless and legitimately dangerous. Courtesy, Joseph L. Miles, Midland, Texas.

1

"A cowboy of the old school"

Nearly forty years ago an esteemed historian offered, "Frontier heroes sprang up as soon as America had a frontier."[1] After making such an uncomplicated assertion, the author then set in motion a competent dissertation highlighting the literary process which catapulted certain Western personalities to the forefront of America's consciousness. Basically three components were requisite for building up, or in selected instances wrecking, real people's reputations. First, it was obligatory for a particular individual to have "actually performed some notable and verifiable exploit," to have at least done *something*.[2] That *something* should be of sufficient buoyancy to support, "literary elaboration"—the second indispensable ingredient for manufacturing champions.[3] Lastly, and almost comically simplistic, the tale had to be repeated. And repeated, and repeated—until myth and legend overtaxed factuality, historical accuracy, and in some cases even common sense.

Conversely, and often seemingly in spite of reality, unless a frontier figure somewhere along the line—during lifetime or posthumously—picked up an engrossed biographer, his or her own story was more often than not relegated to unorganized and un-indexed heaps of historic jumble cluttering courthouse, library, and museum basements. Irrefutably, a cadre of Western characters opted for self-promotion and personal profit, and indeed, a few succeeded in either writing their autobiographies or seeking out someone to do the job in their stead. The overwhelming majority, however, did not. Consequently, as logic would suggest, if no one tells the story, there is no story. The purpose then of this particular narrative is merely to appropriately chronicle another interesting Western frontier lawman's life story, and recapture a glimpse of the role he played in spine-tingling adventures and hair-raising escapades, several of which were indeed noteworthy, catching the eye of inquisitive newspapermen and making national headlines. The saga of W. D. Allison merits impartial and objective biography, especially since so many of the gunfighting genre have purchased enduring fame with counterfeit credentials or have been speciously puffed up by Hollywood script writers.

In her seminal analysis and balanced inspection of one Western hero, Paula Mitchell Marks reports that defining the difference between law and lawlessness could indeed prove challenging, so much so that even many contemporary Westerners themselves found it impossible to distinguish between the good guys and the bad guys.[4] Political positioning, economic competitiveness, unquestioned allegiance to family, and in many cases an ethnocentric loyalty based on race alone, clouded any bright line dividing right from wrong. And even today, the clear-cut differences between the black hats and the white hats can prove elusive and less than precise.

Generically, an overwhelming majority of television addicts and movie-goers, who in their heart of hearts, really believe Tombstone stalwart Wyatt Earp was heroic, would likely stand aghast upon learning just a few historic truths. Surely would be their surprise when reading the words of the preeminent historian for Arizona and New Mexico law enforcement during the *Territorial Period.* Larry Ball's perspective on Wyatt Earp's forced exodus from the Southwestern scene is refreshingly free from unwarranted sentimentality and mythical mistake. Ball simply reports, "It was a unique spectacle; a posse of federal lawmen forced from their district. While the Earps blackened the reputation of the marshalcy in southern Arizona, other marshals earned the regard of the citizenry."[5] Writer Leon Metz, who for years has proficiently researched material relating to Southwestern gunfighters, advises that Stuart Lake, Earp's imaginative and inventive biographer, was forced to settle on Wyatt as a second choice candidate for literary lionization.[6] Prolific writers and southeastern Arizona historians, Lynn Bailey and Don Chaput, refreshingly cut to the chase, "...Wyatt Earp, the most well-known shootist or gunfighter in America's past, was never in a man-on-man gunfight or duel. In fact, it cannot be demonstrated historically that Wyatt Earp ever killed a man...This is indeed a lamentable record for America's premier gunfighter."[7] In her evaluation of Earp's Arizona stopover, Paula Marks asks, had Wyatt "been part of the problem or part of the solution?"[8]

Mentioning the legendary *sometimes* lawman at all in this specific narrative is not meant to launch another assault on Wyatt's questionable character, but rather to frame the larger question, why is the name Earp so well recognized, and W. D. Allison's name is not?[9] Both Allison and Earp were authentic frontier lawmen, Wyatt for a while, Allison for a lifetime; but one garnered modern-era name recognition and the other did not.

Certainly had Allison been drowned in the same pool of printer's ink as Earp, his name would well be just as memorable, for as Allison's valid story unfolds, Wyatt's authenticated history will wither and pale through impartial comparison. The question revolving around popularized name recognition, however, is not unanswerable. Aside from the fact that Allison never attempted self-promotion, it simply boils down to the time period during which he lived.

Unquestionably, at least for a while, most Americans were pleasantly enthralled and caught up in an almost insatiable fascination with the "Old West." Mountain men, cowboys and trail drives, Apaches and Comanches, cavalry campaigns, outlaws, lawmen and shootouts -- it was fun! And it was profitable for novelists, screen writers, and movie-makers. One way or the other, the Wild West was everyone's experience. But there was a stopping point in time.

Generally that stopping point, that time when an exhilarating Western tale ended predated the year 1900, the turn of the century. Somehow it just didn't quite seem as Western—not quite so sensational— once electricity, telephones, and automobiles were incorporated into the scene. Once the Western stage was set with modern trappings it was time to move on to gangster movies and epic war stories. And even serious historians, many specializing in the "Old West," brought their last chapter to a close with the final tick of the century clock, or in the case of Arizona and New Mexico, twelve years later when they shed Territorial skins and slithered into statehood. Sadly, at least from the historic viewpoint, many noteworthy figures and a plethora of significant happenings have been for the most part innocently overlooked, not necessarily by capable historians and archivists, but by the public at large. Make no mistake though, for the first quarter of the twentieth-century, especially in certain geographic areas of southeastern Arizona, southern New Mexico, western Texas, and of course Old Mexico, it was still a wild and woolly Western frontier.

Sure, one could comfortably slouch back reading the latest newspaper to the tune of clickety-clack on the railroad track, or with a tad more adventurous spirit the trip could also be made by pleasantly riding in a convertible automobile—all the way to sunny California. For the time period, however, sticking close to the roadbed or the steel trail was sound advice. Within walking distance, either way, north or south, were steps to be cautiously taken back in time. Away from the scattered communities tethered to faded yellow railroad depots were isolated ranches, big ranches, unfenced ranches—out of the way ranches. The country south, toward the international border with Mexico could be incredibly harsh, crisscrossed with yawning canyons, the backdrop occasionally interrupted with inhospitable and sharp-toothed outcroppings known locally as mountains, but to the well-traveled they appeared to be less than grown, kinda wanna-be mountains, unkempt and pockmarked. Had they committed some past sin and been prohibited from reaching maturity? From the threatening looks of the surrounding landscape it was easy, natural, to presuppose they were being punished for something. To the north, back toward the Llano Estacado? Flat! Flat! Flat! A sea of grass, as far-off as the eye could see, without doubt past the distant horizon, maybe even forever. Gentle breezes or raging winds, the waving stem-tops seemed to give life to the ground underfoot, making it move, agreeably pitching and yawing most of the time. But then an unforgiving frosty blue Norther with hurricane force squalls could straight away capsize the dream of worldly goods—or peacefulness. And on this particular pastoral sea, everyone stayed within an arm's reach of horse or wagon—the literal lifeboat. Welcoming ports were few and far between. Either way, north or south, away from the thoroughfare it was unquestionably still a wildly Western frontier.

The people? The word population seems to carry a connotation of consequential numbers, of which there weren't. Maybe it is best said the land was defiantly inhabited, albeit meagerly, rather than populated. Those that had come to stay, especially those living out on the ranches were tough as the proverbial boot. They had to be. It was a long lonesome ride to see a doctor, and still longer to see sympathy. The men, for the most part were cowmen, fiercely independent, self-reliant, long accustomed to drought, blizzard, and willing to look hard-time square in the eye—without a blink. The women for the most part were cowmen's wives, fiercely independent, self-reliant, and long accustomed to doing without and suffering their man's misfortune—without a tear. One could leave the ranch and ride to civilization, but somehow, civilization just hadn't yet been dragged too far from the well-traveled road. Men still toted guns, despite what lawmakers at State Capitols had to say—in the border country and on that sea of grass there were still real-live bandits, nifty cow-thieves, and although encountered infrequently, sometimes just a damn mad neighbor or maybe an obstinate owl-hoot cowboy. Surely it had been conjured up elsewhere, but the adage, "I'd rather be tried by twelve, than carried by six," were words believed. Up in the sky, on some rare occasion one of those bi-wing flying machines might pass by—on the ground it was still horseback work, catch-ropes, six-shooters, skint' lips, and stubborn pride. Pure and simple, a Western frontier—but it too was changing.

It was a *transitional* frontier, policed by *transitional* lawmen, those intractable men, men still accustomed to gut-wrenching days in the saddle, greasewood campfires, boiled coffee, lumpy bedrolls, and chasing a shot of whiskey with the gurgling pull from a half-empty canteen. Not yet had he metamorphosed into a city detective type. Looking at ground dampened by urine he could tell you if the pursued was riding a horse—or Heaven forbid—a mare. At the right time, simply studying a mama cow's teats could tell a story true since the beginnings of bovine time. Horseshit? A book! And a burnt hide—that could prove a road map for a not so slick thief's trip to the penitentiary. It was a wide-open frontier land where a lawman might have to hurriedly gather a posse and ride hell-bent-for-leather chasing after merciless Mexican bandits, and yes, even a wayward bronco Apache crossing the border for plunder was not entirely out of the question.[10] The revered ranching writer and historian J. Evetts Haley described this species of frontier lawmen as men who were "lured by dalliance with danger."[11]

Yet, that same *transitional* lawman was also comfortably at ease with his hands wrapped around a steering wheel and a new-fangled semi-automatic pistol thrust into his waistband. And he was learning to make use of the telephone as an effective means of gathering and disseminating critical intelligence on criminal matters, even though the instruments were few and far between. Cameras? The gadgets were proving just as valuable for courtroom use as they were at providing snapshot fun at the family reunion. Those gismo typewriters were in vogue too—for a few of em'. In short, depending on exigency the *transitional* lawman was always at home, on the range or driving down a dusty road headed for his next appearance before a Grand Jury at the county-seat. The *transitional* badman? He was still bad!

W. D. Allison, as we shall see, was a sterling example of the *transitional* lawman on a *transitional* frontier. Whether or not he made the switch from a nineteenth-century type lawman to a modern-era crime-fighter willingly is speculation. Unmistakably we know he did, we just don't know his mindset. It would probably be a cinch bet that at least from time to time a smidgen of nostalgia wormed into his consciousness, sending him off into daydreams of once again riding across wide-open ranch country on a honest horse, but dreams are a kind of personal thing, so this then is the factual side of W. D. "Dave" Allison's story.

In presenting Allison's biography it is necessary to correct a few misnomers and honestly made mistakes. The subject of this story was not named William David Allison, although often that error is reported and repeated.[12] Allison's birth name was William Davis Allison.[13] The slip-up would be understandable. Those times when he was signing his name on official documents, as reflected in numerous examples of his signature, Allison used his initials, W. D., and even in voluminous letters to his wife he simply closed with "W. D. Allison." Practically speaking though, throughout the Southwest, he was simply known as Dave Allison.

Dr. John Pryor Allison and family. Dave Allison, standing, second from left. Courtesy, Pat Treadwell, Tahoka, Texas.

Dave's father, John Pryor Allison was born just south of the Tennessee line in Limestone County, Alabama, on August 6, 1832.[14] Dave's mother,

Mary Waters Clive, the daughter of George Waters and Patsy Carr Clive, was born in Abingdon, Virginia on October 17, 1838.[15] At the age of twenty, Mary accepted John's marriage proposal, and the pair were united on May 18, 1858, at Cincinnati, Ohio.[16] The newlyweds tarried not too long in the Buckeye State, as evidenced by the birth of their first child, Ellen, on March 15, 1859, at Fulton, Mississippi.[17] Whether John returned to Cincinnati to complete his education or to began his medical practice is uncertain, but during this, the final Ohio sojourn, on June 21, 1861, the subject of our story was born, named after his paternal grandfather, William Davis Allison, the first son of a now Doctor John Pryor Allison.[18]

With hostilities at hand, and the Confederacy dreadfully in short supply of qualified physicians, the Allison's, a toddler on the apron string and baby Dave still at the breast, returned to Itawamba County, Mississippi, where John P. Allison, M. D. enlisted in the 24th Mississippi Infantry Regiment during September of 1861, and was initially assigned to B. F. Toomer's Company F, popularly known at the Cummings Grays.[19] The 24th Mississippi Infantry was ordered to Charleston, South Carolina, and later to Fernandian, Florida, where several Companies served on small vessels which participated in sailing coastal waters, slipping through an ineffective Union blockade. In the Spring of 1862, the regiment was tagged with the tasks of more traditional foot soldiering, and ordered to Tennessee.[20]

Apparently during his stint with the Confederate Army, Doctor Allison's family remained in Fulton, Mississippi, not too far from Tupelo. It was here that Dave Allison learned to walk, talk, hop, skip, jump, and quite probably as most little boys do, ask a few embarrassing and discomforting questions. Some of which may have well dealt with the arrival of his new little brother, George Clive.[21] After remaining in Mississippi for a while after the Civil War, physician and father John Pryor Allison made the decision to move his family to Houston. And it was here, along the Lone Star's Gulf Coast, that fate somehow twisted the life from Dave's older sister, nine year-old Ellen.[22] Mother Allison, surely heartbroken, had little time to squander on grief, she had her hands full with two boys to raise and another child on the way. At Houston, on October 5, 1869, eight year-old Dave Allison was blessed with a baby sister, Patricia Winston.[23] And again, for whatever reason, financial or otherwise, maybe just a touch of wanderlust, it was time to move once more, this time north of Dallas to McKinney, Collin County.[24]

Collin County, organized in 1846, was much different from the swampy salt-grass coastal country which little Dave had grown accustomed to. The topography was open and rolling, except along meandering creeks which were handsomely decorated with hardwoods, some of which sported trunks so immense it required several men joining hands just to take the measure.[25] During spring, the morning sun could seemingly spin brilliant colors like a kaleidoscope as it began to peek at zillions of immodest wildflowers teasingly dotting undulating hillsides. In the Fall, as the leaves fell, the orange, gold, and red was more brazen—almost brassy—as if crying out an erotic challenge before Winter's breath blew frigid. Dave Allison could have cared less!

At ten years old, perched at the very edge of the 1871 Texas frontier, Dave Allison surely wasn't philosophizing about nature's wonders; no, he was awestruck by features more real, things he could actually touch, say, a six-shooter, bullwhip, bowie knife, or maybe even a gaudily beaded Comanche war-club darkly stained with human blood. Unquestionably he heard others talking about Indian Territory just a hopscotch to the north, and surely he had a question or two regarding eating a buffalo's tongue, an indulgence which most grownups thought delectable. Undoubtedly about this point in time he began asking for a gun of his very own, even a secondhand single-shot, an old one would have been okay. For just behind those picnic spots outside of town were the thickets, the underbrush and brambles, where from their veiled lairs late in the evening scads of deer warily ventured into view. And turkey, scrumptious turkey, deceptive turkeys—seemingly stupid looking turkeys—that is until one was desired for supper. Little boys ached for the hunt—it pushed them to big boy status. Doctor Allison understood.

Biographically, it is often a problematic exercise to offer in detail someone's childhood experiences. But a few reasoned circumstantial deductions are not out of place. Dave Allison came from a reasonably prosperous and well-educated family.[26] It is not unfair to think Dave attended school while in Collin County; certainly his father placed great value on learning, and later, when we have opportunity to examine a few of Dave's personal letters and some of his official law enforcement correspondence, it will be demonstrated that he was well-educated and articulate for his times.[27]

It is safe to presume that at a reasonably early age Dave Allison started developing a proficiency with firearms; certainly his father, a hunter himself, was making sure his sons acquired the necessary outdoor skills for frontier life—it was a rite of passage for a Westerner. Doctor Allison was committed to making sure his children, especially the boys, could pass life's exams—in and outside the classroom.

McKinney, Texas, 1870's, when Dave Allison was there as a youthful aspiring cowboy. Courtesy, Helen G. Hall, McKinney, Texas.

As Dave grew taller, the family grew larger. For it was at McKinney that three more brothers were added to the clan, Luke Pryor, John, and Paul Clifton.[28] It was also in Collin County that Dave, a burgeoning teenager, became absorbed with the cowboy life, just as surely as if some waddie had pitched a loop around his boots, jerked the slack, dallied off, and flipped him in a somersault to the ground. Back East, young men dreamed about becoming cowboys. But Dave didn't live back East. Around Waco the Chisholm Trail split, branching to the right was the Shawnee Trail, almost arrow straight, headed due north to Preston's Crossing on the Red River— right through the middle of Collin County.[29] And it was here, here in his home county, that cowmen, cowboys, trail-bosses, horse wranglers, and cantankerous greasy-faced camp cooks stepped from imagination to reality. Dave Allison didn't have to read books about cowboys, he could hang out in town and see the real thing—brush up against them—listen to music of jingle-bob spurs as they crossed plank walkways—catch a sniff of sweat-stained leather. If he had asked, one of those tanned faces might have looked down, smiled, and actually let him monkey-finger a .45 Colt's revolver, but he didn't ask. Someday he'd have his own cartridge belt and six-shooter, his own set of leggins', maybe even silver trimmed gal-leg spurs instead of jingle-bobs', and someday he too would be a cowboy headed north to the Kansas Cowtowns—no homework, no little brothers, no worries. Never mind the dirty fingernails, the scars, the blisters, and he actually thought that strained gimpy shuffle was smart looking, and he sure enough didn't know yet about cowboy's empty pockets. There was a lot about cowboys Dave Allison didn't know.

What he didn't know he would have to learn somewhere else. It was time for another move. In 1876, while Dave was fifteen, Doctor Allison rounded up his herd, which at that time consisted of a wife, five sons, and daughter Pattie, cajoled his brood toward the southwest, and alighted at Brownwood, Brown County, Texas.[30] At the time McKinney was a metropolis compared to the frontier village of Brownwood. Dave's mother, Mary, was the kind of stick by your man woman that would make a home out of haunt. The boys were elated. There were less people—fewer school teachers. More deer, more wild turkey, and even a few wary panthers.[31] Compounding their excitement was all the hullabaloo still going on, two years later, about John Wesley Hardin and his pals killing twenty-six year-old Brown County Deputy Charles M. Webb during a scorching shoot-out in nearby Comanche County.[32] Hardin was still on the dodge, and rumors as to his whereabouts echoed throughout the countryside as hard-edged Texas Rangers hunted for the fugitive. After sundown, around crackling campfires, no doubt unsentimental cattlemen and tough-as-nails cowboys casually stoked the fire while poking fun at the lawmen's ineffectual rummaging around—Hardin still had friends, good friends—and relatives—in that part of the Texas ranch country. Young boys and teenage apprentice cowhands knew prudence commanded they keep mouths shut, but they listened with awe. Geographically and demographically it was a wilder broken country, stocked with untamed frontier folk.

Founded by the renowned Indian fighter Henrys S. Brown in 1856, Brown County with drainage to the Colorado River, was right at the edge where Texas countryside begins to seductively open into wanton expansiveness.[33] North was Fort Griffin, and the hell-roaring civilian community simply known as, The Flat. To the south lay the beautiful Texas Hill Country. A short distance to the west was the aptly named Western Trail, the longest of all the well-known cattle trails, stretching from the southern tip of Texas all the way to Ogallala, Nebraska, where like the Chisholm Trail it split, the western fork to Montana, the eastern fork to Dakota Territory.[34] By 1879 the Western Trail was the principal thoroughfare for Texas cattle, having "supplanted the farmer-laden Chisholm Trail to the east."[35] Brown County was ranch country, cowboy country, just the ticket for the Allison boys, but most especially for Dave.[36]

Brownwood is where Dave made the leap from mischief to maturity—from adolescence to adulthood. Amid the Brown County mesquite flats is where he fine-tuned his cowboy skills.[37] Where he abandoned academia and mechanically learned to build a loop—and throw it too—with precision. Where he whetted his cow savvy on the spinning grindstone of hard work and hazard. Where he worked for day pay—scanty wages—but cowboy wages. Where towards white-hot embers and red-hot irons he dragged bawling calves, tacky slobber grudgingly clinging to their milk-splashed gums, and where little by little he became acquainted with the stench of scorched hair and burnt hide. And, at some point, incontestably too, he was ordered to the manure painted ground, told to pull out his Barlow and get busy performing cow-lot surgery, throwing samples of a bull calf's manhood into a blue and white speckled wash-pan, and then momentarily hesitating prior to his next move, making sure not to cut identifying notches into the wrong ear. Where effortlessly, or at least seemingly so, he proved a knack for topping off a horse, even a hammerhead—one with white in his eyes, blood in his nostrils, and spiders in his mind. It was in Brown County where Dave Allison learned to read cattle, horses—and men.

By nature and profession the men were a tough lot. Quickly he was corrected, and it was made emphatically clear that men who owned the cattle were not cowboys, they were cowmen. Cowboys worked for cowmen. Whether boss man or hired hand, there was no room for crybabies, not in a crowd where some men in a split-second moment of dumb carelessness had lost a finger or thumb, simply by catching it between a tightly stretched rope and a rawhide covered saddle horn. And, there were even stories about men getting caught on the ground between their horse and a belligerent longhorn steer—somehow entangled—a lariat rope fortuitously draping around their sunburned neck, then bingo—their head cut smooth off. Sometimes there was even a dash of twisted humor squeezed from someone else's wincing pain. Many proudly boasted they worked from can to can't—that is from the time you *can* see first light until darkness finally overhauls another day and you *can't* see nothing. Some were hard drinkers. Some were damn good cussers. Most all carried cigarette fixins' in a vest pocket—"tailor-mades" were yet hard to come by. All knew personal business was guarded with the same passion as personal property—something best left alone. Most all would welcome a stranger with open arms—but always be armed. Six-shooters and five-shooters were worn in holsters, stuffed into trouser pockets, stashed in saddle bags, or secreted in rolled up woolen blankets, but everybody had to have one—or two—because everyone knew if God had wanted men to fight like cats and dogs, He'd givin' em' claws and paws. It was in these Brown County cow-country campgrounds that Dave Allison learned those lessons not taught in front of chalky blackboards. Around the branding fires, and in the brush corrals, step by step, he learned the rules grown men, cowmen and cowboys play by, and how to differentiate between slurred and drunken utterances which were just harmless fun, and prickly challenges more sinister. Wild cattle and men with the bark still on can more often than not prove deceptively dangerous creatures. Book-learning was okay, reading men was critical. Certainly there was a cattle range classroom, a college of long-standing customs, traditions, cow camp etiquette. Doctor John Pryor Allison's eldest son was making a good student.

His sixteenth year, 1877, was a harbinger of consequence for Dave Allison. Besides his birthday in early summer, autumn breezes heralded another new arrival, the birth of his third sister, Clara Belle—the last of the Allison children.[38] And the year was indeed significant in other ways for Dave—though at the time he had not a clue.

For once again in northeast Mississippi, the Magnolia State, just like Dave Allison a few years earlier, a little brown-eyed boy was learning to walk, talk, hop, skip, and jump. And just like Dave, he too, at a point in time would feel compelled to tinker around in the cow business, the Texas cow business. His name was kind of feminine, for a boy. Not many Southern boys, or for that matter, boys from anywhere were named Hillary, but everyone soon enough learned not to dare call him girlish, and none except his mama called him Hillary. He was simply known as Hill Loftis.[39] But in 1877 he still had growing to do. Fate would be patient.

Little could he have realized it then, but while Dave Allison was sweating, riding, roping, and wrangling—piece work cowboying—in Brown County, Texas, events were taking place not too far northeast at Graham, in Young County. There at the county courthouse, or by other accounts under a noble Oak tree, cattlemen, distraught over an unprecedented and seemingly infectious rash of cattle thievery, met to discuss issues regarding mutual protection.[40] Indeed their concern was not ill-founded, the threat was legitimate, simply exemplified by one authentic case. By some accounts Bill Henderson was the leader, by others just a charter member, but by all, he rode somewhere near the front of a band of genuinely tough rascals operating out of the Wichita Mountains near Fort Sill, Indian Territory. The degenerates were jumping back and forth across the Red River with their four-legged plunder, using the boundary line to avoid detection, lawful pursuit, or apprehension. The cattle ranchers and honest townsfolk in Shackleford County Texas were understandably weary, exhausted with an insufficient legal system, worn out with lame excuses. Charley McBride, Jim Townsend, and a guy called Brownlee, a despicable trio of Bill Henderson's good-for-nothing wide-loop buddies, should have realized their misdeeds and transgressions were goading honest men to seek dishonest remedy—but they didn't. Out in the Clear Fork bottoms, just outside Fort Griffin, they were found resting under the shade of a lonesome tree, all three dangling from a substantial limb. Shortly thereafter (June 1876), Bill Henderson and another thug, Hank Floyd, were caught in Kansas with twenty-six head of horses stolen in Texas from a rancher they had murdered. In handcuffs and leg-irons the rogues were returned to Albany, the Shackleford County seat. On nearby Hubbard Creek they too were lynched, and a local editor captioned public opinion, editorializing that if hanging wouldn't put the "kibosh" on criminals "maybe cremation would."[41]

The cattlemen meeting at Graham knew they had a real problem, but they also were well aware vigilante justice was not necessarily an appropriate answer—it was just a stopgap measure—they were seeking long term solutions. The thievery was epidemic. And, in fact, some of the suggestions for dealing with the prickly problem proved to be "such strong measurers" that a few refused to even participate for fear of "retaliation by the lawless element."[42] With a twentieth-century journalistic touch the highly popularized term "rustler" resplendently jumped from sensationalized printed pages of breathtaking Western chronicles, in truth though, from those days long ago to this very day, in real ranch country the term is incredibly seldom applied. There is but one evocative expletive particularly held in reserve for a man that steals cattle. With the invective utterance spoken as if it but were one revolting word, and crediting his total human worth less than a loathsome zero, the man who steals cattle is simply known as nothing more than a "Goddamn cow-thief."[43]

On February 15, 1877, at Graham, for the purpose of "determining the best method of gathering cattle and otherwise protecting the interest of all concerned," forty cattlemen, including C. C. Slaughter and the son of Oliver Loving, J. C. Loving, huddled, developing a workable strategy.[44]

The result? Birth of the Northwest Texas Cattle Raisers Association, the foundation for what would eventually become the Texas and Southwestern Cattle Raisers Association.[45] Soon it would simply be known throughout the Southwest as the Association, and for our purposes, the Association is one of the cornerstones later supporting Dave Allison's irreplaceable story.

According to the newly formulated Association rules, the ranch country was to be divided into separate districts, and "men will be allotted to each district, whose duty it shall be to gather all cattle in their districts, and notify the owners of the same, and hold them until they are called for by their owners."[46] Furthermore stockmen were warned not to in any way molest cattle not their own within district boundaries, until the cattle were rounded up and inspected by persons designated by the Association to control herd movement within the geographically defined range.[47]

As the Association grew, so did their collective political clout, and in one book detailing facts about the cattle industry, it was claimed, "To hold an office in this Association is a mark of great honor and distinction and to become president is to hold a position of but less importance than the civil office of the state."[48] But more of the cow business later.

We may assume that he was learning the cowboy business, but for the next several years little is known pertaining to Dave Allison's maturation process. There is confirmation that the family remained near Brownwood, as clearly substantiated by the United States Census of 1880, and the subject of our story, by now a strapping nineteen year-old was still living at home.[49] Disappointingly those same records, which are only partly decipherable, indicate Dave had quite possibly taken up an apprenticeship of some type, for under the heading *Profession, Occupation or Trade* the word "Assistant" is readable beside his name, however, the next word is illegible. It is not unreasonable to suspect that Doctor Allison was encouraging Dave to seek his fortune with employment more befitting a physician's son, a job more lucrative than one paying cowboy wages. What the elder Allison actually thought, or had to say, will have to remain mere suspicion; Dave Allison's movements, however, will not.

Like so many in the age bracket, by the time he turned twenty-one Dave Allison had moved further west, this time on his own.[50] Those material possessions he actually crammed into saddle bags, stuffed into bedding, or tied to his hull, can be only guessed at, but by the time Dave Allison managed a trip to Midland County, Texas, he possessed two qualities gold coins couldn't buy.

First, he was a cowboy. A top-hand cowboy. A cattleman's kind of cowboy, as noted by one of his contemporaries, himself a noted Western author, who penned that Dave Allison was a "cowboy of the old school."[51] When Dave Allison unlimbered at Midland, he was already seasoned, already well-versed in the intricacies of the then booming Texas cattle industry, not from the standpoint of a budding capitalist, but closer to the ground, a young man with an aptitude for managing livestock, one proficient in getting the day to day work done, and unlike so many of his uneducated cohorts, Dave could keep accounts. For the rest of his life, in one way or the other, Dave Allison would never be far removed from the cow business and those Western characters who were profiting or pilfering therefrom.

Secondly, by the time Dave Allison arrived in Midland County he outright owned a personality trait soon to be recognized by all who knew, or would come to know him. Dave Allison was *fearless*.[52]

ENDNOTES
Chapter 1. "A cowboy of the old school"

[1] **Steckmesser**, Kent Ladd. *The Western Hero in History and Legend.* P. 3. Hereafter cited as **Steckmesser**.
[2] Ibid.
[3] Ibid. The author refers to the "working of the folk imagination."
[4] **Marks**, Paula Mitchell. *And Die in the West.* P. 20. Hereafter cited as **Marks**.
[5] **Ball**, Larry D., *The United States Marshals of New Mexico & Arizona Territories 1846-1912*. P. 125. Hereafter cited as **Ball**.
[6] **Metz**, Leon Claire. *The Shooters*. P. 110. Metz reports, "Prior to Jim's (Manning) death, the well-known journalist Stuart Lake offered to write his biography. Manning declined, and suggested Lake see Wyatt Earp. Thus Earp became famous; whereas James Manning is almost unknown in western annals."
[7] **Bailey**, Lynn **& Chaput**, Don, *Cochise County Stalwarts*, Volume I, P. 114. The general reader may not be informed regarding certain Wyatt Earp truths, therefore the author's concluding paragraph is cited in full. "There is considerable irony here. Wyatt Earp, due to literature, movies, and television, has become the 'leader' of the Earps, but only in the Twentieth Century, not in history. And, irony of irony, Wyatt Earp, the most well-known shootist or gunfighter in America's past, was never in a man-on-man gunfight or duel. In fact, it cannot be demonstrated historically that Wyatt Earp ever killed a man. It is true, that because of his presence (the famous shootout; the Tucson rail yard, etc.) certain dead bodies were found, but how they were killed and by whom has never been established with certainty. This is indeed a lamentable record for America's premier gunfighter." Hereafter cited as **Bailey & Chaput**.
[8] **Marks**. P. 365.
[9] **Bailey & Chaput**, Vol. I, P. 110. "On the other hand, they (Earps) were never among the community leaders, and their important Arizona reputation is based on book, movie, and television portrayals, not on the record." Also see, **Sheridan**, Thomas E., *Arizona—A History*. P. 384., "More ink has been wasted on the shoot-out at the O. K. Corral than on any other subject in Arizona history. Our national fascination with Wyatt Earp, Doc Holliday, and the Clantons has little to do with their historical importance and everything to do with the mythology of the Wild West." Hereafter cited as **Sheridan**.
[10] **Meed**, Douglas., *They Never Surrendered: Bronco Apaches of the Sierra Madres, 1890-1912.* The author presents a captivating and well-researched account of later day Apache/Anglo conflict, which surprisingly, as **Meed** points out, continued well into the twentieth-century.
[11] **Haley**, J. Evetts., "COWBOY SHERIFF," *The SHAMROCK*. P. 2. Summer 1963. Hereafter cited as **Haley**.
[12] **Thrapp**, Dan. L., *Encyclopedia of Frontier Biography*. Volume I. P. 17. Although the author respectfully included Allison in his comprehensive study of notable frontier characters, he, like others, gets Allison's first name right, but because the subject of this biography was generally known as "Dave," he understandably assumed the middle name was David, when in fact it is actually Davis. Other errors made by the author regarding Allison's biographical sketch, some of them indeed quite significant, will be addressed appropriately. Hereafter cited as **Thrapp**.

[13] See United States Census, 1880, Brown County, Texas. Roll No. 1292. Also see, Official Certification from Gaines County, Seminole, Texas, dated April 16, 1923, sworn to by County Health Officer F. J. Richardson, before T. O. Stark, Gaines County Judge. The information concerning Allison's correct middle name was brought to the author's attention by Pat Treadwell, Tahoka, Texas, an Allison relative, the daughter of Thomas "Mitty" Phillips, Dave Allison's nephew. Pat has accomplished a considerable amount of competent genealogical research on "Uncle Dave" Allison, and has graciously shared the family's private papers, photographs, and her personal wealth of knowledge with the author. Additionally, as with any family history, there were several stories or comments about "Uncle Dave" which could not necessarily be proved with paper documentation but, nevertheless, have become a part of family tradition and folklore—there is not reason one to disbelieve or doubt them. There, as will amply be demonstrated, are sufficient primary source materials available to unequivocally take the true measure of William Davis Allison. However, Pat's knowledge of material not wholly sustained by recorded documentation will be shared with the reader and hereafter cited as **Treadwell**. Even at the time of his death, it was *assumed* at the inquest that Allison's middle name was "David," a misnomer which necessitated official correction. .

[14] **Treadwell**.

[15] Ibid.

[16] Ibid.

[17] Ibid.

[18] Ibid. And. The birthplace of Cincinnati, Ohio is more than adequately confirmed in numerous Texas Ranger *Enlistment Papers* and *Descriptive Lists*. Courtesy Texas State Library and Archives Commission, Austin, Texas and the Texas Ranger Hall of Fame and Museum Library, Waco, Texas.

[19] Confederate Army Muster Rolls and Regimental Returns for the 24th Mississippi Infantry, copies courtesy **Treadwell**. Also see, **Howell, Jr**., H. Grady, *For Dixie Land I'll Take My Stand, A Muster Listing of All Known Mississippi Confederate Soldiers, Sailors, and Marines*. P. 41. And see, **Rowland**, Dunbar, *Military History of Mississippi, 1803-1898*. P. 255.

[20] **Walter**, John F., *Unit History, Twenty-fourth Mississippi Infantry*. P. 824-830. Apparently it was determined Dr. Allison's services could best be utilized in the war torn civilian community, for in the family papers is a copy of *Certificate to be Given a Soldier at the Time of His Discharge*, dated August 27, 1862, and signed "B. F. Toomer, Capt."

[21] **Treadwell**. George Clive Allison was born June 5, 1866.

[22] Ibid. The cause of Ellen's death is unknown. Whether or not Doctor Allison believed there was some advantage for his daughter's health by a move to Houston is likewise unknown. Possibly, as later events seem to indicate, the move to Houston may have been intended as a temporary stopover on Doctor Allison's westward migration.

[23] Ibid. Patricia Winston Allison, Pat **Treadwell's** grandmother, as mentioned was born on October 5, 1869, at Houston. She married Thomas Nelson Phillips at Brownwood, Brown County, Texas, on her birthday in 1904, at age thirty-five. Pattie, a professional piano teacher, passed away on May 10, 1928, at Brownwood, Texas.

[24] Ibid. Certainly there exists the possibility Dr. Allison already had relatives in the area. See, **Pitts**, Alice Ellison and **Champ**, Minnie Pitts, *Collin County,*

Texas, Families. Volume II. P. 9-10. However, for our purposes there will be no attempt to identify Dave Allison's relatives other than parents, grandparents, and siblings.

[25] **Kingston**, Mike, (**editor**). *Texas Almanac, 1994-95.* P. 179. Both the county-seat, McKinney, and the county itself were named for pioneer settler Collin McKinney. Collin County was created from Fannin County. Hereafter cited as **Kingston**. Also see, **Hall**, Roy F. and Helen Gibbard, *Collin County—Pioneering In North Texas*. "The big forest were too much for the settlers and no attempt was made to clear any land of forests." P. 43. And see, **Gournay**, Luke. *Texas Boundaries—Evolution of the State's Counties.* P. 48. Hereafter cited as **Gournay**.

[26] **Treadwell**. Allison family genealogical records reveal that one of Dave's brothers followed in his father's footsteps and became a physician, another brother became a pharmacist, one sister was a career school teacher, and as previously mentioned his sister, Pattie, was a professional piano teacher. Certainly education was an important factor in Doctor Allison's house. In truth, it appears that Dave probably had the least formal education of any of his surviving siblings.

[27] Numerous indeed will be the examples to support a contention that Dave Allison received a degree of formal education as a youngster, although reports cards or diplomas are lacking. Many of his official reports to the Texas Adjutant General are available for examination, as well as letters he wrote to his wife and daughter, several of which will be quoted later in detail. All clearly demonstrate a reasonably respectful level of education.

[28] **Treadwell**. Luke Pryor Allison was born May 24, 1871. John Allison on May 17, 1873, and Paul Clifton Allison on April 11, 1875.

[29] **Stephens**, A. Ray and **Holmes**, William M., *Historical Atlas of Texas*. P. 43. Hereafter cited as **Stephens & Holmes**. Also see, **Drago**, Harry Sinclair., *Great American Cattle Trails.* P. 30-31. Hereafter cited as **Drago**. And see, the excellent, *The Chisholm Trail—High Road of the Cattle Kingdom* by Don **Worcester**. P. 3-16. Hereafter cited as **Worcester**. Also see, **Stambaugh**, J. Lee & Lillian J., *A History of Collin County, Texas*. P. 109. "For many years it was also the principal trail over which cattle were driven to markets as they came through, or by Dallas to Preston and on to the north. During the Civil War, traffic over it was greatly reduced but boomed again after the fighting ceased. It is estimated that from 200,000 to 260,000 head of cattle crossed at Preston in the spring and early summer of 1866. Traffic again decreased after the construction of the Houston and Texas Central Railroad from Dallas in 1872." Admittedly, during the time of Allison's childhood in Collin County the Shawnee Trail was in decline. See, *The New Handbook of Texas*, Vol. I, P. 1004, "The new route (Chisholm Trail) to the west of the Shawnee soon began carrying the bulk of the Texas herds, leaving the earlier trail to dwindle for a few years and expire."

[30] **Treadwell**.

[31] **Smith**, Tevis Clyde, *Frontier's Generation, The Pioneer History of Brown County with Sidelights on the Surrounding Territory*. P. 35-36. "The panthers were a nuisance to the stockmen; they killed many valuable cattle."

[32] **Metz**, Leon., *John Wesley Hardin, Dark Angel of Texas*. P. 138. Hereafter cited as **Metz**. Also see **Marohn**, Richard., *The Last Gunfighter, John Wesley Hardin*. P. 71-85. Hereafter cited as **Marohn**. Brown County Deputy Sheriff Charles M. Webb, a former Texas Ranger, was born on May 2, 1848 and killed at Comanche, Texas on May 26, 1874.

[33] **Kingston**., P. 169. And see, **Gournay**, P. 69.
[34] **Forbis**, William H., *The Cowboys.* P. 145.
[35] *The New Handbook of Texas*, Volume VI, P. 894.
[36] Ibid., Volume I, P. 780. "Because Brownwood lay on a feeder line of the Western Trail, stores and saloons served the needs of the cowboys who drove the herds through town."
[37] Certainly there is no attempt to fool the reader, and therefore acknowledgment must be made there is not authenticated documentation to indicate just when Dave Allison developed his skills with cattle, horses, and firearms. The *assumption* is being made the process began during his teenage years, as it did with most young men of the era, because as will be explored, by the time he reached adulthood he was a well-seasoned cowboy, remained closely connected with the cattle industry for the remainder of his life, and was exceptionally noted for his expertise with weapons—all facts later supported by primary source materials.
[38] **Treadwell**. Clara Bell Allison was born October 24, 1877, at Brownwood, Brown County, Texas.
[39] **Fenton**, James I., "Tom Ross: Ranger Nemesis," *Quarterly of the National Association and Center for Outlaw and Lawman History.*(NOLA) Volume XIV, No. 2. P. 4. Hereafter cited as **Fenton**. The author reports Loftis born in 1872 in northeast Mississippi. **DeArment**, R. K., "Bloody Easter," *Old West.* Spring 1994. P. 14., gives Hillary Loftis's birthday as January 11, 1871. Hereafter cited as **DeArment**. Texas Prison records on file with the Texas State Library and Archives Commission, Austin, Texas, confirm the birthplace as Mississippi, but give the year of birth as 1873. Although it is of no actual importance to the Dave Allison story, and serves only to further confuse the issue, on his Death Certificate, Loftis (under the name Tom Ross, alias Chas. Gannon) is recorded as being 54 years old at the time of his death, February 3, 1929. Courtesy, Sylvia **Berkram**, Glacier County Clerk & Recorder, Cut Bank, Montana.
[40] **Spiller**, E. B. (editor), "The Texas & Southwestern Cattle Raisers' Assn.—Its Origin, Purpose, Brief Resume of Activities," *The Cattleman.* March 1923. P. 75.
[41] **Robinson III**, Charles., *The Frontier World of Fort Griffin.* P. 99-114. Also see **Cashion**, Ty., *A Texas Frontier, The Clear Fork Country and Fort Griffin, 1849-1887.* P. 213-233. And see, The *New Handbook of Texas*, Volume I, P. 1041. "With county seats far apart, grand juries disinclined to indict, and trial juries reluctant to convict, early cattlemen often had to take law enforcement into their own hands in dealing with rustlers."
[42] *The New Handbook of Texas.* Volume VI, P. 418.
[43] **Clarke**, Mary Whatley., *A Century of Cow Business, The First Hundred Years Of The Texas and Southwestern Cattle Raisers Association.* P. 15. Apologetically, it must be made emphatically clear that the author, in her treatment of the subject simply used the terminology "damn cow thief," however, on the cattle ranges, around the campfires, and at today's livestock sale-barns, away from ladies' hearing, someone guilty of altering a brand or stealing cattle is purely and simply a "Goddamn cow-thief" or a "son-of-a bitchin' cow-thief." And assuredly, even today, a "Goddamn cow-thief" is not politely referred to generically as a "rustler." And even author **Clarke** acknowledges, "From that day to this, Association members still so described the cow thief, refraining from calling him a dignified name like 'rustler', 'mavericker', etc. They leave those names to fiction writers." Of the old-timers at the meeting the author rightly extols the cattlemen as being "...fearless and sincere men who were not afraid to

'stick their necks out' in a movement for law and order by establishing the sanctity of the brand." Hereafter cited as **Clarke**.

[44] **Murrah**, David J., *C. C. Slaughter, Rancher, Banker, Baptist.* P. 39-53. Hereafter cited as **Murrah**. And see, *The New Handbook of Texas*, Volume VI, P. 417.

[45] Ibid.

[46] **Clarke**, P. 16.

[47] Ibid.

[48] Ibid., P. 23. Quoting, *Cattle Industry of 1895.*

[49] United States Census 1880, Brownwood Justice Precinct No. 1., Brown County, Texas. P. 379, Line 5.

[50] **Treadwell**. As would be reasonably suspected an exact date for Dave Allison leaving home and heading west cannot be established, however, family remembrances passed down through the years assert that by the time he was twenty-one he was own his own and living at Midland, Texas. **DeArment** simply states, "...(Allison) went west at an early age and cowboyed in west Texas." P. 12.

[51] Charles A. Siringo to Dave Allison, January 1, 1921, Roswell, New Mexico. Complete details cited in Chapter 9.

[52] As will amply be demonstrated by direct primary source quotations throughout Dave Allison's biography, if there were but one word to serve as a common denominator for all the characterizations made about our subject, that word would be, *fearless*. Such assessment is also made from numerous secondary sources, such as the excellent Master of Arts Thesis, "Tom Ross: Outlaw Stockman," prepared for The University of Texas at El Paso, 1979, by James I. **Fenton**. P. 85. "Allison, for example, was reputed to be 'one of the very best peace officers the Southwest ever produced.' He was noted for being absolutely fearless, a quality that no doubt stood him in good stead in the numerous gunfights in which he participated." Hereafter cited as **Fenton (II)**. **DeArment** comes close to using the term *fearless*, "All who knew him (Allison) attested to his bravery and skill as an officer and investigator..." P. 13.

2

"We ain't got no guns like that."

Formally, Midland County was created in 1885, with the city of Midland garnering the shire-town honors. The frontier settlement, like so many other Western communities could trace beginnings directly to a railroad, this one, the Texas & Pacific operating between Fort Worth and El Paso, and the town was named because it squatted right at that midway point between the two cities.[1] Most people just passed through. A handful of vigorous visionaries, however, had already come to the well-substantiated Texas presumption, in the wide-open spaces where stands a scrub-oak, there too should stand a cow. From all points on the compass, from all four sides neighboring this West Texas whistle-stop spot, there were miles, and miles, and miles, of wide-open spaces, sinfully stunted scrub-oaks, and dust-coated cows.[2] Neighbors? Just a few.

Midland, Texas. Christmas Day, 1895. Dave Allison was Sheriff. Courtesy, The Petroleum Museum, Abell-Hangar Collection. Midland, Texas.

In a brief thumbnail sketch, one well-regarded Western writer casually mentions Dave Allison, "...went west at an early age and cowboyed in West Texas."[3] The biographical account is correct, but a smidgen more detail will prove indispensable in understanding Dave Allison's story.

The fact that Dave Allison landed in Midland was not by happenstance. When Dave Allison left home he was in fact a top-notch cowboy and talented horseman.[4] As they say though, the skids had been greased. He was well-connected. Connected with local Midland County powerhouses W. E. and G. H. Connell, E. H. Estes, and John Scharbauer, two of whom still owned property in Brown County, Texas.[5] Illustrative of their close ties with the Texas beef business, and their financial standing in the fledgling far-flung county can be found in a certification by Midland County Clerk, A. B. Rountree. He guaranteed that, "W. E. Connell is a merchant and Banker—G. H. Connell is a Banker and (emphasis added) *has a Large Cattle Ranch* as also John Scharbauer is a Banker and *Heavy Cattle Dealer* and that E. H. Estes is *invested heavily in cattle raising...*"[6]

Elisha Hamilton "Lish" Estes. A Midland pioneer, ranching powerhouse, and one of Dave Allison's surety bondsmen and a steadfast political backer. And Nancy Caroline (Lee) Estes, wife of "Lish" and the first Anglo female to drink from Monument Springs. Courtesy, Nancy McKinnley, Midland, Texas.

Although there is no hard evidence as to exactly why Elisha Hamilton "Lish" Estes cast an approving eye in the direction of youthful William Davis Allison, *perhaps* there is a slight clue. No doubt both had tramped over some of the very same ground, for when he was but twenty years old, Estes "went to Brown County where he was a wage worker and rode the range looking after cattle and guarding homes against Indian depredations."[7] Later after marrying Nancy Caroline Lee, and establishing several West Texas ranches, Estes moved to the Midland area where his brand, the **7Z7**, became well known.[8] "Lish" Estes stubbornly carved out an enviable working ranch at Monument Springs, New Mexico Territory and, in fact, it can be reported his wife Nancy was the first white woman ever to partake of refreshing waters flowing from the reliable spring.[9] In time, "Lish" Estes became one of the leading cattlemen in the Southwest. For whatever reason, "Lish," and the others, liked what they saw in young Dave Allison. And just maybe, Dave Allison found it fortunate to have fallen in with an influential and commanding clique, one which an old-timer tagged, "that old Brown County bunch."[10]

Reasoned deduction in the case of Dave Allison logically points to but one conclusion. Doctor Allison's standing in the Brownwood community portended a warm introductory reception for his westward-bound son. Dave Allison went to work for the Connells.[11]

It was work! At the time, that part of West Texas ranch country was Open Range. Some places were flat as a simmering pancake in a blackened cast-iron skillet, at other places the geography appeared uneven, sort of lumpy, like the golden crowns of cathead biscuits momentarily imprisoned in a wire-handled Dutch oven. And just as back strap is sharply cut from the bone, this country too was carved, slashed by sandy draws and abrupt arroyos. Midland by most standards wasn't pretty, though it was mesmeric. In the mountainous ranching country to the north and northwest, cattlemen contended with snowdrifts, but in the Midland country, when daytime skies grew so dark it prompted chickens to roost, and after the bitterly howling winds had skipped through, it was sand that blanketed town and required shoveling—not snow![12] It was unfenced country for the most part, that is excepting around garden-plots. It was still that part of the Western country where, "…the philosophy of fencing had reverted to the ancient custom of enclosing fields to keep livestock *out*, rather than enclosing pastures to keep livestock *in*."[13] It was un-owned cow country, reasoning Midland County Clerk Rountree to comment, "…that no one in our county have much real estate…"[14] It was that big and lonesome kind of country. Country so big a cowboy could ride across it from dawn till dusk, dismounting only to answer nature's call, never having to climb down and fiddle with a bothersome wire gap.

It was that country where a soon to be mama cow would hide like a bank-robber, seemingly melting into a puddle of zilch, until days later, with a newborn calf closely tracking her every hoof-print, she would reclaim instinctive social status with her utterly unconcerned herd mates. Until almost blue in the face, Dave Allison counted cows. Looked for cows. And counted cows again. Everyday! He reunited wandering strays, roped and doctored the sick, and no doubt sporadically shot a lobo wolf. When he found a cow creature stuck, bogged down, he tied his lariat rope to the saddle hard-and-fast, then with artistic skill deftly tattooed a loop around the horns, and gently if possible or otherwise if necessary, persuaded his horse to pull with freight-train might—the command was rare though, there wasn't much mud in Midland. Pencil after pencil he sharpened with his trusty pocketknife, as he counted and marked in the tally-book. The Connell's were making watchful note too—Dave Allison had more potential than most young men, who were content with just drawing cowboy pay.

BANG! Unexpectedly and unforgivably the rifle simply went off, the spent ball traveling mere inches before puncturing Doctor John Pryor Allison. During a fun-filled hunting outing, somehow, Doc Allison climbing through a fence accidentally shot himself. Dutifully his bewildered companions rushed the seriously wounded Allison to Brownwood for medical treatment. Unquestionably, Dave, cowboying in Midland County was notified, but whether or not he managed the trip back to Brownwood in time remains elusive. Initial diagnosis seemed to indicate the doctor's wound survivable, spirits were elevated, but blood-poisoning developed, and on March 31, 1882, Doc Allison died.[15] Later, Dave's daddy, a true pioneering Texas physician was interred with military honors befitting a Confederate Army Veteran at the Greenleaf Cemetery in Brown County.[16]

The loss was exceptionally difficult for Dave, not necessarily because he loved his father any more than the others, but simply for the reason he was the oldest. Thankfully, from the historic approach Dave's footprints can be traced with reasonable accuracy. For the next decade Dave remained in Midland, while the rest of the family divided their time between that place and Brownwood.[17]

The Connells amplified Allison's responsibilities by turning over to him wide ranging clerical duties.[18] By some accounts Dave maintained records for the family's mercantile business interests in Midland, by others he rode herd around the mountains of paperwork connected with the ranching operations—likely, a combination of duties were employed.[19]

Meanwhile, a certain character trait was leading Dave Allison toward law enforcement. Later one of Dave's bosses would remark, "Cool as ice he was, and he'd left school before ever he learned to spell as far as the word *fear*."[20] A contemporary newspaper editor would mention Allison as being "…noted for *fearlessness* and intelligent devotion to duty."[21] One of the cattlemen who actually knew Dave reported "…he was a brave, *fearless*, upright man."[22] Another cowman simply penned Dave Allison was "brave and *fearless*."[23] In yet another descriptive account of Allison it was written that "…he was noted for being absolutely *fearless*…"[24] During the course of historical investigation, noted historian and author, James Irving Fenton, exemplified the general public's opinion of Allison by way of the characterization, *fearless*[25]. Another well-respected Western writer and researcher, R. K. DeArment, says, "All who knew him attested to his bravery…"[26] And, if one reads between the lines just a little, another chronicler confirming Dave Allison's courage replaces the word *fearless* with *splendid*.[27].

Whether or not Dave on a particular occasion acquitted himself well in some fractious cow camp shoot-out, or in some other fashion bested the situation with a rowdy adversary, somehow capturing the favorable notice of Midland County cattlemen, is, and, probably forever, will remain undetermined. Was there a singular scorching moment when Dave proved how much pluck he personally owned? *Perhaps* so. *Maybe* not. But without reservation, Dave Allison had amassed those qualities which were recognized by his cow-country cohorts as prerequisites for a promising political future. First, even if he had not previously been forced to show a reservoir of raw nerve—his backers thought he had it! Secondly, Dave Allison was intelligent, smart with numbers, and displayed amazingly good common sense for a young man. Lastly, he was a well-liked cowboy and, since he was a cattle-country product, he could be counted on to lend a sympathetic ear and offer a sensitive way of thinking toward cattlemen's wants. While but twenty-seven years old, William Davis "Dave" Allison was nominated for Midland County Sheriff.

During the elections held on November 6, 1888, Dave accomplished two admirable distinctions. He captured Midland County's top law enforcement job, becoming the county's second sheriff, and, Dave Allison was now the youngest sheriff in the whole state of Texas.[28] Immediately the Connells, E. H. "Lish" Estes and John Scharbauer pledged a surety bond in Dave Allison's behalf. The bond was approved by the Texas State

Comptroller, John D. McCall, and the newly elected Midland County Sheriff was in business.[29]

Dave Allison as Midland County Sheriff, 1893, pictured second from right, from an old newspaper clipping. Courtesy, Nancy McKinnley, Midland, Texas.

In the tax collecting business![30] The popularized image of town-taming Western two-gun sheriffs is for the most part a twentieth-century phenomenon journalistically designed to promote profit and indulge vicarious fantasies. In Texas, and indeed throughout the early West, election to the office of sheriff resulted in the assumption of a myriad of duties which were in most cases positively routine, and lacked any hint of the rousing shoot-outs which today are laminated and twisted into the job description. Collecting taxes was but one of those tasks. The actual truth is hammered home by Larry Ball: "That the sheriff chose to collect taxes rather than to perform the chores of policeman was not uncommon. Of the two very different jobs, tax collecting was obviously more politically sensitive and certainly more lucrative. If pressed to publicly choose between the two, the incumbent would almost certainly select the tax office. While it is impossible to judge from the perspective of today, this tendency to slight the very important tasks of the shrievalty may have harmed the overall efficiency of frontier law enforcement."[31] Another law enforcement historian, Frank Prassel, corroborates, "Sheriffs served in many jurisdictions as the tax collector, a duty which at times appeared to occupy most of their time."[32] With legitimate concerns linked to the assessment and collection of taxes hanging in the balance, little room is left for doubt that adherents on behalf of major economic enterprises took a decided notice of just who was aspiring to become the county sheriff—and *their* tax-collector. Why not have your own man? Cattlemen from the mushrooming livestock industry, financially fixed railroad powerhouses, and heavily-invested mining speculators were but three representatives from commercial ventures dominating development of the American West, each vigorously backing political contenders who could be counted on to fastidiously safeguard specific interests.[33]

Noticeably, as Dave Allison's story continues to unfurl, his particularly warm relationship with two of the acknowledged special interest congregations will be underscored. Categorically, Dave Allison's adoption by West Texas cattlemen is not, in and of itself, necessarily adverse to an impartial imposition of the law, but make no plain mistake, Dave was a cattleman's candidate. The economic influence and political clout of early livestock producers, especially after the birth of organized stock associations, cannot be underestimated.[34] Within the Lone Star State, Texas and Southwestern Cattle Raisers Association leadership was particularly proficient at expanding their sphere of legislative leverage, keeping association coffers crammed full, broadening their public relations message, unashamedly defending their membership, and with overwhelming successes were unconditionally committed to prosecuting obstreperous outlaws and "sons-a-bitchin' cow-thieves."[35] A religious Saint might have been able to walk on Pecos River waters, but in West Texas, if he failed to have the Association's blessing he couldn't have been elected to doodley-squat. Dave Allison had it!

An inordinate amount of Dave Allison's time may have been concentrated on the less than sensational duties of tax collecting, but, the sheriff as a conscientious conservator of the peace had always to stand ready for the unexpected. Peacekeeping was a sheriff's responsibility too. Many sheriffs prided themselves on wheeling and dealing among townsmen unarmed, reserving the right to retrieve their revolver from a desk drawer at the office."[36] Plentiful are historic Western stories where the county's top lawman is caught without his six-gun. Southwestern Sheriff Romulo Martinez of Santa Fe, on one occasion in attempting to affect an arrest was forced to chunk rocks at a suspect.[37] During his career, New Mexico lawman Dee Harkey unashamedly begged proposed arrestee Carl Gordon, "…I am an officer and want to arrest you, but I left my gun this morning at the wagon, and that is my hard luck." Exhibiting a healthy portion of common sense, Gordon turned over his six-shooter to Harkey, complaining, "Here take mine, I can't hit anything with it anyway."[38] Clearly, some sheriffs went unarmed, some of the time. Apparently Dave Allison wasn't one of them. As of yet, but one known photograph of Dave Allison while Midland County Sheriff has surfaced, and it unmistakably reveals the young lawman wearing a Colt's six-shooter on his right hip.

Llano Hotel, Midland, Texas, and celebrating cowboys come to town. Courtesy, Haley Memorial Library and History Center, Midland, Texas.

The youngest sheriff in the Lone Star State may have had a badge pinned to his vest, a revolver appended to his side, and a handful of court process to serve, but the promising days of Dave Allison had not been foreshadowed by a yearning jaunt down the matrimonial aisle—yet. Just how and exactly when, Dave Allison met an admittedly eye-catching eighteen year-old, Lena Lea Johnston, is indeterminate—but he did. Possibly it was at one of the local dances or parties which were the young societies "greatest amusements."[39] Whether or not Dave Allison attended the youthful merrymaking bashes is uncertain, but for sure, Lena, one of Midland's *belles*, with a delicate presence graced the festivities as she politely awaited a gentlemanly invitation to promenade out onto the dance-floor.[40]

Political expediency mandated Dave Allison's appearance at some Midland shindigs. Mrs. R. E. "May" Estes remembered, "We always had a big barbecue on the 4th of July. Everyone came. The cowmen donated beef for the barbecue. Ladies would bake cakes and pies, and make various kinds of salad. The men cooked beans in a huge iron kettle and 'son-of-a-gun', a West Texas delicacy. After eating, we would have speeches by all the candidates who were running for office. At night we had dances. Some of the men would call for the square dance. The young people would have a dance of their own, there they did the waltz and two-step. The preachers had a great time preaching about the sins of dancing the round dance. They predicted that young people who danced the waltz and two-step were bound for Hell."[41]

Lena, the daughter of Robert Washington and Lucy Ann Johnston, had been born in the Red River country of northeast Texas at Honey Grove, Fannin County.[42] Precisely when Lena made the move with her parents to West Texas, or as some chose to phrase it "the country God had forgotten," is uncertain, but unquestionably by the time Dave Allison meandered into the scene or onto the dance floor, the Johnstons were among Midland's prominent pioneering families.[43]

In 1888, the same year Allison was elected sheriff, the Connells, and John Scharbauer, three of Dave's four bondsmen, in response to the growing need for some type of financial institution to accommodate the booming West Texas cattle business had organized a private banking service. "From this hub of a financial structure, The First National Bank of Midland came into being."[44] One of the signatories on the *Organization Certificate* for the new bank was R. W. Johnston.[45] And it wasn't too long before Midland was "called the richest little town in Texas."[46] All because of the livestock business! A show made somewhat obvious by remarks made by a prolific frontier newspaperman, who penned "…Midland which is said to be the home of more wealthy cattlemen than any other town of several times its size in the United States."[47] Aside from his banking interests, as would be expected, R. W. Johnston was an area cattleman, with a registered brand, **J** on the left jaw, and a — on the left shoulder.[48] Although well-fixed, he wasn't a stuffy capitalist, but a cowman.

Details pertaining to the romance and courtship are scanty. Politically well-connected Sheriff William Davis "Dave" Allison, the son of an esteemed pioneering Texas physician, measured up—if any son-in-law could—to the high standard R. W. Johnston had set for his only girl child. When Dave Allison proposed marriage, asking for Lena's heart, he got it, and when from R. W. Johnston he effectively attained her hand and a fatherly blessing, the sacred promise was preserved. On February 21, 1889, at Midland, Texas, the renowned cowboy circuit riding preacher, L. R. Millican, a Minister of the Gospel, joined Dave Allison and Lena Johnston in Holy matrimony.[49]

Scandalous morsels concerning whether or not Dave and Lena were forced to suffer any cow-country frivolities on their wedding night are markedly hidden behind the bedroom door. Certainly it would not have come as a surprise to either had they been the target of what some knew as an old-fashioned "Belling," however, others just called the outrageous monkeyshines "fun". On one such occasion, Dave Allison *may* have participated, *maybe* not, but one of his deputies did, as well as his personal friend and area cattleman, John Scharbauer. An unidentified bullwhacker married one of the chambermaids of the Llano Hotel. After dark, with nary a cow creature to lasso, an owl-hoot to chase, or anything bordering on productive to do, an irreverent assemblage of pranksters painstakingly proceeded to the bridal-chamber door. Finding, not unsurprisingly, that it was locked—down it came! A nearly naked groom lunged for a shotgun, the half dressed blushing bride scooted further beneath the bedcovers. The bridegroom was physically restrained—a impotent prisoner of wedding night war. Scharbauer and Jim Flanigan, assisted by Dave Allison's deputy, Lod Calohan grabbed sheep man Ike Gronski and hurled him into the wedding bed with a screaming and scantily clad bride, which caused a "great commotion." Realizing the precariousness of the then current state of diplomatic affairs, and sizing up the strength of the enemy, the freshly married freighter acquiesced, stridently declared an unconditional surrender, hurriedly dressed, and good spiritedly treated all the valiant warriors to drinks at Worley's Saloon.[50]

The legitimate absence of a bride and groom was not necessarily just cause to cease the capricious cutting up. Again, as when most mischief is typically done, after dark, a squadron of jokesters literally picked up Henry Rohlfing's eight foot by ten foot peanut and candy store, moved it across the street, and then stealthily slinked back into the protective womb of night's darkness. The next day, Henry, full-well knowing it was better to laugh than to cry, affably stood for drinks at Worleys, and it wasn't too long before the little store was placed back on its proper foundation.[51]

Sometimes awkward attempts at tomfoolery would boomerang. Such was the case when Jeff Cowden roped the smokestack of a Texas & Pacific locomotive. The upshot? Incontrovertibly predictable! "He was almost killed, horse's leg broke and saddle tore to bits. Jeff never put his rope on any more engines, only maverick calves thereafter."[52] Every now and then a youthful cowboy's crack at humor or his dim-witted effort at venting pent-up frustrations took on darker tones—sometimes bordering on absurdity. "We were watering the herd in Brown and Youngblood's range one day, and it was quite a job to keep out strays. Bill Gates was having trouble with a 'Long S' cow. She finally headed for a water hole and Bill fore footed her just in time to roll her in the water hole. He jumped off his horse, grabbed her by the horns, and proceeded to water her. When he got through, she was well watered, never to need water any more."[53]

"Boys will be boys," so goes the saying, but from time to time what started out as coarse good-natured rowdiness, often seasoned with a splash or two of whiskey, frenziedly spiraled out of control, and sorrowfully ended in calamity. One of these led to murder, and an early arrest by Dave Allison.

W. L. "Lod" Calohan, renowned West Texas range detective and one of Dave Allison's first-rate "riding" deputies. Courtesy, Haley Memorial Library and History Center, Midland, Texas.

Noting that good manners were commonly in short supply during mealtimes at cow-camp chuck wagons, and disgusted with the inexplicable practice calling for cross-legged cowboys to seemingly spit something—somewhere—between each and every bite, a Midland hotel proprietor took it upon himself to assure proper etiquette had been dragged along the railroad tracks to West Texas. To partake a meal at his table required proper apparel, a coat. No jacket—No supper! To what level Ed Bunch's gills had been primed with neat whiskey is undetermined, perhaps he was quite full, maybe he was sober as a judge but, regardless, he observed the mandate to "dress for dinner." He donned a garment his compadres called a "fish," but many others simply referred to the yellow raincoat as a "slicker." Into the hotel dining room he stepped, formally attired, at least so he thought. And likewise, to just what degree an amber current had diluted and was flowing in Tom Murphy's blood is unknown, however, he took offense at Bunch's disrespectful shenanigan. For a few seconds sizzling words stewed, but then the fiery pot boiled over, and Ed Bunch plunged a knife into Tom Murphy's gut.[54]

Sheriff Dave Allison, accompanied by Midland County Deputy Sheriff Lod Calohan, rushed to the little hotel, made quick investigation, without fanfare arrested Ed Bunch, and attained medical help for the copiously bleeding Murphy. Later, as was common practice, Bunch's cattleman boss posted bond for his badly behaved cowboy, and the knife-wielding assailant was released pending Grand Jury action. Sadly, as a result of the stabbing, three weeks later Tom Murphy died.[55] On November 15, 1892, before a Midland Justice of the Peace, Sheriff Dave Allison swore out a complaint stating, "with malice aforethought (Bunch) did kill and murder one Thos. J. Murphy by stabbing him, the said Thos. J. Murphy with a knife, the same being a deadly weapon."[56]

With a murder charge now in the works, Dave Allison and deputy Calohan headed out to locate and re-arrest Ed Bunch. With knowledge his outfit was working cattle on the range northwest of Midland, the lawmen proceed to the vicinity "under the hill right east of Eunice," New Mexico Territory. In the distance, far off, Bunch's sympathetic boss man could see the two approaching riders. With rumor of Murphy's death already blowing in the wind the cowman rode up to Bunch who was riding a "big blaze hammer leg horse" and with a nod of his head and a wink, authoritatively suggested, "Why don't you ride over and turn those cattle a little to the left toward the draw." Ed Bunch wasn't a dummy and he nonchalantly coaxed the strays as directed, toward the depression and entirely out of sight.[57] Whatever had happened between two grown men was their own personal business the cowman mused, and from a no-nonsense standpoint he full-well knew Ed Bunch wasn't no "Goddamn cow-thief." That's all that really mattered!

When the pair of lawmen finally reached the cattleman, who had already planted himself squarely on the rocky ground, they remained glued in their saddles until politely invited to dismount. To foster good-will, Deputy Calohan produced a quart of whiskey, and the trio exchanged pleasantries, visited, and imbibed. After a while, the cowman looked west toward the fast fading brilliantly orange sun, and inquired, "Dave do you want Ed?" Sheriff Dave Allison, a cowboy at heart, with seeming indifference casually replied, "Yes, Murphy is dead and I thought I would go and get him. I saw him riding into the setting Sun just as I taken that drink of whiskey" Lazily the law enforcement confab lasted. With ease, Ed Bunch "just kept riding."[58]

According to one report, if it is to be believed, while Dave Allison and Calohan were out on this mission, scouring the range for Bunch, they happened upon "an old half-Indian," Eph Campbell, and for some undisclosed charge, arrested him. Returning to Midland and caught in a nasty blizzard, the arrestors and the arrestee holed up at a handy ranch house. "Old Eph taken an awful case of bowel trouble, and kept bothering them to go out with him…It was cold and they didn't think he would go off in his underclothes, and he just kept going. They lost him. He went off in his underclothes."[59]

Although it may come as surprise to modern-day readers, especially those entertaining idealistically romantic notions of just how imposition of the criminal justice system does, or was supposed to work, in truth it was not at all uncommon, and in some cases even downright predictable for law enforcers to adopt a somewhat lethargic way of doing things. In the grand scheme, Sheriff Dave Allison knew Ed Bunch would have to answer for his alleged crime—sooner or later—when that time came there was not the slightest doubt in Allison's mind that he had sufficient sand in his system to get the job done. Out on the range, away from town, things weren't always as they might first appear. It was in some ways a game—with rules. And in cow camps throughout the American West it would have been untenable, an indefensible violation of the unwritten covenant for a cowboy's boss to cooperatively turn him over to lawmen. A cattleman or foreman that would do that, well, they themselves might suffer personnel recruiting dilemmas at the next Spring roundup. There was no profit to be had from grazing cattle absent cowboys to gather, work, herd, and ship the bellowing beeves. Cowboying was by tradition transitory. Treat one right and he'd die defending the ranch brand, treat one wrong—he'd be gone. In the cow business, smart managers of men made it—fools suffered consequences. When Bunch's employer tipped him off to approaching man hunters he was fulfilling his part of the cowboy's contract. When Ed Bunch silently slipped away, causing no undue commotion and not stirring up the herd, taking his personal troubles on down the road, he was living up to his end of an unspoken bargain. After a reasonable time had been allowed to pass, the cowman had made forthright inquiry as to the sheriff's mission, at the same time he *pointedly* looked toward a sinking western sun, suggestively giving a tacit clue—doing his civic duty—but still able to truthfully swear before an all knowing God and any skeptically minded cowboys that he hadn't "talked!" If Sheriff Dave Allison had hastily jumped to his feet, charged after, and then straight away captured the wanted man, Ed Bunch and all his buckaroo buddies would have surmised the boss snitched off his whereabouts—the word would have spread. True or not, damage to the cowman's reputation would have been done. Dave Allison understood how the game was played.

Patience reaps reward. Later, over in Arizona, just as Sheriff Dave Allison knew would eventually happen somewhere, fugitive Ed Bunch got nabbed. The Territorial Governor issued an *Executive Department Extradition Warrant* authorizing W. D. Allison to "forthwith take and transport said Ed Bunch to the line of this Territory…"[60] So in the end, discretion proved a not unwise course, the Blind Mistress of Justice had her defendant—neither a lawman nor a bad guy was gratuitously gunned down—a West Texas cattleman still owned his good name while he hobnobbed and warmed his hands with the hired-help at cow-camp cook-fires scattered across the Staked Plains.

Nine months after their Midland marriage, on November 24, 1889, William Davis "Dave" and Lena Lea Allison were blessed with their one and only child, a girl, and baby Hazel became the absolute apple of her father's eye.[61] It would be a good place to raise a youngster. Like so many Western communities, Midland, although forlorn looking at first glance was in fact thriving, due largely to a booming cattle industry and the sustaining connection with the rest of the world provided by the railroad.[62] Residents could well depend on modern conveniences, provided they were possessed with a smidgen of sensible patience. Had there been a horrendous train wreck delaying delivery of delicious foodstuffs nobody would have starved or been forced to skip too many meals. Even though the surrounding landscape had an unfruitful appearance, for a proficient human predator the hunting harvest could indeed prove bountiful. Hunger could be sated with healthy portions of rabbit, quail, plover, venison, antelope, and of course beef—beef—and more beef—which in turn provided fresh milk and butter which could be cooled in a box of running water above windmill tanks. Not only could the skillful huntsman put game on his own table, were he so inclined, he could sell any overkill to butcher Albert Lee, who advertised in the local newspaper, "we will buy all the game you will bring in, and pay the best market price of the same."[63] One early resident didn't mince words, "We had good food."[64] Full of pride Midlandnites could boast of merchants, mechanics, medical practitioners, magnanimous money men, meticulously mannered socialites, ministers, maybe even a few mendacious attorneys, and a couple of persnickety but professionally proficient schoolteachers. Midland was on the move! There were, however, no bragging rights regarding water. It was in short supply! Thankfully, windmills offered a solution, and Midland became known as a "windmill city."[65] On balance, Dave and Lena Allison knew Midland was just the place, the right place for Hazel to grow up.

It was just the right place for Dave Allison too. By all accounts he was exceedingly well respected and subsequent events will clearly reveal he was popular with an electorate who returned him to office time and time again.[66] Additionally, aside from his own background, he married into a well-respected and financially secure Midland family. Since much of the ranching was carried out on Open Range, although the use of barbed wire fencing was steadily increasing, the exact extent of Dave Allison's cattle operations cannot be precisely documented. Whether or not he ranched with his father-in-law, cattleman and financier R. W. Johnston is undetermined, but in Midland County Dave Allison registered livestock brands under his own name. A running **A** to be branded on both shoulders of cattle, and a **P** on the left jaw of horses, as well as a — on the left thigh.[67] His position as County Sheriff and Tax Collector, coupled with his involvement in the cow business, seems to offer evidence that Dave Allison while at Midland was believably prosperous, and is further evidenced by his $600.00 purchase of, "all of block number one hundred and seventeen (117) in Southern addition to the Town of Midland..."[68]

Sprouting cattleman or not, on occasion Sheriff Dave Allison was obligated to saddle up and assume the role of a frontier lawman. In one such case, Allison, along with Texas Rangers, chased after brigands who had stolen horses and saddles from Bob Beverly and Bill Welch while the boys had been in delightful attendance at a big "*baile*" at Comstock, down in the Devil's River country west of Del Rio. After an extended trip of rough riding over exceptionally torturous topography, Allison and the Rangers forcefully, but safely, captured the loathsome thieves near Pecos City, in the broken country southwest of Midland. The prisoners were held tightly manacled in custody until Val Verde County Sheriff Jones managed train connections, finally arrived at Pecos City and officially latched on to the "damn horse-thieves." The two stolen horses were quickly reunited with their owners.[69]

Chasing after West Texas horse thieves and brand-blotchers may seem like stirring fun, a great open-air adventure, but in actuality it was dicey business. Sheriff Dave Allison's working relationship with the State Forces was beneficially reciprocal, professionally productive, and carried forth with warm and cordial individual friendships. *Possibly* he was personally acquainted with Texas Ranger Charles H. "Charley" Fusselman, and *maybe* the young lawman was one of those who from time to time assisted Sheriff Dave Allison in running odious livestock thieves to ground; *perhaps* not. Unquestionably though, the Midland County Sheriff was shocked when word traveled back down the line. On April 17, 1890, at El Paso, Fusselman, in town for a criminal court case, was notified by Mundy Springs rancher John Barnes that Mexican outlaws had made off with some of his horses and cattle.[70] El Paso city policeman, George Harold, himself a former Texas Ranger, and a veteran of the Round Rock, Texas, shoot-out with the notorious bandit, Sam Bass, volunteered to accompany Fusselman in pursuit of the outlaws.[71] Fusselman, Harold, and cattleman Barnes charged forth. Knowing the thieves would make for New Mexico Territory and then across the international line, the diminutive three-man posse scurried north out of town and into the inhospitable and craggy looking Franklin Mountains. Headlong after the fleeing banditos, the squad of lawmen finally caught up with Ysidoro Pasos, who was serving as a rear guard.[72] Taking custody of Pasos, who had been caught napping on the job, the lawmen unrelentingly quickened their pace in the frantic race. Unbelievably, Fusselman, who had been riding the fastest horse cleared a ridge line and inadvertently blazed and blundered right into the outlaw's momentary camping spot. Bullets zinged! Realizing the fat was already in the fire, Fusselman yelled, "Boys, we're in it, so let's stay with it."[73] Unremittingly levering his Winchester, brigand Geronimo Parra at last managed to put a bullet into Fusselman's head. The twenty-four year old Texas Ranger died in the saddle. A withering fire caused Harold and Barnes to scramble for cover, lose control of prisoner Pasos, and hasten their retreat back to El Paso for reinforcements.[74] Later, ten years later, there would be a pay back for Geronimo Parra.[75] Over in Midland County, Sheriff Dave Allison full-well knew catching crooks could prove a dangerous occupation, and Fusselman's death accentuated his resolve. Take no chances!

That Sheriff Dave Allison lived up to the categorization of *fearlessness* is indisputable, but recklessly foolish he assuredly was not. During one incident, again accompanied by his sometimes deputy, Lod Calohan, who has admirably and accurately been described as "a good rough and tumble cowman" and a "good hand on the range," one who "knew all the men that was stealing and all the men that wasn't," Sheriff Dave Allison took out after a gang of damn troublesome horse-thieves. Somewhere, between mudless Midland and the winding Pecos River, Allison and Calohan caught sight of the hard-ridin' miscreants, and pressed the chase. Unbeknownst to the two weary officers, the pursued party was armed with the latest model .30-.30 caliber smokeless powder Winchester rifles, capable of much more effective long-range accuracy than the lawman's seemingly short barreled .44-.40 caliber saddle-ring carbines. Neither Dave Allison or his deputy had ever run up against such technologically superior weaponry. When the bullets started flying in their direction, zinging by all too close for sensible comfort, Lod complained to his boss, "We ain't got no guns like that," and cognizant that there was indeed advantage in living to fight another day, Dave simply remarked "Lets go back to town."[76] Which they did!

The records are sparse, lacking details, but they still reflect that Sheriff Dave Allison's arrest minutes ran the gamut of what would typically be anticipated of a conscientious frontier lawman. There are incarcerations for Keeping and Exhibiting a Gaming Table and Bank; Unlawfully Carrying a Pistol; Aggravated Assault; Murder; Passing as True a Forged Instrument; Disturbing Public Worship; and undoubtedly to the obdurate happiness of the Texas and Southwestern Cattle Raisers Association, a vigorous sampling of arrests for stealing livestock—cattle and horses.[77] And, although the details are hopelessly inadequate, an examination of these old arrest records reveals that the sheriff himself was arrested. The *complaint* simply stated that "W. D. Allison and J. H. Brown …with force and arms, did then and there unlawfully fight together in a Public place."[78] Which combatant actually bested the other remains historically elusive, as does the disposition of the case, although reasonable *speculation* suggests that both *probably* paid a nominal fine. What is not speculative, however, is that on another occasion, Sheriff Dave Allison was forced to arrest his esteemed deputy, Lod Calohan, for the very same offense.[79]

To satisfactorily comprehend Sheriff Dave Allison's everyday activities, he and other Western sheriffs of the time period operated under a fee system, and did not draw a predetermined monthly salary. Specifically, Dave Allison as Midland County Sheriff, received $1.00 for making an arrest, $.50 for serving a summons, $1.00 for approving a bail bond, $2.00 per day for attending a prisoner, and was paid $.05 per mile on the out trip to make an arrest or to serve court papers, but should he return with a reprehensible prisoner in tow, he was compensated at the rate of

$.25 per mile for travel by private conveyance, or if traveling by train with the prisoner he was paid at the rate of $.15 per mile.[80] As but one example, in Midland County Criminal Case Number 93, *The State of Texas vs. Juan Beuabrdes*, the defendant was charged with murder. Sheriff Dave Allison traveled to the vicinity 30 miles from Fort Stockton, Pecos County, Texas, made the arrest and returned via Horsehead Crossing on the Pecos River. At Midland, court process was served on potential witnesses, and after the Sheriff's fees were totaled for the case, Dave Allison billed the county in the amount of $109.25.[81] A not insubstantial amount for the time period, although in the majority of cases the compensation was much less. Nevertheless, a hard working county sheriff could make a decent living, and those possessing political savvy could usually parlay their social, business, and governmental contacts into other lucrative positions. Sheriff Dave Allison, as old Midland County records reveal, was industrious, and he plainly maintained the knack for getting along in a Western frontier community—especially one comprised of cowmen, cowboys, and the capitalizing citizens who were catering to their wants, needs, and desires. The sheriff's job at Midland now and again was dangerous, periodically mandated strenuously tiring travel, and at all times was a nightmare of paperwork, fiscal figuring, and boundless bureaucratic business. Sheriff Dave Allison needed a little help.

"The sheriff looked for certain qualifications in a deputy. The candidate for a deputyship had to be a person of known bravery, possess proficiency with guns, be able to ride horseback for long periods, and be familiar with the countryside."[82] In Lod Calohan, Sheriff Dave Allison had a darn good one, a deputy especially knowledgeable of cattle brands, because from early on, as Bob Beverly asserts, he had an insight to the open range country—all that open range country—where there were no fences—while he worked for Dave Allison.[83]

Following a common frontier practice, Dave Allison gave deputyships to his little brothers, John and George Clive, no doubt subscribing to the adage "blood is thicker than water."[84] Historian Larry Ball offers the sheriff's rationale, "Not only did the county lawmen desire to provide relatives with economic opportunities to better themselves, but the sheriffs feared political enemies were always trying to compromise their deputies. Deputies with family or marriage ties to the chief lawman provided additional bonds against such threats…Family appointments probably took place in most county shrievalties, although some sheriffs were more enthusiastic about this than others."[85] Sheriff Dave Allison *probably* tasked the young deputies with serving routine court process and maintaining an official presence in administrative positions at the courthouse office. Regardless of assignment, both were legit lawmen and were required to swear under oath that they would:

> …faithfully and impartially discharge and perform all the duties incumbent upon a Deputy Sheriff of Midland County Texas according to the best of my skill and ability, agreeably to the Constitution and Laws of the United States and of this State; and I further solemnly swear, or affirm, that since the adoption of the Constitution of this State, I being a citizen of this State, have not fought a duel with deadly weapons within this State, nor out of it, nor have I sent or accepted a challenge to fight a duel with deadly weapons, nor have I acted as second in carrying a challenge, or aided, advised or assisted any person thus offending; and I furthermore solemnly swear, or affirm, that I have not, directly or indirectly, paid, offered or promised to pay, contributed not promised to contribute, any money or valuable thing, or promised any public office or employment, as a reward to secure my appointment as such Deputy, *so help me God!*[86]

On another occasion, J. H. Mims swore in an affidavit that he had "reason to believe and does viably believe that his life is in danger, and that he makes this affidavit for the purpose of obtaining permission from the Sheriff of Midland County to go prepared to defend himself—under the law against any danger that might arise against the defense of his person." Dave Allison, not necessarily expecting any law enforcement work from him, nevertheless deputized Mims so that he might legally go armed during his day to day activities, and not suffer public humiliation, possibly having to "tuck tail and run."[87] In West Texas there was no duty to retreat!

Another example of Allison handing out a deputy sheriff's commission raises intriguing questions and leaves sufficient room for conjecture. At least for awhile, according to two sources, Dave Allison tendered a Midland County Deputy's badge to Mannie Clements, Jr., son of Emanuel (Manning) Clements, Sr. who had been shot and killed by Sheriff Joe Townsend at Ballinger, Runnels County, Texas, during an 1887 hell-to-pop episode.[88] Suffice to say that Mannie Clements, Jr. was a notorious character in his own right, considered by many in the Southwest to be a notable "sporting" or "race horse" man, and not just a few thought him a conspiratorial partner in more than one baffling murder.[89] That Sheriff Dave Allison associated with Clements there is no doubt, as evidenced by an excerpt from a letter he wrote to a disreputably known Huntsville ex-convict and man-killer, John Wesley Hardin, regarding the likely forfeiture of John Denson's bail bond:

> *...Manning Clements is at my home this evening, wounded in right hip. "Flesh Wound" from an accidental discharge of his pistol, While it is painful, yet it is not dangerous and he shall have good Care. and attention, He Sat down on a cott* (sic), *and pitched his pistol on a palate on The floor. And the hammer being on a cartridge, it was discharged...*[90]

Whether or not Mannie Clements ultimately had any undue harmful influence on Dave Allison will always remain a mystery, but clearly from any legitimate viewpoint, if true, it was an ill-advised law enforcement appointment.[91] An additional state of weird affairs involving a notorious character and Dave Allison was an unhelpful newspaper blurb; but in truth, the matter was perfectly explicable.

It seems an iniquitous Martin Mroz of southeastern New Mexico fame, in the congenial company of his beloved common-law companion, Helen Beulah, who was depicted as "a wild, hard, heavy, good looking blonde," had somehow deduced that a short vacation from their regular stomping grounds around budding Eddy and wicked Phenix, New Mexico, was in order. The trip would be made all the more pleasurable, considering that Mroz was wandering about just one wretched step ahead of the law. Although pathetically minor (possible theft of livestock feed), nevertheless, the criminal charges were real, and upon learning of his whereabouts about twenty miles north of Midland, Sheriff Dave Allison was obliged to make an arrest. Upon Martin Mroz's solemn promise that formal legalistic extradition proceedings weren't really necessary, and since his bail bond in the case would amount to but a paltry $300, an agreement was reached whereas the dog-tired couple could comfortably overnight at a private Midland hotel, rather than occupy a public financed cold-steel cell. Sorry to say, and much to Sheriff Dave Allison's chagrin, when he called upon on the pair next morning, he sadly discovered the lovebirds had flown the coop and were steadily ridin' like hell, diligently focused on earning their very own wayward pages in Old West history books.[92]

Aside from deputizing two of his brothers, Dave Allison was no doubt exceedingly proud of another brother, who had by hard work and self-discipline managed a medical education. By the year 1893, Dr. Luke Pryor Allison was licensed to practice medicine at Midland, and sometime later he was named the County Physician. During 1897, after noting a case of Scarlet Fever, Dr. Allison established a rigid quarantine, scrupulously guarding against an infectious catastrophe of epidemic proportion.[93]

At thirty-one years of age, the auburn-haired Dave Allison applied for an appointment as a Special Texas Ranger, "to serve the State without pay" subject to the orders and authority of the Texas Adjutant-General's Office.[94] Under special provisions, a number of Special Ranger commissions had been authorized and allocated to the Texas and Southwestern Cattle Raisers Association.[95] With the blessings and official endorsement of Association Secretary J. C. Loving, son of cattle industry pioneer, Oliver Loving, the youngest sheriff in the state of Texas was commissioned a Special Ranger.[96] Certainly Dave Allison did not abdicate his throne as king of Midland County lawmen, but armed with the Special Ranger Commission, wherever he went in search of those "Goddamn cow-thieves," all over the gigantic Lone Star State, his peace officer status was best not challenged, nor the gargantuan authority that went with it. To the uninitiated in cattle-country custom, it might seem somehow inappropriate for a wholly private organization, one tightly bound with the cords of economic special interests, to possess and pay their very own cadre of officially commissioned and state sanctioned peace officers, but such was, *and is*, the magnanimous weight of the beef business in Texas.[97]

The practice of cross-deputization was in fact quite common on the Southwestern frontier, the most common example being between deputy United States Marshals and local sheriffs.[98] "It made sense for a sheriff or deputy sheriff to be vested with federal authority."[99] Clearly when a sheriff or deputy rode out into the wild reaches of sometimes huge jurisdictional areas to serve county court process, it was only smart to empower them to conduct federal business on the same mile-racking trip.[100] Eastern New Mexico lawman Dee Harkey may have set the record. "I said I had six sets of duties. I was sheriff J. D. Walker's deputy and United States deputy marshal, from the time I went over and talked to the Phoenix bunch about behaving themselves. I had been elected constable and then I was made cattle inspector for the Cattle Raisers' Association of Texas, and the same for the Cattle Sanitary Board of New Mexico, and to complete the list I was appointed town marshal."[101] Sheriff William Davis Allison's primary allegiance, unquestionably, was to the law, but a little work for the Association from time to time no doubt added financial and political capital to his account. A sheriff needed both.

From the best accounts of old-timers and through imprints of genealogical lore passed from one Allison generation to the next, it can generally be said that Dave was iron-willed, unreservedly determined, and as previously documented in this biography, absolutely *fearless*. One such example of family lore, told by a descendent with authority, is that on one manhunt Sheriff Dave Allison, deep in the dead of a bitterly and dangerously cold winter, doggedly tracked a fugitive for four days and nights. After finally making an arrest, and deep-freezing the prisoner at the jailhouse, Dave Allison returned home and family members had to literally pry the frozen leather reins from his gloved hands, and actually chip away ice from his saddle so that the near frozen lawman could finally dismount and thaw out before a welcoming fire.[102]

Fortunately, however, in telling Dave Allison's story there are primary source materials that may be counted on to augment frostbitten family remembrances, no matter how truthful and attention-grabbing they may be. One of which was the *Knowles News*, in New Mexico Territory, which editorialized that Dave Allison "was one of the very best peace officers the Southwest ever produced."[103] Of the young Texas sheriff, another out of state newspaper, the *St. Louis Post-Dispatch* reported:

> Dave Allison had been a man of much experience in gun fights. Though according to repute he was inclined to peace, as Sheriff and Ranger he had found it necessary to engage in many hand-to-hand combats. It is of record that during his 12 years as Sheriff of Midland County he never went after a man he did not get, though as a rule he took his prisoners alive. Men sought by Sheriff Allison knew his reputation for coolness in emergencies, and he was not an officer to be resisted by men who care to keep their hides intact.[104]

A *Roswell Daily Record* editor characterizes Dave Allison as being *fearless* in one story, and follows up in another saying the prominent lawman "was recognized as one of the most efficient officers of the Southwest."[105] Closer to home, a reporter for the *El Paso Times* credited Allison as being one of the best pistol shots in the Southwest, an appraisal echoed by none other than the "Border Boss" himself, Texas Ranger Captain John R. Hughes, who depicted Dave as being "absolutely *fearless*."[106] Dan Thrapp, in his three volume *Encyclopedia of Frontier Biography*, although mistaken on a few specific material facts about the subject of this particular biography, offers in summation that Dave Allison was "considered the most efficient sheriff in the history of the Lone Star state."[107] A modern-era professional educator looking in on Dave Allison's law enforcement life has determined, "Allison knew how to use a gun and was not afraid to do so when the need arose."[108] Area cowmen, through their rightful and understandably partisan voice, *The Cattleman*, of Dave Allison's tenure as Midland County Sheriff remarked, "…he made a record surpassed by none as a peace officer…"[109]

But more telling than any sugar-coated accolades heaped on Dave Allison are the justifiable fears of his enemies, who thought Allison was a man of "…violent and dangerous character" and a man "reasonably calculated to execute any threats made…"[110] For a true-grit, no BS Southwestern lawman, admiration from honest folk was fine and dandy, but an earned loathing from the conniving criminal crowd was a badge to be worn with distinctive honor, especially if a few of em' were "Goddamn cow-thieves."

Sadly, and unfortunately the details are scant, but on April 19, 1895, Dave Allison's little brother, John, just short of his twenty-second birthday, passed away from an undetermined cause at Midland.[111] Assuredly John's death, right in the very prime of life, overwhelmed Sheriff Dave Allison who without question loved his younger brother, but also looked upon him as a working partner and police protégé.

Another young man, however, was alive and very much kicking. That Mississippi boy, Hillary U. Loftis, at any early age had made it to Texas, and for awhile cowboyed for Dan Waggoner's Three **DDD** (reversed) brand up in the Red River country, north of Vernon, Wilbarger County.[112] John Allison, before he died, had ridden his pony up to that career line, turned to the right, and headed down the law enforcement trail. Hill Loftis went the other way. For whatever reason, and little does it really matter, Hillary Loftis had joined up with Dalton/Doolin gang veteran, George "Red Buck" Waightman and his little band of cutthroats.[113] On December 24, 1895, a passel of the murderous misfits, comprised of "Red Buck," ex-Motley County Sheriff Joe Beckham, castaway cowboy Elmer "Kid" Lewis, and the hooligan trainee, Hillary Loftis, robbed and pistol-whipped "nearly to death" a clerk at Waggoner's company store."[114] Leaving him on the floor to die, gurgling in his own blood, the killers desperately fled the crime scene, but only a short time later hijacked Alf Bailey's store and post office at Rondie (Ronda), Texas making off with "cash, stamps, and merchandise worth $700."[115] After their gutless skullduggery, the mounted gangsters hightailed it north, frantically running from the lynch law in pursuit.

Fighting bitterly cold weather a twenty-two man posse, composed of Texas Rangers, local lawmen, and a few citizens, all under the command of Ranger Sergeant W. John L. Sullivan blasted off into a howling North Texas wind.[116] Eventually determining the outlaws were "holed up" in a line rider's dugout twenty miles to the north, near the Red River, the platoon of frosty fighters late in the evening began closing in on the predator's lair. Forewarned by an alert sentinel, volley after volley of horrific rifle-fire was unleashed on the advancing lawdogs. Scampering for cover on hard frozen ground posse men laid siege, and answered shot for shot, killing their horses to cut off any attempt at escape.[117] Perhaps it's true or maybe it's a dash of West Texas folklore, but a newspaperman penned, "…that Joe Beckham, who was a fiddler of the old-time type, sat on a bunk in the dugout when he got tired of shooting at the flashes and played tunes on his fiddle. A bullet from down the draw hit against the door jamb, when somebody inside had opened the door a bit to do some shooting. The bullet glanced and hit Joe Beckham in the eye, killing him in the midst of a merry fiddle tune that he never finished."[118] As darkness fell, so fell the temperature. Lower and lower it dropped, making unworkable fingers and Winchester levers, alike. It was a bone-chilling game, and even though the law were superior in numbers, this deadening winter night the outlaws had Old Man Winter on their treacherous team—the lawmen were forced to forfeit the field.[119] Returning to the arena of battle next day under only lukewarm solar rays, lawmen tallied the scorecard. Bad guys? Four dead horses! One dead crook! Joe Beckham laid lifelessly stretched on the dugout's dirt floor, icicle stiff. "Red Buck" Waightman, "Kid" Lewis, and Hillary Loftis? Off somewhere to play another day.[120]

And, to be sure, that panicky Mississippi boy would have to go off somewhere, somewhere far off, because his outlaw activities had managed him a reserved spot in the next edition of the *Ranger Bible*, a list of wanted fugitives:

> Wanted for highway robbery, Hill Loftis. Age about 32, height 5 feet 9 inches, weight 160 pounds. Has a very peculiarly shaped head, being very long behind with a

> high forehead. Occupation, cowboy. Probably in New Mexico. Indicted in 1896. Reward by sheriff of Wilbarger County.[121]

Sheriff Dave Allison was accepted by Midland County voters who rewarded him with the title of Sheriff on six separate occasions. And every now and then, he got more than just a little help from cattle country cohorts, some of whom weren't necessarily even Midland County residents, a detail explained by tireless ranch country historian J. Evetts Haley, "Barnes Tillous, the famous Quien Sabe boss, was passing Midland in 1896 with a herd on the trail, and all the cowboys rode in to vote for the re-election of Dave Allison as sheriff."[122]

From an earnest evaluation of existing evidence it is clear Dave Allison was an upright family man—a loving husband—a good daddy. However, to coin a popular phrase, Sheriff Dave Allison "wasn't living at the foot of the Cross." Dave Allison liked to gamble! The cow business was in fact a gamble, and policing at times could prove a frantically exhilarating win or lose game, but candidly it must be admitted, a dispassionate inspection exposes that Dave Allison craved more.[123]. Sheriff Dave Allison, it was alleged, messed up Midland County Sheriff's Office books—$10,000 worth by one account.[124] In another version, Sheriff Dave Allison simply had "official troubles of his own."[125] Did he embezzle tax-payer's funds? On the sly, did he for the short term miss-appropriate Midland monies, having in mind to refill county coffers later? Was it just a case of bungled bookkeeping? Family emergency? Did he let some cattle-country chums skate on their tax bills?

In the final objective analysis, there seems an ample measure of ambiguity in the official resolution proffered by the Midland County Commissioner's Court regarding Dave Allison's decision to voluntarily surrender the Sheriff's job. In part it reads:

> "...Be it resolved by this Court that Midland County has lost a faithful and efficient officer, who, during his long term of office has ever been faithful in the discharge of all his official duties..."[126]

It is worth noting that during this same chancy time period, Dave Allison was arrested and charged with Gaming, a case in which he ultimately paid a fine and court cost.[127] Had the *fearless* Sheriff verily overplayed his hand?

As subsequent events will make plain, Dave Allison, despite the Midland County controversy, continued to retain the admiration and approval of most local cowmen, fellow West Texas peace officers, and probably most importantly, the Texas and Southwest Cattle Raisers Association. During February 1898, William Davis "Dave" Allison officially resigned as Midland County Sheriff and relinquished his local law enforcement commission.[128]

ENDNOTES
Chapter 2. "we ain't got no guns like that"

1 *The New Handbook of Texas*, Volume IV, P. 706. "Because other towns in Texas were already named Midway, the site was renamed Midland to get the post office." And see, **Kingston**. P. 246. Also, **Gournay**, P. 107.
2 Ibid. "By 1890 it had become one of the most important cattle shipping centers in the state…"
3 **DeArment**. P. 12. The author once again completes a thoroughly competent effort at brief biographical sketches of Allison, his partner H. L. Roberson, and the men who killed them.
4 Numerous are the examples of Dave Allison's cowboy skills, as have been and will be cited. Remarks regarding his horse training abilities can be found in the remembrances of Arizona old-timer Arcus Reddoch and will be specifically addressed during this narrative when chronologically appropriate.
5 *Schedule of Property*, Midland County, Texas. On November 13, 1888, W. E. Connell declared that among other property he owned 108 acres of land in Brown County. E. H. Estes cited that he owned 320 acres in Brown County. Courtesy Texas State Library and Archives Commission, Austin. And see, *The New Handbook of Texas*, Volume II, P. 271. "He (W. E. Connell) entered the ranching business at the age of fourteen and, working with his father's cattle during most of the year, attended school only in the winter."
6 *Certification of Surety Bonds*, by Midland County Clerk A. B. Rountree, November 14, 1888. Courtesy Texas State Library and Archives Commission, Austin. John Scharbauer had come to the Midland area in 1880, and after first prospering as a sheep raiser, he later switched financial investments to the cattle business and became a remarkably prominent West Texas rancher. *The New Handbook of Texas*, Volume V, P. 913.
7 **Kerber**, Frances, (**Consultant**). *The Pioneer History of Midland County, Texas,1880-1926*. Hereafter cited as **Kerber**. P. 79. Elisha Hamilton "Lish" Estes was born on November 19, 1849, in Navarro County, the son of Tennessee native, Aaron Estes, and his wife Elizabeth. "Lish" grew up in the cow business and after maturing past "wage work," established ranches near the Colorado River at the mouth of Oak Creek, later in Mitchell County, then Yellow House Canyon and in 1885 moved to the Midland area, establishing a large ranch at Monument Springs, New Mexico Territory. Still later he ranched in "Old Mexico," but returned to Midland area and joined up with another of Allison's bondsmen, John Scharbauer in a successful cattle operation. Estes became "one of the best known of the pioneer cattlemen in Texas." Still later, and the fact will prove important in the telling of Allison's story, Estes moved to Van Horn, Culberson County, where he founded a large ranch near Victoria Canyon in the Van Horn Mountains. Information on E. H. Estes to the above titled volume was the contribution of Nancy R. **McKinley**, Midland, Texas.
8 Ibid.
9 Interview with Nancy R. **McKinley**, the granddaughter of "Lish" and Nancy Estes at Midland on March 11, 2001. Monument Springs is located in Lea County, New Mexico about 12 miles southwest of the city of Hobbs. See, *The Place Names of New Mexico* by Robert **Julyan**. P. 233. Hereafter cited as **Julyan**.

---

[10] Transcript. Bob Beverly to J. Evetts **Haley**. June 27, 1946. And see, Beverly to **Haley**, June 23, 1946. "...He (Allison) came here with that Brown County bunch. You see there were two factions in Midland always—one was the Brazos River bunch and one was the Colorado River bunch...The Brazos bunch, that was the Baptist bunch. They all come in out of the Palo Pinto and that country, you know, in the early days and then the other bunch come in the Esteses and all that bunch out of Coleman, Brown (Brownwood) and the Colorado River country..." Courtesy, The Nita Stewart Haley Memorial Library and The J. Evetts Haley History Center, Midland.

[11] That he went to work for the Connells at Midland is part of Allison family lore, and is also confirmed by the remarks of Texas and Southwestern Cattle Raisers Association attorney Dayton Moses. See, "Closing Argument For The State In Cause No. 592, *The State of Texas vs. Tom Ross*, 72nd Judicial District of Texas," by Dayton Moses. Copies of these closing arguments are contained in numerous collections, ie., Texas and Southwestern Cattle Raisers Association Archives, Fort Worth; Southwest Collection—Texas Tech University, Lubbock; The Nita Stewart Haley Memorial Library And The J. Evetts Haley History Center, Midland; The Texas Ranger Hall of Fame and Museum Archives, Waco; as well as the personal collections of Pat **Treadwell**, Tahoka, Texas; and Bill **O'Neal**, Carthage, Texas, the author of numerous titles on Western history, one of which is the acclaimed, *The Arizona Rangers*. The *Closing Argument* will hereafter be cited as **Moses**.

[12] **Kerber**. P. 6. Article contributed by Betty **Luther**. "It was so sandy that people shoveled drifts away from fences."

[13] **McCallum**, Henry D. and Frances T., *The Wire That Fenced the West.* P. 12.

[14] Letter to Texas State Comptroller, Austin, Texas from Midland County Clerk, A. B. Rountree, November 14, 1888. Courtesy Texas State Library and Archives Commission, Austin.

[15] **Treadwell**, Allison family genealogical papers.

[16] **Bishop**, Lorene., *In The Life and Lives of Brown County People—Civil War Veterans Biographical Sketches—Book Ten.* P. 3. And, **Treadwell**, Allison family genealogical papers.

[17] **Treadwell**, Allison family genealogical research and papers. Dave's sister Pattie died in Brownwood, Texas as did his brother Luke Pryor "Doc" Allison. Dave's mother, Mary, and his brother, John, died at Midland, Texas, and his youngest sister, Clara Belle Allison Watson died at Ranger, Texas.

[18] **Moses**.

[19] **Treadwell**. Generally it is believed by family members that after "Uncle Dave" quit cowboying in Midland he kept the books at an area hardware store. Other reports, although unverifiable, indicate he was charged with keeping ranching business records.

[20] **Rynning**, Thomas H., *Gunnotches,* P. 293. Hereafter cited as **Rynning**.

[21] *St. Louis Post Dispatch*, July 29, 1923.

[22] *The Cattleman*, May 1923. "Cattle Thieves Kill Two Association Inspectors". Quotation from a letter to the Texas and Southwestern Cattle Raisers Association. The letter writer is not identified. P. 16.

[23] Ibid. Excerpt from a separate letter, and once again, the letter writer is not identified.

[24] **Bean**, Tom and **Hawley**, Scrub. "Rustler Tom Ross Died Young, But Still Years Past His Time," *Livestock Weekly*. 1996.

---

[25] **Fenton (II)**. P. 85
[26] **DeArment**. P. 13.
[27] **Pettey**, Weston A., "Seminole Incident," Unpublished Typescript. P. 19. Courtesy Nita Stewart Haley Memorial Library & J. Evetts Haley History Center. Midland. The published version of this manuscript appeared in the 1980 *West Texas Historical Association Year Book* and will hereafter be cited as **Pettey**.
[28] *Certificate of Election*, certifying W. D. Allison's election to Sheriff and Tax Collector of Midland County, Texas, dated November 12, 1888. And see, *Governor's Proclamation*, reflecting W. D. Allison's election as Midland County Sheriff, signed by Texas Governor L. S. Ross, dated January 16, 1889. Courtesy, Texas State Library and Archives Commission. Austin. And interview with Nancy **McKinley**, Midland County Historical Society. The other Midland County officials were County Judge E. B. Lancaster; A. B. Rountree, District and County Clerk; W. J. Mosley, County Attorney; J. F. Collona, County Treasurer; H. J. James, County Surveyor; C. A. Winborne, Hide and Animal Inspector; and A. S. Hawkins, Justice of the Peace. See *Midland Gazette*, November 9, 1889 as reprinted in the *Midland Reporter-Telegram*, Special Centennial Edition, 1985.
[29] *Schedule of Property to Accompany Bond of Tax Collector, Midland County*. Also see, Certification of Midland County Clerk A. B. Rountree. And *Approval of Bonds*, signed by Texas State Comptroller, John D. McCall, dated November 19, 1888. Courtesy, Texas State Library and Archives Commission. Austin.
[30] *Certificate of Election*, dated November 12, 1888. The *Certificate* reflects Allison's election to the office of "Sheriff and Tax Collector." Interestingly, and indeed indicative of the sparse population in West Texas at the time is the fact that Dave Allison received 74 votes, yet still carried the majority, was the victor, and was installed in office. Courtesy, Texas State Library and Archives Commission, Austin.
[31] **Ball(S)**, P. 35. Although the author is primarily focused on sheriffs in Arizona and New Mexico during the Territorial period, his remarks relating to tax collecting duties are also appropriate for early Texas sheriffs. For a thorough discussion see **Ball(S)** Chapter 12, "Ex-Officio Collector," P. 246-264. And see, **Ball's** article "Frontier Sheriffs at Work," *Journal of Arizona History*, No. 27., P. 284. "As ex-officio tax assessor and collector, he collected license fees and taxes." Hereafter cited as **Ball (F)**.
[32] **Prassel**, Frank Richard., *The Western Peace Officer, A Legacy of Law and Order*. P. 101. Hereafter cited as **Prassel**.
[33] **Ball (S)**. The author particularly notes the interests that mining, railroads, and the livestock industry played in early day sheriff's contests. P. 61- 64.
[34] Ibid. "The livestock industry also became a powerful force in the shrievalty campaigns." P. 63. And see, **Benner**, Judith Ann. *Sul Ross, Soldier, Statesman, Educator*. P. 189. "While addressing the Twentieth Legislature, Ross, (Governor) again stressed the importance of the livestock industry and recommended passing laws to favor and protect the stock raiser."
[35] **Biggers**, Don. *Buffalo Guns & Barbed Wire, Two Frontier Accounts by Don Hampton Biggers*, Introduction by A. C. **Greene**—Biography by Seymour V. **Connor**. P. 161. "The cattle raisers' association is a great organization and has perfected the most complete system of co-operation ever known. The executive committee supervise all routine work. They employ the attorneys who attend to all legal matters in which the association is interested, but their chief service is in prosecuting parties charged with stealing cattle from any member or members of

the association. About the worst complication a man can get into is to be indicted for stealing an animal belonging to this organization, and the last thing the wise professional does is to allow himself to be thusly embarrassed…" Hereafter cited as **Biggers**.

[36] **Prassel.** "Most sheriffs and deputies rarely encountered violence and many found it quite unnecessary to carry firearms…" P. 110.

[37] **Ball (S)**. P. 181.

[38] **Harkey**, Dee., *Mean as Hell, The Life of a New Mexico Lawman*. P. 162. Hereafter cited as **Harkey**. According to the author, Gordon was an elected constable for awhile, and still later, like the subject of this biography, served for a time as Chief of Police at Roswell, New Mexico.

[39] **Kerber**. P. 14. Article contributed by Elza **White**.

[40] Ibid. **White** names many of the youthful participants at Midland area dances and parties. One of which was "Lena Johnson," which unquestionably in fact would have been Lena Johnston.

[41] Ibid. Contribution of Mrs. R. E. "May" **Estes**.

[42] Lena was born at Honey Grove, Texas on August 24, 1871. Much of the information on the Johnston family, Lena's subsequent marriage to Dave Allison, the birth of the Allison's daughter, Hazel, and later migration of the Johnston family to Roswell, New Mexico, as well as a wealth of other genealogical material was graciously furnished by relative Linda Stockley **Weiler**, Roswell, New Mexico. Hereafter cited as **Weiler** for interview material, and **Weiler (II)** for information gleaned from her article "The Story of Our Old House" as it appeared in Vol. IV, No. 4, of *Old Timer's Review.*

[43] **Kerber**. P. 16. Article contributed by Beth **Fasken**. Interestingly, Ms. **Fasken** offers remarks on her first trip to West Texas, "All was well until we left Ft. Worth. Trees began to disappear. Shrubs kept getting smaller, Wide open spaces. Nothing else. And then we passed through a small town called Ranger with numerous small shacks. Close to the railroad track was a two-story, wooden hotel with a large sign saying, 'We have the best salt and toothpicks in the country.' My doubts began then." Evidence reflecting Johnston family prominence is profuse.

[44] Ibid., P. 37-38. Article contributed by Alva D. **Butler** and Conrad **Dunagan**.

[45] Ibid., The authors, report the signatories as W. E. Connell, A. W. Hilliard, John R. Hoxie, William H. Cowden Jr., Herman N. Garrett, W. P. Mudgett, John Scharbauer, and R. W. Johnson. The latter should read R. W. Johnston. Also see, *The New Handbook of Texas*, Volume IV, P. 706. "The First National Bank of Midland was chartered in 1890, and the city began to serve as a regional financial center."

[46] Ibid., P. 6. Contribution by Betty **Luther**.

[47] **Biggers**, P. 186.

[48] **Kerber**., P. 27. Courtesy, Darla **Bushman**, Special Collections, Midland County Public Library. Midland.

[49] Ibid., P. 152. Appendix B. Midland County, Texas Marriages, 1885-1926. Compiled by Helena Coleman **Grant** and Ruth Waldrop **Hord**. In another account, Millican's initials are given as I. R. and it is reported he was pastor at the Baptist Church. Also see, *Death Rides The River—Tales of the El Paso Road* by Robert S. **Bolling**, P. 3. Hereafter cited as **Bolling**. Patricia **Bramblett**, County-District Clerk, Hudspeth County, Sierra Blanca, Texas reported in an interview with the author that L. R. Millican was noted throughout West Texas as a highly

respected circuit riding preacher and was especially fondly thought of by cowboys and cattlemen.

[50] Ibid., P. 14. Contribution by Elza **White**.

[51] Ibid.

[52] **Kerber**, P. 6 & 14. Contributions by Betty **Luther** and Elza **White**.

[53] Ibid., P. 46. Contribution of T. O. **Midkiff**.

[54] Transcript, Bob Beverly to J. Evetts **Haley**, March 24, 1945. Courtesy, The Nita Stewart Haley Memorial Library and The J. Evetts Haley History Center, Midland.

[55] Ibid. Although the name Ed Burch is used throughout the typed transcript, in fact, the subject's true name was Ed Bunch, as will be evidenced in a following citation. Even the typist preparing the transcript noted "(or Burk or Burl. Can't get name certain)".

[56] *Information* No. 288 filed by W. D. Allison, Sheriff, on November 15, 1892 charging Ed Bunch with Murder. Courtesy Marla C. **White**, Chief Custodian of Records, Midland County Sheriff's Office, Midland, Texas.

[57] Transcript of Bob Beverly to J. Evetts **Haley**, March 24, 1945. Courtesy Nita Stewart Haley Memorial Library and The J. Evetts Haley History Center, Midland. And see, **Chesley**, Hervey E., *Adventuring with the Old-Timers, Trails Traveled—Tales Told.* P. 118. Hereafter cited as **Chesley**.

[58] Ibid.

[59] Ibid.

[60] Territory of Arizona, Executive Department, *Extradition Warrant of Arrest and Authorization For Movement*, Ed Bunch, made out to W. D. Allison. Courtesy, Arizona Department of Library, Archives, and Public Records, Phoenix.

[61] **Weiler**. Family genealogical papers. And, Headstone, South Park Cemetery, Roswell, New Mexico. Hazel's birthday and the particularly close relationship between Dave Allison, his wife, and their daughter are likewise confirmed by **Treadwell**. Additionally, Dave Allison's letters to Lena and Hazel are most affectionate and extraordinarily respectful, even though he does indeed sign them with formality, "W. D. Allison," rather than a much more personal, "Dave" or "Daddy."

[62] Midland, at the time, enjoyed daily train service from the Texas & Pacific Railroad. Two trains arrived each day, one eastbound and one westbound.

[63] *Midland Reporter-Telegram*, 1985 Centennial Edition reprinting article from November 9, 1889 edition of the *Midland Gazette*.

[64] **Kerber**., P. 6. Contribution of Betty **Luther**.

[65] **Clarke**., P. 40. Regarding windmills the author reports, "Some towns were described as 'windmill cities'. Midland was in that class since it was located on the plains. Major W. V. Johnson of Lubbock County was said to have drilled the first ranch well to supply stock water and also 'figured out' the windmill system with its necessary complement of reservoirs for storage. He accidentally discovered the best method of building the common earthen tank when building a cement-lined reservoir. He let the windmill pump water into the basin, then turned the cattle into it until the ground was well trampled. He then had a tank 'that would hold water like a jar.'" Divers & Crowley, wholesale and retail merchants, advertised, "a full and complete line of windmills, horse powers and water supply material." And see, *The Handbook of Texas*, Volume IV, P. 706. "At this time the city's residents obtained their water from wells with windmill

pumps; virtually every house had a windmill in its yard, and Midland became known as 'the Windmill Town.'"

[66] Before eventually leaving Midland County, Texas, Dave Allison would be elected to the office of Sheriff on six separate occasions: November 6, 1888; November 4, 1890; November 8, 1892; November 6, 1894; November 3, 1896; and November 8, 1898. Courtesy Texas State Library and Archives Commission, Austin. And Midland County Clerk records. Also list of *Sheriffs of Midland County*, courtesy current Midland County Sheriff Gary **Painter**. Dave Allison did not usually run unopposed, as clearly illustrated in the October 24, 1896 edition of *The Western Eye Opener*, which listed his opponents for the 1896 sheriff's contest as J. H. Knowles and D. C. McCormick. Allison defeated both candidates.

[67] Brands recorded with the County of Midland. Also see **Kerber**., P. 23 & 27.

[68] *Release of Vendors Lien*, July 31, 1891 to W. D. Allison. Courtesy, County Clerk, Midland, County, Midland, Texas.

[69] Transcript, Bob Beverly to J. Evetts **Haley**, June 23, 1937. Courtesy, The Nita Stewart Haley Memorial Library and The J. Evetts Haley History Center, Midland.

[70] **Croce**, Antonio., "In The Line of Duty," *The Texas Gun Collector*, Fall 1996. Hereafter cited as **Croce**. Charles H. "Charlie" Fusselman was born in Williamson County, central Texas, on July 16, 1866. At age twenty-two he enlisted in the Texas Rangers on May 31, 1888 in Duval County. Later he was assigned to the Big Bend country of far West Texas. By the time he was involved in this chase after Mexican outlaws he had already proved his mettle in a vicious Winchester and six-shooter duel with Donanciano Beslanga. Beslanga died with eight bullet wounds in his body. Fusselman was exonerated at the coroner's inquest. Also see, **Martin**, Jack., *Border Boss, Captain John R. Hughes—Texas Ranger*. P. 88-92. Hereafter cited as **Martin**.

[71] **Croce**. And see, **Stephens**, Robert W., *Texas Ranger Sketches*. P. 59-61. George Harold (Herold, Harrell) was born May 9, 1840, near Richmond, Virginia. During the Civil War he served in "T. T. Teel's Company of Texas State Troops, which later became the Second Texas Field Battery, an artillery unit...he participated in the shoot out with the Sam Bass gang at Round Rock, Texas, July 19, 1878. Some sources credit him with killing Bass while others acclaim Dick Ware as the Ranger who fired the fatal shot, but the proof is inconclusive." Known throughout the Southwest as an efficient and capable lawman, after a lengthy stint with the El Paso Police Department, Harold died of natural causes on December 12, 1917. Hereafter cited as **Stephens**. Also see, the excellently researched, *Sam Bass & Gang* by Rick **Miller** for a precisely detailed biographical sketch. P. 373-374.

[72] Ibid.

[73] Ibid. Apparently the words shouted by Fusselman were later reported to newsmen by participant George Harold.

[74] Ibid. "Harold tried desperately to reach out and get a hold of Fusselman, but the gunfire was too intense. Turing his horse, he shouted to Barnes 'Let's get the hell out of here.' Barnes agreed, but while turning, lost his grip on the reins of Pasos' horse. His prisoner escaped and both men had to shoot their way out in a fast retreat."

[75] **Meed**, Douglas V., "Daggers on the Gallows, The Revenge of Texas Ranger Captain 'Boss' Hughes," *TRUE WEST*. May 1999. P. 44-49. Ten years later Geronimo Parra was hanged for killing Texas Ranger Charles Fusselman. **Meed's**

adept reporting of this saga is indeed a story in and of itself, involving such notables as John Hughes and Patrick Floyd Garrett of New Mexico Territory.
[76] Transcript. Bob Beverly to J. Evetts **Haley**, September 13, 1945. Courtesy, The Nita Stewart Haley Memorial Library and The J. Evetts Haley History Center, Midland.
[77] *Minutes of Sheriff's Accts*., Courtesy, Gary **Painter**, Midland County Sheriff, Midland. And *Criminal Fee Book, County Court*, Midland County Clerk. Also see, *Criminal Docket, County Court*, Midland County Clerk.
[78] *Affidavit For Information*, No. 310. The State of Texas vs. W. D. Allison, filed July 24, 1893. Courtesy Marla C. **White**, Chief Custodian of Records, Midland County Sheriff's Office, Midland.
[79] Ibid. No. 358, Dated June 5, 1895.
[80] *Minutes of Sheriff's Accts*. The schedule of fees is a part of the printed format on the document *Minutes of Sheriff's Accts*.
[81] Ibid.
[82] **Ball (S)**, P. 27.
[83] Transcript. Bob Beverly to J. Evetts **Haley**, September 13, 1945. Courtesy, The Nita Stewart Haley Memorial Library and The J. Evetts Haley History Center. Midland.
[84] That John Allison, at least for a short while, served as a deputy is confirmed by examination of Sheriff Dave Allison's official Midland County stationary, on which the sheriff's brother's name is a part of the printed letterhead. Courtesy, Texas State Library and Archives Commission, Austin. And see, **Ball (F)**, P. 285. "In so politically tense an environment sheriffs practiced nepotism blatantly, even flagrantly."
[85] **Ball (S)**, P. 33-34.
[86] Deputation files. *Deputation* for G. C. Allison dated January 2, 1891 and *Deputation* for John Allison dated February 8, 1892. Courtesy Marla C. **White**, Chief Custodian of Records, Midland County Sheriff's Office, Midland, Texas.
[87] Ibid. *Deputation* for J. H. Mims, dated September 19, 1892.
[88] **Thrapp**, Dan L., *Encyclopedia of Frontier Biography*, Vol. I, P. 282. "In 1894 he was deputy under Sheriff Dave Allison at Pecos City, Texas, and is said to have worked under Jim Miller at one time as a town officer." And see, **Hunter**, J. Marvin and **Rose**, Noah H., *The Album of Gunfighters.* Hereafter cited as **Hunter & Rose**. Also see, **Stephens**, Robert W., *Manning Clements—Texas Gunfighter*. P. 77. The author clearly places Mannie Clements, Jr. in Midland during the time-frame Dave Allison was sheriff, however, he does not award him with a deputy's badge. Mannie Clements, Jr., as history has well recorded, was a notorious Southwestern "sporting man," and all around "shady character" heavily involved in horse racing, and suspected by some in a murder conspiracy resulting in the death of Patrick Floyd Garrett in 1908, near Organ, New Mexico Territory. On December 29, 1908, at El Paso's Coney Island Saloon, Mannie Clements, Jr. was shot in the back of the head. He died on the spot. The bartender, Joe Brown, was tried and acquitted for the murder, and a local attorney amplified public opinion when he remarked, "It is a surprise to me that Clements was not killed sooner." Hereafter cited as **Stephens (II)**. Also see' **Metz** and **Marohn**.
[89] **Stephens (II)**. P. 78.
[90] *Letter* from Sheriff W. D. Allison to John Wesley Hardin, June 16, 1895. Courtesy, Southwestern Writers Collections, Albert B. Alkek Library, Southwest Texas State University, San Marcos, Texas.

---

[91] As of publication, the author of this narrative has been unable to locate any official Midland County documentation which would confirm Clement's appointment as a Midland County deputy sheriff. Records at the Midland County warehouse and archives are voluminous, and the fact that Clement's deputation has not been located, as of yet, is not conclusive. Other persons that Dave Allison deputized, aside from those listed in the text were; R. H. Williams; S. B. Tillous; George E. Cowden; N. B. Jones; Enoch Powell; J. W. Holt; C. A. Winborne; and Lew Murphy. Naturally, this listing is not all inconclusive.

[92] *El Paso Herald*, May 7, 1895. And, interview with Dennis **McCown**, Austin, Texas. Also see, *Eddy Current*, May 5, 1895. And see, **Marohn**, P. 223, "Mroz was apprehended while on his way to Mexico near Midland, Texas, but he and his female companion escaped, stole some horses, and continued their flight." And see, *El Paso Daily Herald*, May 7, 1895.

[93] **Kerber**. P. 39. An article prepared by Ada M. **Phillips**.

[94] *Application and Oath of Office for Special Ranger Commission*, signed "W. D. Allison," dated August 8, 1892. Courtesy, Texas State Library and Archives Commission, Austin.

[95] **Clarke**. P. 51-61.

[96] *Descriptive List*, Company B, Frontier Battalion, signed by "W. H. Mabry," Texas Adjutant-General, dated August 12, 1892. On Allison's application as cited above, J. C. Loving, Secretary for the Texas and Southwestern Cattle Raisers Association, is one of the individuals who were "recommending the appointment" and "vouching for the good character" of William Davis Allison. Courtesy, Texas State Library and Archives Commission, Austin. The document titled *Descriptive List* was in fact a Ranger's official commission and had the following notation: "This Descriptive List, for identification, will be kept in possession of the Ranger to whom it refers, and will be exhibited as a warrant of his authority as such, when called upon, and must be surrendered to his Company Commander when discharged." Mike **Cox**, *Texas Ranger Tales—Stories That Need Telling*, says, "Special Rangers were not paid by the state, though they generally were on someone else's payroll, often as inspectors for the Texas and Southwestern Cattle Raisers Association. On paper the authority of a Special Ranger was somewhat limited in comparison with members of the Frontier Battalion, but the qualifier 'Special' did not get much attention. Along the border the word people paid attention to was 'Ranger.'" P. 137. Hereafter cited as **Cox**.

[97] Today in Texas and Oklahoma the Texas and Southwestern Cattle Raisers Association employs approximately thirty-five Field Inspectors charged with investigating the theft of livestock and ranch related property, ie., saddles, stock trailers, portable loading chutes, etc. In Texas the Field Inspectors carry Special Texas Ranger Commissions, are state licensed Texas Peace Officers, and are paid by the Association, not with public funds. In both Texas and Oklahoma the Field Inspectors maintain an excellent working reputation with their fellow dedicated law enforcement officers, providing valuable service and make significant contribution to the overall operation of the criminal justice system, especially in those communities economically welded to the cattle industry. Additionally, the steadily growing interest in equine activities in urban areas is mandating that Field Inspectors also direct their time and efforts toward capturing "citified crooks" and returning stolen horses, tack, and related equipment to appreciative complainants.

[98] **Ball (S)**. P. 34.

[99] Ibid.

---

[100] Ibid.
[101] **Harkey**. P. 72-73. The author's reference to Phoenix (Phenix) was not the city in Arizona Territory, but rather a community near Carlsbad, New Mexico.
[102] **Treadwell**. To be sure, at least for anyone who has spent time horseback in wet wintry weather, the story, at least the portion about "sticking" to the saddle, has the ring of bitter truthfulness. In *Forts & Forays*, James A. **Bennett**, a nineteenth-century Dragoon, in a journal entry wrote of men frozen in the saddle, "At least 20 men were unable to dismount from their horses and had to be taken down by others." P. 21. Stories of almost gruesome West Texas winters are legion. In fact, the record low temperature for Texas was recorded at Seminole, Gaines County, just north of Midland in 1933—23 degrees below zero. See, **Stephens** and **Holmes**. P. 5.
[103] **Fenton (II)**. Quoting the April 22, 1910 edition of the *Knowles News*, published at Knowles, New Mexico. The author continues with his own assessment of Allison, "He was noted for being absolutely fearless, a quality that no doubt stood him in good stead in the numerous gunfights in which he participated." P. 85.
[104] *St. Louis Post-Dispatch*, July 22, 1923.
[105] *Roswell Daily Record*, April 4 & 5, 1923.
[106] *El Paso Times*, April 3, 1923.
[107] **Thrapp**., Volume I, P. 17.
[108] **Fenton (II)**. P. 86.
[109] *The Cattleman*. May 1923. P. 13.
[110] *Fort Worth Star-Telegram*. June 18, 1923.
[111] **Treadwell**. Family genealogical research, at least at the time of this writing, has failed to adequately determine John Allison's cause of death.
[112] **Fenton**. P. 4., And **DeArment**., P. 14. Also see, **Clarke**, Mary Whatley, "Bad Man…Good Man?," *The Cattleman*. Vol. LVIII, No. 7. Hereafter cited as **Clarke (II)**. And see, **Gournay**, P. 82. Wilbarger County was named for Josiah Pugh Wilbarger and brother, Mathias Wilbarger. "Josiah Wilbarger was shot, scalped, and left for dead by Comanche Indians. He was found the next day, still alive, and managed to recover and live another twelve years."
[113] Ibid. And see, **Pettey**, P. 136. For more information on George "Red Buck" Waightman see, **Thrapp**, Vol. III, P. 1495. Also see, **Hanes**, Bailey C., *Bill Doolin, Outlaw O. T.*
[114] **DeArment**, P. 14 and **Fenton**, P. 4. Also see, **Sterling**, William Warren., *Trails and Trials of a Texas Ranger*. P. 377-381. The author identifies Lewis as Elmore rather than Elmer, and he describes "Red Buck" Waightman as a person "who was so wantonly murderous that neither the Dalton nor Doolin gangs would let him ride with then." Hereafter cited as **Sterling**.
[115] For the account of the robbery of Waggoner's and Bailey's stores, the work of **Fenton**, **DeArment**, and **Clarke** was blended. Also see, **Sullivan**, W. J. L., "Twelve Years In The Saddle for Law and Order on the Frontiers of Texas," *Old West*. Spring 1967. **Fenton** refers to Rondie, Texas—**Clarke** says Ronda, Texas. All are in basic agreement, and assuredly all accounts place Hillary Loftis at the scene of both crimes.
[116] **Fenton**, P. 4., **DeArment** P. 14, and see, **Paine**, Albert Bigelow., *Captain Bill McDonald—Texas Ranger*. P. 176-178. Hereafter cited as **Paine**. **DeArment** lists the posse men as "…six Texas Rangers under Sergeant W. J. L. Sullivan; Wilbarger County Sheriff Dick Sanders and his deputy, John Williams; Billy

Moses, former Motley County sheriff; Vernon City Marshal Charles Sanders; and Constable Tom Pickett of Wichita Falls." **Paine** adds Jack Harwell and Ranger Captain Bill McDonald's nephew, W. J. McCauley. **Fenton** reports, "William J. 'Bill' McDonald, one of the 'Four Great (Ranger) Captains' of the period, was quickly notified; however, not fully recovered from a wound sustained in a shoot-out, he sent his deputy, Sergeant W. John L. Sullivan, to handle the chase. Gather a posse of twenty-two local officers and citizens, Sullivan approached the outlaws' hideout on Christmas Eve."

[117] Ibid. Three of the lawmen's horses were killed before the decision was made to thwart any escape attempt, and put the outlaws afoot by killing their horses. And see, **Sullivan**, W. J. L., *Twelve Years in the Saddle with the Texas Rangers*. P. 119-126.

[118] *St. Louis Post-Dispatch*, July 15, 1923. Also see, **Warren** C., "Joe Beckham, The Outlaw Sheriff," *Real West*, August 1983. P. 29.

[119] **Fenton** and **DeArment** both concur that it was so bitterly cold that lawmen could not operate their weapons. **Paine** asserts that McCauley and Harwell remained behind, but by morning were "nearly dead from exposure, were in no condition to charge it (the dugout), alone."

[120] **DeArment** reports Waightman wounded in the fight. **Fenton** concurs, but adds, "…one had been killed; Red Buck and another, slightly wounded." P. 19. Unquestionably it seems Hill Loftis managed to escape the blistering winter shoot-out untouched. For an account of Waightman's death, see, **Steele**, Phillip, "The Woman Red Buck Couldn't Scare," *The West*, April 1971. And see, **Boren**, Sanford, "End of the Trail for Red Buck," *Frontier Times*. July 1970.

[121] **Sterling**, P. 377. The list of Lone Star State fugitives was also known to Texas Rangers as the *Black Book* or the *Preferred List*.

[122] **Haley**., P. 4.

[123] **Rynning**, P. 293. The author who was one of Allison's later law enforcement bosses, refers to Dave's fondness for gambling, a quotation cited later in full. Also see, Bob Beverly to J. Evetts **Haley**, March 24, 1945. Courtesy, The Nita Stewart Haley Memorial Library and The J. Evetts Haley History Center, Midland.

[124] Beverly to **Haley**, March 24, 1945.

[125] **Haley**., P. 4.

[126] Midland County Commissioner's Court, February 14, 1898. Book II. Courtesy, Todd **Houck**, Director of Archives, The Petroleum Museum Library and Hall of Fame, Midland. Dave Allison was succeeded by H. W. Wells.

[127] *Criminal Fee Book, County Court*. Courtesy Marla C. **White**, Chief Custodian of Records, Midland County Sheriff's Office, Midland, Texas.

[128] Midland County Clerk's notation to W. D. Allison biographical files in the collection of Bill **O'Neal**, Panola College, Carthage, Texas.

3

"We forgot about the body unless it showed up downstream."

Three years earlier, in an administrative effort to maintain tighter control, Texas Adjutant General Woodford H. Mabry had asked that Special Rangers appointed under provisions of Special Order No. 6 surrender their commissions. Sheriff Dave Allison had complied.[1] That the action had been taken for administrative or non-partisan political reasons, and was not a personal repudiation of Dave Allison's character is evidenced by his next move in an admittedly confusing string of job hops. At thirty-eight years of age, the veteran Lone Star sheriff enlisted in Company D, Frontier Battalion, Texas Rangers, at Ysleta, a drowsy downriver hamlet south of El Paso on the American bank of a ceaselessly troublesome international line, the Rio Grande. On October 1, 1899, the legendary Texas Ranger Captain John R. Hughes approvingly welcomed Dave Allison into Ranger ranks.[2]

Although Company D was charged with protecting the most dangerous part of Texas, the year 1899 proved reasonably peaceful. A Texas Ranger historian, in speaking of the relatively calm year, unceremoniously remarks, "…the company made numerous quiet arrests..."[3] For the reporting period of 1898-1899, of which Dave Allison barely caught the tail end, Company D made 348 scouts and traveled over 57,000 miles, safely making 395 arrests without serious bodily injury to either a beleaguered badman or a risk-taking Ranger.[4] Private Dave Allison was a participating member on at least a few of these arduous and adventurous border country patrols, as evidenced by an inspection of Company D *Monthly Returns.* His first assignment as a rookie ranger was to assist Captain Hughes and a fellow private, J. W. Matthews, in guarding the El Paso County Jail against an anticipated assault from an angered mob. The rangers' presence forestalled the expected riot. On another occasion Dave Allison investigated a West Texas train wreck, racking up an impressive 1000 miles from start to finish. Unrelated to the wreck, Dave and Captain

Hughes were forced to arrest a rowdy and quarrelsome trio, Jalau Baria, David Madrid and Jose Ariauas, safely locking them away in the same El Paso County jail.[5]

Dave Allison's tenure as a regular Texas Ranger under this particular enlistment was short-lived. It seems that Texas and Southwestern Cattle Raisers Association leadership had flexed a little political muscle and had squawked into influential and powerful State lawmaker's ears. Certainly it is *speculative*, but undoubtedly Dave Allison had been forewarned of the pending legislative maneuvering. On December 18, 1899, Private W. D. "Dave" Allison resigned from the Texas Rangers, was honorably discharged, and Captain Hughes certified the now ex-Ranger was due $18.00 from the State piggy-bank for services rendered since the 1st of December.[6]

Back at Midland, Dave Allison forthwith turned right back around and submitted a written application to the Texas Adjutant General for another appointment as a Special Ranger, again "to serve the State without pay..."[7] In response to a printed question designed to ascertain why the commission was being requested, Allison stated, "That I may be instrumental in Suppression of Crime, and bringing to justice Criminals."[8] Additionally, before a local Justice of the Peace, Dave Allison swore that he was "sober and temperate" in his habits, and that he had never "been convicted of any crime."[9] On December 28, 1899, with a legible handwritten notation "Recommended by Cattle Association," Dave Allison's application was approved and for a second time he was appointed a Special Texas Ranger.[10] Whether or not Dave Allison was getting sound advice "from inside sources" is unanswerable, but unquestionably his timing in resigning from the famed Frontier Battalion was appropriate and not financially unwise. A taste of Association monies could surely prove palatable, especially when down in Austin, at the State Capitol, the Texas Rangers as a constabulary organization was literally choking on half-baked legal technicalities, force-fed by cunning and devious lawyers. In short, the State of Texas gave him a commission, the Cattle Association gave him a salary.

At its 1874 inception, as would naturally and only rightly be anticipated, the famous Frontier Battalion had drawn enforcement authority from the legislatively constituted state statutes; an indispensable public safety measure, a law, which in part, stated that officers of the Frontier Battalion would have all the powers of a peace officer.[11] Clearly, lawmen comprising the famed Frontier Battalion and more centrally located Texas Rangers were Lone Star peace officers. Not necessarily! A lawyer bit down on an unintended statutory tid-bit, and ferociously held on until other legal-beagles from the pack could catch up to the feeding frenzy. Wholly disregarding public order and common sense, and putting honest citizen's security on the back burner, the word-wolves challenged with their own convoluted and opportune interpretation of the law—as it was written—that the word *officer* meant just that, an *officer*. Therefore, as everyone should then well know, Texas Ranger noncommissioned officers and privates were not themselves lawful peace officers and, in fact, they were guilty of what amounted to kidnapping if they arrested anybody at all. From their self-serving scraps of putrid logic, only the Ranger Captains were in fact Texas peace *officers*.[12] The rancid fight had a very real upshot, the bone of contention resulted in, "...many charges of false imprisonment were made against the Rangers in different parts of the state, and warrants were issued for their arrest."[13] It was a gristly and raw beefsteak battle. Predictably, the Governor was compelled to submit the distasteful question to the Attorney General for a definitive and legally binding answer. On May 26, 1900, defense-lawyers hungering for greenbacks, greedily salivated as they digested the legal opinion. "Attorney General Thomas S. Smith decided the language of the act was specific and allowed only officers to make arrest. Smith's was a very narrow ruling based on a definition of the term 'officer' to mean only commissioned personnel as opposed to 'police officer' or 'peace officer.' In effect, the ruling said that almost every arrest made since mid-1874 had been illegal."[14] At Midland, Dave Allison no doubt was flabbergasted and predictably perturbed when he heard the news from Austin.

Political pressure, prompted Attorney General Smith to issue a stop-gap measure. A Ranger reorganization recipe was judiciously concocted which allowed for the temporary creation of four six man companies, and allowing privates to *assist* commissioned *officers* in making arrests and enforcing the law.[15] By July 8, 1901, nonetheless, new legislation was written and put into effect, allowing for the Texas Governor to organize a "ranger force" for the "suppression of lawlessness and crime throughout the state."[16] Wording in the new law was not ambiguous: Texas Rangers were peace officers, all of them.

During this period of Texas tomfoolery, Dave Allison's awareness had been diverted to a train robbing caper miles away, as was the probing attention of most Southwestern lawmen. On the evening of February 15, 1900, at Fairbank, Cochise County, Arizona Territory, shameless hijackers challenged a gritty Wells, Fargo and Company messenger, Jeff Milton, for the express safe key. Thankfully historic accounts abound, and fortunately for rapt readers the well-celebrated J. Evetts Haley penned a biography of Milton, while the saga of Burt Alvord, the criminal mastermind, has been eloquently preserved by accomplished wordsmith, Don Chaput.[17] Only a brief recap of the breathtaking story is requisite for impacting on Dave Allison's story.

During a blistering exchange of gunfire, Jeff Milton received gunshot wounds, shattering his left arm.[18] Lying in a pool of blood, Milton was a goner for sure, at least so thought train robber, "Three-Fingered Jack" Dunlap. He was dead wrong! Eleven pellets from Milton's double barrel shotgun pole-axed him to the ground, while other shot struck a partner in crime "Bravo Juan" Yoas in the seat of the pants—and beyond.[19] Realizing carefully crafted blueprints for immediate wealth had gone awry, the three other bandits, brothers George and Louis Owens, and West Texas cowboy Bob Brown, scooped up their wounded pals and dashed into a dark desert night.[20] The five wayward brigands may have been dim-witted in the first place, thinking they could rob the train while it was stopped at the crowded Fairbank's depot, but for sure, they knew a hard-ridin' posse with revenge on the brain would soon overhaul them, if they tarried. Splitting up, the quartet abandoned "Three-Fingered Jack" to suffer whatever Fate had in store. In the end, he was caught (found) at Buckshot Springs. He snitched, naming the devoted pals that deserted him, as well as others, including Burt Alvord and Billy Stiles, cunning schemers who had established alibis elsewhere, and then he died.[21] The rest of the gang, along with Matt Burts and Bill Downing, arrested for a previous robbery, and Alvord and Stiles were soon rounded up and thrown into the jailhouse at Tombstone.[22] It does seem, however, that the thirty-four year old blue-eyed Texan, Bob Brown, made good with his escape and hightailed it back to familiar country, at least for a short stopover, before moving over to Arkansas for a spell.[23]

According to J. Evetts Haley's historical informant, Bob Beverly, Brown indeed made it as far as Arkansas, where he stayed for awhile before he "got broke and sick."[24] According to Beverly, under the weather and near destitute, Bob Brown wrote a letter to Dave Allison asking for money, "and Dave went out there and got him and sent him to the penitentiary…"[25] Western writer DeArment offers further clarification, "Allison's detective work reportedly ended the career of a notable Arizona criminal. Bandit Bob Brown fled the territory after involvement in an attempted train robbery at Fairbank in February 1900. Allison traced him to Arkansas, arrested him, and returned him to Arizona where he was convicted and sentenced."[26] Don Chaput's investigation seems to somewhat confirm the story, "In early June, (1900) Bob Brown was found, while trying to hide in his native Texas. He was arrested and shipped to Tombstone."[27]

There would be jail breaks, courtroom ballyhoo, gunshots, prison sentences, and Presidential Pardons before the Fairbank's robbery story was finally in the wraps and, for sure, the yarn is a dandy but, for the most part, William Davis Allison's participation ended with the capture and arrest of a penniless cowboy gone bad, Bob Brown. Perhaps, candidly speaking, there wasn't actually too much sleuthing involved, if in truth, Brown did write a letter giving away his whereabouts, or maybe that was just a face-saving excuse for being foolish enough to assume Dave Allison would ignore criminal violations as significant as train-robbery and attempted murder. That Special Ranger Dave Allison was indeed a "hard-charger" can be extrapolated by a quick glance at one of his seventeen-day, 1000-mile "scouts" through Crockett and Concho counties. On this trip he nabbed suspected cow thieves Will and P. W. Herren, and also arrested Henry Green for "assault with attempt to commit murder." Apparently all the lawless infractions had taken place further back west as Dave locked all three up in the El Paso County Jail. On another trip, Dave maneuvered to Midland in search of Wash Barker, but this time after the 592 mile trip he came up empty-handed, for the time being.[28] Involved detective work or not, William Davis Allison caught approving adulation from Arizona lawmen, cowmen, and ever posturing politicians.

That it was undeniably a *transitional frontier*, policed by *transitional lawmen* is aptly divulged in Webb's concisely descriptive remark about the newly forged force, "The Rangers were still mounted men, though they frequently traveled—often with their horses—on the trains which now penetrated all parts of the state. They furnished their own horses and horse equipment; but they wore no uniform and carried no badge."[29] Certainly cowboy and cattle-country cop Dave Allison had his own horse, and notwithstanding all the tumultuous hubbub about Midland County's balance-sheet, he maintained the reputation of a rock-solid, loyal, and unwavering peace officer, no doubt in large part due to his fortunate relationships with area beef-barons. Under the new law creating the Rangers, the Governor appointed the Company Commanders, who in turn were allowed to hand-pick their own men, and promote their preference for first-sergeants. John R. Hughes, who had tenaciously held on to his Captaincy, hunted recruits who he knew were "courageous, discreet, honest, temperate, and of good families."[30] Additionally he placed great emphasis on their qualifications as peace officers, and "recruited only those capable of capturing outlaws by their brains as well as by their bullets and brawn. A good detective, or a good fighter, was not enough—he wanted only men who were both."[31] One of those men he sought out was William Davis "Dave" Allison.

Hazel Allison, Dave and Lena Allison's only child. Courtesy, Pat Treadwell, Tahoka, Texas.

On October 19, 1901, Dave Allison re-enlisted for a two-year hitch in the regular Texas Rangers at Fort Hancock, Texas. He was forty years old.[32] Dave Allison, before El Paso County Notary Public William Hamilton, took the following oath:

> I do solemnly swear (or affirm) that I will faithfully and impartially discharge and perform all the duties incumbent upon me as a member of the Ranger Force until August 31, 1903, unless sooner discharged, according to the best of my skill and ability, and agreeably to the Constitution and laws of the United States and of this State. So help me God.[33]

Dave Allison was posted at Marathon, Brewster County, Texas.

By city standards, Marathon wasn't too much of a town.[34] By county standards, Brewster was one hell-of-a county. Created in 1887, it was, *and is*, the largest county in Texas, over 6000 square miles, about the size of Connecticut and Rhode Island combined.[35] It is the magnificently rugged Big Bend Country, slashed by seemingly bottomless canyons and capped with distinguishing mountains that serve to protect inaccessible basins and tiny, trickling underground springs. On the south, its border is the meandering and mysterious Rio Grande. Back to the north, about a hundred miles or so, Brewster County breaks into immense tableland. Betwixt and between? Habitat for a natural world embracing creatures owning venomous fangs, arched stingers, and sharp teeth, and camouflaged desert plants bristling with dagger-like spikes. Other lurking marauders would hack with a machete or spit out bullets. Brewster County was bandit country.[36]

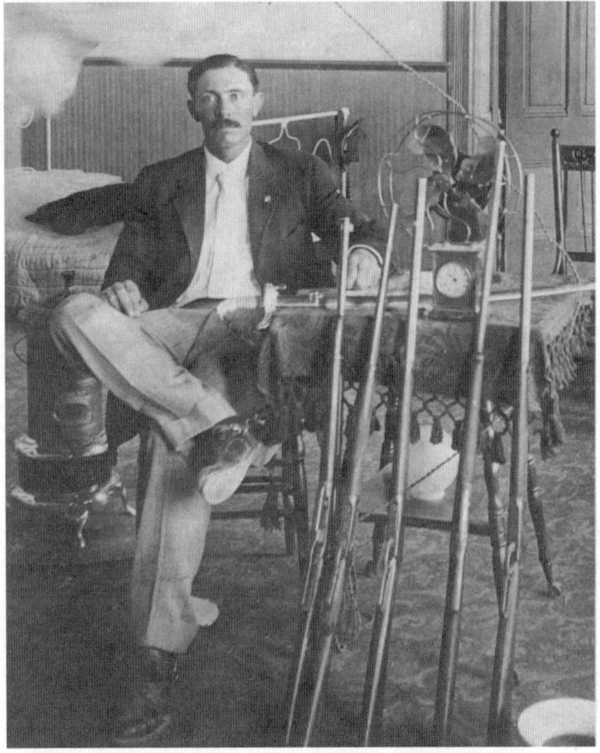

An early hero of the Mexican Revolution, Pascual Orozco would end his days on the run, horseback, in West Texas. Courtesy El Paso Library.

On the west, just across a surveyor's precise but hard to find line, Brewster County had a little sister, Presidio County. She took her Spanish name from Presidio del Norte (fort of the north), and was nearly 4,000 square miles of rugged topography that included some of Texas' tallest mountains.[37] And she, too, sometimes harbored bad guys and bandits.[38]

Texas Rangers. Standing first from left, Private Herff A. Carnes, who would later become a redoubtable United States Mounted Customs Inspector, and a faithful partner of Dave Allison during a vicious shoot-out with Mexican Nationals. Seated far right, Ranger Captain John R. Hughes, the legendary Texas Ranger and a strong supporter of Dave Allison. Courtesy, Texas Ranger Hall of Fame and Museum. Waco, Texas.

At Marathon, in all probability Dave and Lena Allison were somehow trying to placate twelve-year old Hazel, for surely she was questioning why a blossoming soon to be debutante had been pried from Midland's relative culture, yanked away from her schoolroom friends, and dragged to this God-awful country. Much further to the south, in the Mexican frontier state of Chihuahua, another quizzical mind was trying to take a peek at life's riddles and Fate's plans. Pascual Orozco, Jr., near San Isidro, had already been through the learning to walk, run, hop, skip, and jump phases of his childhood, in fact, he had "acquired a rudimentary knowledge of reading and writing during his four or five years of primary education."[39] Having soaked up whatever formal education was available for a rural middle-class boy, and it has been described as "woefully inadequate," Pascual followed in family footsteps and went to work in his father's store. But there was something missing for Pascual Orozco, Jr., who in his very heart and soul ached for more. While yet a teenager, he married, and by the time the Allison family had migrated to Marathon, Texas, Pascual Orozco, Jr. on the Mexican side of the border, was swathed in crisscrossed bullet-filled bandoleers, and proudly adorned with well-oiled six-shooters. Orozco was a muleteer, a guard, for the valuable ore shipments securely lashed onto cross-buck packsaddles, which in turn were tightly cinched atop long-eared donkeys, or sometimes mules. These pack animals were prodded down sharply winding hairpin trails through the rugged western Chihuahua mountains. Dangerously infested mountains. The state of Chihuahua too, had bad guys and bandits. Pascual Orozco, Jr. was making a name for himself—a good one—he, too, was fearless, and was but twenty years old.[40]

At Marathon, newly arrived Hazel Allison, at least from time to time, must have casually focused her stare back to the North and the seemingly more civilized setting, privately pondering her prospects for the future—Pascual Orozco, Jr. did too!

Midland area cow-country. Courtesy, Haley Memorial Library and History Center, Midland, Texas.

That Big Bend country, that Brewster and Presidio country, was big ranch country. One writer succinctly says, "The Big Bend was cut out to be a cattle country…where cattle are kings, and the cowman, cowboy, Mexican laborer, banker, and the townspeople all swear allegiance to them."[41] Texas Ranger Dave Allison's kind of country. And it was Association country.[42] Those Association tentacles were many, and they were far-reaching. The Lone Star State was known world wide as a Cattlemen's Kingdom, and the Association would make sure the message was not trampled over, not rubbed out, not by railroad men, not by mining men, and positively not by a few of those haplessly lucky quick-rich oil men. The Association's common cord needled right through membership like the thread stringing cranberries for a Christmas tree decoration. Pulled firmly it joined the few into a whole, deftly applied and jerked tightly it could prove devastatingly strong. Dave Allison was an Association man.

Robert W. "Bob" Johnston, Dave's father-in-law, was an Association man too. A dyed-in-the-wool Texas cattleman, but in 1901, when the Allison family moved to Marathon, Bob and his wife, Lucy, migrated to Roswell, New Mexico Territory.[43] Reportedly the move was for medical reasons, and that is indeed historically plausible since at that time Roswell was being highly touted as a healthful place to live due to temperate Southwestern weather.[44] For $1225, Bob Johnston purchased the east half of Block 24, West Spring River Addition from B. T. Ware.[45] At what ultimately turned out to be Roswell city address, 700 North Lea Avenue, the "prominent cattleman from Midland" built a spacious Queen Ann style home with handsome lathe-turned columns and an all-embracing wrap-around porch.[46] Before an encroaching city pleasantly surrounded the house, the Johnston home was the site for a small farm and a delightfully delicious fruit-tree orchard.[47] Additionally, R. W. Johnston acquired New Mexico cattle ranches, one just northwest of Roswell, the other sixty-miles north-east near Elida.[48] No doubt while he piddled about in his orchard, or when he occasionally napped on the veranda, his fond memories drifted back toward Texas, and his darling granddaughter, Hazel.

In that country, where a smuggler or bandit might be shot and nothing "official" ever reported, some things were just best left unsaid. Texas Ranger Dave Allison didn't need a publicity agent, the "Border Boss" was already irrevocably convinced and damn-well happy with his personnel selection, an assessment echoed in the writings of a proficient West Texas historian who remarked that Allison, "…had more bravery than most men."[49] On February 7, 1902, Captain John R. Hughes, who from past knowledge was thoroughly acquainted with Dave's reputation for *fearless* courage and uncompromising resolve, promoted private W. D. Allison to 1ST Sergeant, D Company, Ranger Force.[50] New stationary was ordered, printed, and put into use. The left margin letterhead read:

HEADQUARTERS COMPANY "D"
STATE RANGERS
FOR HANCOCK, TEXAS

JOHN R. HUGHES, CAPTAIN

———————

W. D. ALLISON, 1ST SERGEANT[51]

As a Ranger Sergeant, Dave Allison's duties were diverse. On the one hand, he was clothed with responsibilities of a "down in the trenches" Texas peace officer; on the other, he was burdened with the chafing saddle of administrative and logistical drudgery. One letter from Sergeant Allison to Texas Adjutant General Thomas Scurry said, "*I have just returned from El Paso. Where I went to make some necessary purchases—and spent three days—Saturday, Sunday and Yesterday. Yours To Command. W. D. Allison, Sgt.*"[52] That Dave Allison's jurisdictional area was still rugged frontier country can be extracted from another of his letters to the Adjutant General. *"I am going to start on an 8 or 10 days scout down the Maravillas Creek, and back through the Chisos Mountains. With two objects in mind—'viz'—one to subpoena a witness in a criminal felony case, the other to effect the capture of two deserters from the U. S. Army at Ft. Sam Houston. Private Earl Buster will accompany me—Yours to Command, W. D. Allison, 1st Sergt. Co. 'D', R. F.*"[53] Whether or not he located the witness is unknown, he did, however, succeed in finally tracking the two deserting soldiers, taking them into custody to be held for military authorities.[54]

Texas Rangers had sworn to uphold the laws of the state of Texas, but they too had personal lives, and from time to time had to tend to important family business. Dave Allison was not exempt. In late March 1902, the Allison's were notified that Lena's father, R. W. Johnston, was gravely ill at Roswell. Dave Allison, Lena, and little Hazel, caught the next train. At Sierra Blanca, Dave dropped off his saddle and rifle, intending to reacquire the gear upon a quick return trip and chase after a suspected murderer from San Saba County, Texas, a rogue, reportedly roaming around in the general vicinity. Dave Allison proceeded to Roswell with an apprehensive wife, playful daughter, and a Colt's six-shooter unobtrusively thrust into his waistband.[55] Later in the month, after his father-in-law's health had stabilized, Ranger Sergeant Dave Allison returned to his Marathon post of duty.[56] He had legitimate law enforcement work to do, but Dave Allison having picked up a rumor in Roswell, which was later confirmed in newspaper reports, had something else on his mind. An examination of his letter can support a conclusion that he was reasonably articulate, and also, it further substantiates where his cattle-country sympathies lay:

> *Marathon Texas. April 24, 1902*
> *Adjt. General Thomas Scurry, Austin Texas.*
>
> *Dear Sir:*
>
> *It has been said that 'a stitch in time saves nine'. I have just noticed an account in "The West Texas Stockman" of Colorado, Texas—to the effect that Col. J. C. Loving would not again be a candidate for the position of Secty. To the "Cattle Raisers Assn. of Texas". Therefore next month at the Convention, which is to convene in El Paso—his successor is to be elected. And while I desire to serve the great State of Texas, to the best of my ability—and want to continue in the Ranger Service, yet it is my further wish, duty and privilege to further my own interests. I want to enter the contest for the office above referred to, and my idea is original, to loose, but little time in making my wants known to the members of the Cattle Raisers Assn., and other influential men. Please sir, is there any impropriety on my part or objection on behalf of the Governor and yourself to my making an effort and still retaining my position? Of course if there is the least, I shall desist, otherwise I shall begin. I have also written my Capt. John R. Hughes.*
>
> *Yours to Command*
> *W. D. Allison*
> *Co. "D," R. Force*[57]

On April 28, 1902, Texas Ranger Sergeant Dave Allison made the trip to Company D headquarters at Fort Hancock to personally confer with

Captain Hughes regarding official law enforcement business, and no doubt, also discuss the pending labors at lining up political support for his bid at becoming the politically powerful Secretary for the Texas and Southwestern Cattle Raisers Association.[58] While in the area, it's a reasonably safe bet Dave Allison sought out some of his El Paso County cow-owning buddies.

Unquestionably, Dave Allison expended time contacting past acquaintances, reaffirming friendships, shoring up any weak spots, glad-handing, and politicking in general, but not at the cost of neglecting Texas Ranger duties. During the month of May, Sergeant Dave Allison, *probably* again accompanied by private Buster, made a lengthy scout along the Rio Grande and deep into the imposing Chisos Mountains. And as typical of Allison's official reports, details are scarce, but the grueling dragnet paid off, "*...we went to capture Bill Burns—for theft of one mule—I have delivered him to the Sheriff of Brewster County in person at Alpine last night.*"[59] On another arduous scout, this time traveling with Texas Ranger private J. B. Townsend, Dave Allison was back in the Chisos country chasing after an ex-sheriff and his son-in-law for stealing horses from a Reeves County rancher.[60]

For whatever the reason, Dave Allison did not land the job he had hoped for with the Association. J. W. Colston was named to the politically influential Secretary's post during the annual meeting of the Texas and Southwestern Cattle Raisers Association at El Paso.[61] Back to work it would be for the Big Bend lawman.

The following month Sergeant Allison and private Townsend were again scouting the border, probing for New Mexico train robbers, striking the Rio Grande country somewhere between Terlingua and Boquillas and then traveling harsh country eastward, at last arriving at Sanderson. There the weary lawmen finally loaded jaded and footsore horses into an available cattle-car, and catnapped as the locomotive chugged along the line back to their post of duty at Marathon.[62] The worn-out Rangers had not located any train robbers, but the arduous horseback scout once again proved Texas Rangers were in the area—for keeps. Ranger Sergeant Dave Allison stayed busy.

Busy or not, nothing remains static—for too long. Company D, Texas Rangers was transferred from Fort Hancock in far West Texas to Alice, Nueces County, deep into the belly of the Texas Rio Grande Valley. A small detachment, under Sergeant Dave Allison was sent even further south, to Brownsville, Cameron County, at Texas' uttermost tip—a rowboat ride from the Gulf of Mexico's salty, shark infested waters.[63]

Whether or not moving Company D to the South Texas stage was a direct result of behind the scenes choreography conducted by the Texas and Southwestern Cattle Raisers Association's leadership is guesswork, but the "Goddamn cow-thieves" were "givin' em' hell" in South Texas, as evidenced by Webb's comment, "There was little to do at Alice except to watch for stolen stock that might be driven there for shipment."[64] According to Captain Hughes, however, at Brownsville, where Sergeant Dave Allison was posted, conditions were "entirely different," cattle were being stolen "all the time." Webb quotes from the Ranger Captain's report, "At one time we brought in 100 head of cattle to Brownsville. Most of this stock was identified and claimed by citizens of the town and country thereabouts. There were many calves among the herd, stolen from the milk pens. The citizens brought their children, little boys and girls, down to the corral where the Rangers held the cattle. The children went into the corral, called the calves by their names, caught them and led them out and home. Many of the cattle were branded, but the brands had been burned by the thieves."[65]

Bob Brown, one of the infamous Fairbank, Arizona, train robbers. Captured by Dave Allison. Courtesy, Yuma Territorial Prison State Park, Yuma, Arizona.

Captain Hughes' biographer, Jack Martin, also pointed out the distinctions between law enforcement work "in the more peaceful surroundings of Alice" and that area around the mouth of the Rio Grande and Brownsville. Texas Rangers frequently "found time heavy on their hands," however, the country neighboring Brownsville and its sister community across the border, Matamoros, was a hotbed for "marauding bands of outlaws" who made "frequent raids" upon area ranches, and the Rangers "often engaged them in gun-fights."[66] Texas Rangers often made piercing scouts into the gloomy thickets bordering the River. Some simply referred to the geography as brush country, others knew it as the *brasada*, but all knew it to be the address for landlubbering pirates, bandits, remorseless killers, and home base for not just a few "sons-of-a-bitchin' cow-thieves." Some of the cutthroats were native Spanish speakers, others just butchered the Queen's English, but regardless of nationality, they all carried fully-loaded Winchesters, six-shooters, long-ropes, running-irons, and, to the man, an unqualified loathing for all law, Mexican or American. That country below the Nueces River—all the way to the border—was in a fashion similar to the Big Bend, or even that out-of-the-way Llano Estacado, each owned a flake of recorded history, but it was based only on stories men opted to tell. Despite what a few well-intentioned, but sometimes idealistic scholars might wish to think, simply because there is no written record doesn't mean it didn't happen. Some goings on were best unmentioned. Bodies buried in unmarked graves or left rotting in the sun for a buzzard's feast were best just disregarded and smartly forgotten. Although most old-time border lawmen unflappably shrugged off inquires of *too* specific a nature, one in fact chose to write, "If a smuggler was killed at night and fell in the river, we forgot about the body unless it showed up downstream on the American side."[67] Dead men tell no tales. No witness—No foul! At least some so thought.[68]

Undeniably, augmenting the woefully small and inadequate law enforcement contingent and transferring a few familiar Texas Ranger faces out of the area, and replacing them with newcomers, was not wholly inappropriate. Earlier in the year, Ranger Sergeant A. Y. Baker had shot and killed suspected brand-blotcher Ramon De La Cerda. The Mexican community was incensed and inflamed, egged on by small partisan Spanish language newspaper editorials which were accusing the Texas Rangers as being nothing other than low-caliber murderers. The repugnant racial wound festered, and from both camps insensitive malcontents pushed and poked the stick of insolent contempt into the inflamed sociological sore. The situation was worsening rapidly, forcing Texas

Ranger Captain J. A. Brooks to proclaim, "My men are crack shots and I am not afraid of them getting the worst of anything."[69] Apparently he spoke a smidgen too soon, for on September 9th, Texas Ranger Sergeant Baker and Private W. E. Roebuck, along with a King Ranch cowboy, Jesse Miller, were ambushed—the charge of buckshot connected—Roebuck fell from the saddle—dead. Six men were ultimately arrested by the Texas Rangers, and one who was actually released from jail after posting the required bail bond was later killed by Ranger Sergeant Baker. A witness with testimony in Ranger Baker's behalf was assassinated. And the bloody turmoil raged! Texas Governor J. D. Sayers, in the end, was forced to send Adjutant General Thomas Scurry to the scene, who not unexpectedly exonerated the Texas Rangers, but did in all candor acknowledge they had indeed "cuffed" some of their Hispanic antagonists "without gloves."[70] With the *probability* of the Association hollering for more Texas Rangers, and the *certainty* of Hispanics screaming for a set of different Texas Rangers, Sergeant Dave Allison found himself drowning in the midst of manpower re-deployments.

With prospects of repositioning the Texas Rangers from Company D becoming enduring reality, rather than a temporary duty assignment, Sergeant Dave Allison, from his Post of Duty at Brownsville, tendered his resignation to the Texas Adjutant General at Austin. Primarily, Allison listed three reasons why he could not, or would not, accept being permanently posted along the Gulf Coast at Brownsville. First, he declared his wife, Lena, for health reasons could not "*survive*" at the low altitude in the steamy and balmy semi-tropical climate of the lower Rio Grande Valley. Secondly, Dave Allison simply declared he had too much "*household effects to move from Marathon to the Valley*," and that "*…it would cost me too much freight money to move our things*." Lastly, with a hint of racial undertones, Sergeant Dave Allison declared, "*This is strictly Mexican* (Brownsville) *and I do not speak the language—therefore am at a great disadvantage*."[71]

It is understandable that Lena, who preserved a particularly close bond with her parents, was hesitant to move even further from her ailing father. And, in the same vein, if human adolescent behavior is at all conventional, odds are that Hazel too had chimed in with whining resistance at being uprooted once again.

On December 20, 1902, Captain John R. Hughes, accepted the resignation and honorably discharged W. D. "Dave" Allison from the Texas Rangers.[72] The action was voluntarily, and as subsequent events will clearly reveal, Dave Allison didn't burn any bridges when he quit the Texas Rangers—one more time.

ENDNOTES

Chapter 3. "We forgot about the body unless it showed up downstream."

[1] Sheriff W. D. Allison to Adjutant General W. H. Maybry, February 16, 1895. Courtesy, Texas State Library and Archives Commission, Austin.
[2] *DESCRIPTIVE LIST*, dated Oct 8, 1899. Signed "John R. Hughes, Capt., Commd'g Co. D, Front. Batt." Courtesy, Texas Ranger Hall of Fame and Museum Library, Waco. Also, see *Monthly Returns,* Company D. Frontier Battalion (Texas Rangers), October 1899. Signed "Captain John R. Hughes." Courtesy, Texas State Library and Archives Commission, Austin.
[3] **Wilkins**, P. 340.
[4] Ibid. For this reporting period, Company D led all other Frontier Battalion companies in the number of arrests.
[5] *Monthly Returns*, Company D. Frontier Battalion, October & November 1891. Courtesy, TSLAC.
[6] W. D. Allison's discharge papers from Company D., Frontier Battalion. Dated December 18, 1899, signed "John R. Hughes, Capt. Commanding Company." Courtesy, Texas Ranger Hall of Fame and Museum Library, Waco.
[7] *Application to the Adjutant General, State of Texas for Appointment as Special Ranger*, signed "W. D. Allison" dated December 23, 1899. Courtesy Texas State Library and Archives Commission, Austin.
[8] Ibid.
[9] Ibid. The application was executed before J. M. Johnson, Justice of the Peace, Precinct No. 2, Midland County, Texas.
[10] Ibid.
[11] **Webb**., P. 453. "Each *officer* of the battalion…shall have all the powers of a peace officer, and it shall be his duty to execute all criminal process directed to him, and make arrests under capias properly issued of any and all parties charged with offenses against the laws of this State."
[12] Ibid.
[13] Ibid., "The fact that they had been operating under the law for more than a quarter of a century, during which time they must have imprisoned thousands of criminals, had no effect on the situation."
[14] **Wilkins**, P. 345.
[15] **Webb**, P. 457. Each of the four companies were comprised of three commissioned officer and three privates. A force woefully inadequate.
[16] Ibid. Also see, **Martin**, P. 175.
[17] **Haley**, J. Evetts, *Jeff Milton—A Good Man With a Gun*. Hereafter cited as **Haley (II)**. And, **Chaput**, Don, *The Odyssey of Burt Alvord, Lawman, Train Robber, Fugitive*. Hereafter cited as **Chaput**.
[18] **Haley (II)**, P. 306.
[19] Ibid. **Chaput**, P. 72., describes "Three-Fingered Jack's" wounds. "He had seven wounds in all, and those in his stomach and groin were deep."
[20] Ibid., P. 73.
[21] **Chaput**. P. 75. And see, **DeArment**, Robert K., *George Scarborough—The Life and Death of a Lawman on the Closing Frontier*. P. 222. Hereafter cited as **DeArment (II)**.
[22] **Haley (II)**, P. 311. "After he confessed, the officers swept over into Sulphur Springs Valley to take the Owens boys at their ranch. They picked up Bob

Brown. They went on to Willcox and put Downing, Stiles, Burts, and Alvord under arrest." **DeArment (II)**, P. 222. "Scarborough, who had once again rushed to Cochise County, joined Sheriff White in a sweep through the Sulphur Springs Valley, which netted them Brown and the Owens brothers. Yoes was captured later in Mexico. The prisoners talked and named as planners of both the Cochise and Fairbanks holdups the Pearce and Willcox officers Stiles, Alvord, and Downing, aided by a pal named Matt Burtts. Sheriff White and Scarborough descended on Willcox and took all four into custody."

[23] **Chaput**, P. 75. "In early June, Bob Brown was found, while trying to hide in his native Texas. He was arrested and shipped to Tombstone." And, P. 80, "The stage was being set for trials and penalties. Not only Alvord and Downing, but also the Owens brothers and Bravo Juan were in the Tombstone jail; Brown was still at large in Texas, and "Three-Fingered-Jack" was in a pauper's grave." Also see, **Thrapp**, Volume I, P. 17. "Allison followed one bandit to Arkansas and brought him back to face charges in Arizona." Comments concerning Brown's physical description can be found, *Territorial Prison At Yuma, A. T., Description of Convict*. Courtesy, Linda **Offeney**, Yuma Territorial Prison State Historic Park, Yuma.

[24] Bob Beverly to J. Evetts **Haley**, March 24, 1945. Typescript. Courtesy, The Nita Stewart Haley Memorial Library and The J. Evetts Haley History Center, Midland.

[25] Ibid.

[26] **DeArment**, P. 12.

[27] **Chaput**, P. 75. And, Beverly advised J. Evetts **Haley**, "Bob (Brown) and I sat down and went over the whole thing, about six months before he died, on the court house steps in Midland." And see, Edwards, Harold L. "Burt Alvord, The Train Robbing Constable" *Wild West,* October 2002, ". . . William D. Allison arrested Robert Brown without incident in Bonham, Texas." P. 51. Also see, *Monthly Returns*, Company D, Frontier Battalion. May, 1900. This primary source document clearly illustrates that Special Ranger W. D. Allison arrested R. E. Brown for "attempt to rob a train," and subsequently the accused was released to "Deputy Sheriff of Tombstone, Arizona." Courtesy, TSLAC.

[28] *Monthly Returns*, Company D., Frontier Battalion. December 1899 & January 1900. Courtesy, TSLAC.

[29] **Webb**, P. 457.

[30] Ibid., 457-461. That Hughes sought out Allison is *speculative*, but seems to not be unreasonable due to the quick enlistment date, and the supposition is somewhat confirmed by Allison's subsequent fast-track promotion within Texas Ranger ranks.

[31] **Martin**., P. 158.

[32] *Descriptive List*, W. D. Allison, October 19, 1901. Signed "John R. Hughes." Courtesy, Texas Ranger Hall of Fame and Museum Library, Waco. And see, John R. Hughes to AG Scurry, February 5, 1902. Courtesy Texas State Library and Archives Commission, Austin.

[33] *Texas Ranger Oath of Office*, W. D. Allison, October 19, 1901. Courtesy, Texas State Library and Archives Commission, Austin.

[34] Upon arrival of the Galveston, Harrisburg and San Antonio Railroad in 1882 Marathon blossomed as a shipping and supply point for area ranchers. Two years later the town population was estimated at fifty and by 1896 the town's population had doubled to 110. Prisoners were chained to a support leg for a windmill

erected in the middle of a Marathon street, that is until they could be moved to Alpine. "Later, a one-room adobe house behind French's Store served as a jail but, after several escapes, was replaced by a rock jailhouse. Eventually, used cells from the Alpine jail were installed." *The New Handbook of Texas*, Volume IV, P. 499. And see, **Wedin**, AnneJo P., *The Magnificent Marathon Basin—A History of Marathon, Texas, its people and events.*

[35] **Kingston**., P. 168. Also, **Gournay**, P. 108. "…making it the largest county in Texas, with an area of 5, 935 square miles."

[36] **Tyler**, Ronnie C., *THE BIG BEND, A History of the Last Texas Frontier.* P. 157-187. Hereafter cited as **Tyler**. Also see, **Raht**, Carlysle Graham, *The Romance of the Davis Mountains and Big Bend Country.* Hereafter cited as **Raht**. And see, *The New Handbook of Texas*, Volume I, P. 729. "The isolated position of many of the mining and industrial settlements that grew up in southern Brewster County made them tempting targets for raiders from Mexico, especially during the turbulent early years of the Mexican Revolution."

[37] **Kingston**, P. 260. Presidio County was created in 1850 from the Bexar District and organized in 1875. Also see, **Gournay**, P. 61. It is the fourth-largest county in Texas. Brewster County was formed from Presidio County real-estate and some could rightly claim that since she (Presidio) was the older of the two counties she should not be cast as a "little sister." To present day Presidio County residents who might take offense, a journalistic apology is proffered.

[38] *The New Handbook of Texas*, Volume V, P. 332. "Raids by Mexican bandits and paramilitary forces invited fierce and sometimes excessive retaliation by the United States military and by the Texas Rangers."

[39] **Meyer**, Michael C., *Mexican Rebel, Pascual Orozco and the Mexican Revolution, 1910-1915.* Orozco was born on the Hacienda de Santa Isabel near San Isidro, Guerrero, Chihuahua, on January 28, 1882. P. 15. Hereafter cited as **Meyer**.

[40] Ibid.

[41] **Madison**, Virginia., *The Big Bend Country of Texas*. The author explains, "The financial condition of the Big Bend is determined by the physical condition of the cattle. When rain is plentiful, the grass is good, the cattle are fat, and the people are happy. But when the drought comes and the grass gets short, the whole face of the region is lined with worry." P. 126. Hereafter cited as **Madison**.

[42] Ibid.

[43] **Weiler (II)**, P. 4., Also see locally published, *Treasures of History, Historic Buildings in Chaves County, 1870-1935*, by the Chaves County Historical Society, Roswell, New Mexico. P. 17. Hereafter cited as ***Treasures***.

[44] ***Treasures***., P. 17. **Weiler** confirms that family tradition supports a contention the Johnstons originally relocated to Roswell for health reasons. And clearly, as will be later explored through examination of Dave Allison's personal correspondence, at Roswell several years later, R. W. Johnston was indeed suffering poor health.

[45] *Roswell Daily Record*, August 2, 1901.

[46] ***Treasures***, P. 17.

[47] Ibid. The old Johnston home, 700 N. Lea Avenue, Roswell, New Mexico is still standing, still inhabited, and has been designated a recognized Historical Landmark home.

[48] **Weiler**. Lena Allison's younger brother, Will Johnston managed the cattle ranch at Elida, New Mexico.
[49] **Means**, Joyce E., *Pancho Villa Days at Pilares*. P. 87. Hereafter cited as **Means**.
[50] W. D. Allison to Texas Adjutant General, February 20, 1902. Courtesy Texas State Library and Archives Commission, Austin.
[51] There are several examples of this particular letterhead used in Ranger Sergeant Dave Allison's official correspondence. Courtesy, Texas Ranger Hall of Fame and Museum Library, Waco. Also see same, Texas State Library and Archives Commission, Austin.
[52] W. D. Allison to Texas Adjutant General, March 25, 1902. Courtesy Texas State Library and Archives Commission, Austin.
[53] W. D. Allison to Texas Adjutant General, May 5, 1902. Courtesy Texas State Library and Archives Commission, Austin. Private Earl Buster, at age twenty-two, originally from Wilson County, Texas, enlisted with the Texas Rangers on April 17, 1902. He supplied his own horse, which at the time was valued at $50.00. *Descriptive List*, courtesy, Texas Ranger Hall of Fame and Museum Library, Waco. The Chisos Mountains are a part of the Big Bend National Park, located in southern Brewster County. See, *The New Handbook of Texas*, Volume II, P. 90.
[54] W. D. Allison to Texas Adjutant General, May 13, 1902. Courtesy Texas State Library and Archives Commission, Austin.
[55] W. D. Allison to Texas Adjutant General, March 31, and April 2, 1902. In the second letter Allison mentions that he left his "saddle and gun" at Sierra Blanca. For the time period, the term "gun" meant a rifle, not a revolver, which was quite often referred to as a six-shooter, six-gun, thumb-buster, or Peacemaker. Despite Hollywood and television's misguided hype, a rifle was the preferred weapon of lawman and outlaw alike.
[56] W. D. Allison to Texas Adjutant General, April, 15, 1902. Courtesy, Texas State Library and Archives Commission, Austin.
[57] W. D. Allison to Texas Adjutant General, April 24, 1902. Courtesy, Texas State Library and Archives Commission, Austin.
[58] W. D. Allison to Texas Adjutant General, April 29, 1902. Courtesy, Texas State Library and Archives Commission, Austin.
[59] W. D. Allison to Texas Adjutant General, May 23, 1902. Courtesy, Texas State Library and Archives Commission, Austin.
[60] W. D. Allison to Texas Adjutant General, July 6, 1902. Courtesy, Texas State Library and Archives Commission, Austin. J. B. Townsend, was 23 years-old when he enlisted in the Texas Rangers at Fort Hancock on November 20, 1901. Prior to his service with state forces he had served as a night watchman, probably at his hometown, Oakland, Texas. Courtesy, Texas Ranger Hall of Fame and Museum. Waco.
[61] **Clarke**, P. 50.
[62] W. D. Allison to Texas Adjutant General, August 4, 1902. Courtesy, Texas State Library and Archives Commission, Austin.
[63] **Webb**, P. 461. At the time of the transfer Alice was indeed in Nueces County, however, today the city is county seat for Jim Wells County, located east of Corpus Christi, Texas.
[64] Ibid.
[65] Ibid., P. 462.

[66] **Martin**., P. 171

[67] **Perkins**, Clifford Alan, *Border Patrol, With the U. S. Immigration Service On the Mexican Boundary 1910-1954*. P. 42. Hereafter cited as **Perkins**.

[68] **Rynning**, P. 288. "The boys of the Ranger force had an oath amongst themselves—not par of the official oath—that they'd get anybody that ever killed a Ranger outside of fair fight. As near as I know they always kept that promise."

[69] **Webb**., P. 464.

[70] Ibid., P. 465. Cameron County Judge Stanley Welch supported the Ranger's actions.

[71] W. D. Allison to Texas Adjutant General, November 5, 1902. Courtesy, Texas State Library and Archives Commission, Austin. Allison's remark that Brownsville was "strictly Mexican" and that he was at a "great disadvantage" because he didn't speak the language seems in truth but a lame excuse. Especially in light of the fact that Dave Allison spent his entire career in the Southwest, much of it in country along the Mexican border, an area with significant Hispanic population, and as will be chronologically explored, in one career move he even accepted employment south of the border in "Old Mexico." Realistically speaking, Dave Allison, for whatever reason, did not want to relocate to the Rio Grande Valley of Texas—and he didn't!

[72] *Certificate of Discharge from Frontier Forces—State of Texas*. Dated December 20, 1902 and signed "John R. Hughes," Capt. Commanding Company D. Courtesy, **Treadwell**.

4

"a grand party in any kind of a scrimmage"

For a short while after surrendering his Texas Ranger Commission and state issued property Dave Allison's authenticated footprints fade from historical observation.[1] Conceivably a diligent search for Allison's trail would lead to 700 North Lea Avenue, Roswell, New Mexico Territory. Whether or not father-in-law Robert W. Johnston offered Dave Allison any type of permanent position connected with one of his several ranching enterprises is undetermined. To be sure, their personal relationship was amicable. Dave had the requisite cow-country know-how, and Bob Johnston had the cows, but if a real job was in fact tendered, Dave outright turned it down. Dave Allison was a lawman at heart—he had the calling—it was in his blood. And, dissimilar to particular and self-promoting Western frontier characters with much more recognizable twenty-first century names, many of whom continually wafted back and forth over that line separating law from lawlessness, internally Dave Allison had forevermore already chosen sides: he was born to police.

If in fact Dave Allison remained at Roswell for awhile, it wasn't for too long. On April 27, 1903, at Douglas, Cochise County, Arizona Territory, forty-two year old William Davis "Dave" Allison enlisted once again as a Ranger—an Arizona Ranger.[2] One writer, in a not inaccurate capsule commentary, concludes that Ranger Captain Thomas H. Rynning, who had in fact hired Dave Allison, "quickly recognized his abilities."[3] In truth, due to his lengthy tenure as Midland County Sheriff, coupled with his service in the vastly publicized Texas Rangers, and because of his favorite-son status with the politically potent Texas and Southwestern Cattle Raisers Association, Dave Allison already owned credentials as a genuine Southwestern frontier lawman, a signal fact noted on his Arizona Ranger enlistment papers, which identified him by occupation as a "Peace-officer."[4] A sampling of what he did do as a legitimate Arizona Ranger must be for the moment put on historic hold, while a quick explanation is made concerning something he didn't do.

In Dan Thrapp's ambitious *Encyclopedia of Frontier Biography*, among other things, Arizona Ranger Dave Allison is credited with killing "Three-Fingered" Jack Dunlap following the blistering shoot-out and botched train robbery at Fairbank, Arizona Territory. Factually, the shooting did indeed take place as previously noted, but on February 15, 1900, before Dave Allison had managed to meander across New Mexico Territory and into Arizona. What was the source for the erroneous data? Thrapp must have tapped into information mistakenly printed in numerous southern Arizona newspapers. One was the *Tombstone Daily Prospector*, which incorrectly reported, "It was Allison who killed 'Three Finger Jack' in the chase after the robbery of a train at Fairbank."[5] Apparently noted frontier lawman Jeff Milton, and/or his pals rightly hollered foul, and insisted on corrective satisfaction. A retraction was immediately printed, and years later was seemingly innocently overlooked by Thrapp. In part the press renunciation declared, "In an article published yesterday…it was erroneously stated that Allison killed 'Three Fingered Jack'. The exact details of the shooting of 'Three Fingered Jack' were obtained here today from Jeff Milton, immigration inspector at Fairbank, who ended the bandit's career in a gun fight on board a train that the bandit and his comrades attempted to rob."[6]

Unequivocally, William Davis "Dave" Allison did not kill Jack Dunlap, and when chronologically appropriate, it will be ironically noted there was another notorious character also answering to the moniker "Three-fingered Jack," and he too was sashaying about, stirring up his own brand of havoc in the southeastern Arizona neighborhood, a fact which may very well have contributed to the newspaper columnist's confusion.[7]

Even cursory inspection of an authentic history of the Arizona Rangers adds but another arrow to the quiver in pointing out, that in a wide-ranging overview the *transitional lawman* has once again traveled a rather lonely and somewhat artlessly unnoticed path. Unquestionably there have been several capable and competent dissertations highlighting the quantifiable contributions and valued service of Arizona Rangers, but the bare-bone fact is, except for devoted scholars and a progressively shrinking pool of Western law enforcement aficionados, the general reading and movie-going public has little knowledge regarding this state police organization. Without doubt the Arizona Rangers, as players on the grandiose Western stage, have reluctantly assumed the role of understudies, while top-billing and spotlight attention was focused on the Texas Rangers. Certainly one dynamic ingredient for this phenomena is simple longevity. Texas Rangers have crossed two century dividing bridges, while the Arizona Rangers were in truth but a short-lived outfit, historically and politically corralled during the first decade of the twentieth-century. With such ceaseless endurance, complemented by a considerably larger supporting cast of practiced publicity agents, there should be little doubt as to why Texas Rangers have overshadowed other badge-wearing brothers standing in the wings. Aside from affirmative Texas Ranger history, which in most cases is richly deserved, the disparity of interests between the two troupes can be credibly traced to the signal fact—time wise—one transcended frontiers, the other functioned solely on a *transitional* frontier.

From ground-level, however, lawmen had not time nor the inclination to worry about straddling century-mark dividing lines. By birth Dave Allison inherited his spot on a *transitional frontier*, but by conscious choice he was a lawman, and when engaged in chasing after crooks and depriving criminals of their liberty, some arbitrarily defined time-line made not a whit of real difference. From the earliest days of Texas Ranger crime fighting, right across that *transitional frontier*, through today, and on into tomorrow, on occasion legit lawmen pull the cinch from deep within, gut up, doing what has to be done. Arizona Ranger Dave Allison did too!

With a readable journalistic touch, while setting the Southwestern stage for a definitive study of the Arizona Rangers, Bill O'Neal, captures with words part of Dave Allison's *transitional frontier* surroundings: "There were telephones now throughout the West, along with ice cream parlors, bicycles built for two, Coca-Cola, hot dogs, and toothpaste in a tube. Adventurous young men who yearned to follow frontier ways had few places to 'hear the owl hoot' at the turn of the century, but Arizona still offered far horizons and a sense of freedom and exuberance…Bank and train robbers, murderers, rustlers, and other law-breakers with a fast horse stood a reasonable chance of remaining free from arrest…Individuals with the instincts of a man hunter could find a rare challenge remaining in Arizona. A man could pin on a badge, climb into the saddle and, in the righteous cause of justice and the territorial statutes, gallop into the mountains and canyons and deserts in pursuit of society's enemies. There were still plenty of wrongs to right in Arizona."[8]

The Arizona Rangers were born during March 1901, the midwife was the Twenty-first Territorial Legislature, and the delivery was long overdue—the labor pains intense! From conception, some thought the progeny might prove to be a bastard child of scheming politicians, causing one critic to comment, "the primary activity of all the rangers he had known was to go camping around the country making coffee."[9] Texas Rangers?

The baby cried, so to speak, and officially the nursery was filled with fourteen newborns—a captain, a sergeant, and twelve privates.[10] From infancy, toys, however, were to be furnished by the babes themselves, and they "…were to provide their own arms, mounts, and all necessary accouterments and camp equipage."[11]

And unlike their earlier dutiful counterparts in the Lone Star State, throughout the territory they were given unambiguous authority to arrest lawbreakers, with clear cut instructions to turn the miscreants over to local peace officers to be jailed pending prosecution.[12]

Unlike their state police counterparts in the Lone Star State, the Arizona Rangers were a direct byproduct of exertions brought to fruition by economic special interests groups. First and foremost were the cattlemen but, almost as importantly, chasing close behind were the buzzing financial heel-flies heavily invested in mining and railroad speculation. One writer adds another element to the equation, but in the end acknowledges the importance of the cattle culture specter, "The growing desire for statehood and the pressure from the cattlemen forced the governor and legislators to act."[13] Even the Territory's Chief Executive was later to proudly, although a tad prematurely, brag that "bands of cattle thieves were demoralized and driven out of the Territory…Stockmen to-day are protected on every hand…"[14] A prominent Arizona historian without hesitation freely admits, "the principal work of the Rangers was protection of the livestock industry."[15] Acknowledging the newly organized batch of territorial lawmen were recruited from "tough but trustworthy cowboys…," one report characterizes the Arizona Rangers as a hybrid cross between the Mexican *Rurales* operating south of the border and the no-nonsense Texas Rangers hard-charging north of the Rio Grande.[16] Another writer simply said of the new recruits, they "had to be good riders, ropers, and shooters."[17] Unquestionably *fearless* Dave Allison was qualified but, as history records, at the birthing of Arizona Rangers he was gainfully employed elsewhere as 1st Sergeant, Company "D," Texas Rangers.

During 1903, the Arizona Territorial Legislative Assembly modified the laws dealing with their territorial police force, which in part read:

> That the Governor of this Territory is hereby authorized to raise and muster into the service of this Territory and for the protection of the frontier of this Territory and for the preservation of peace and capture of persons charged with crime one company of Arizona Rangers, to be raised as

> herein after prescribed, and to consist of one captain, one lieutenant, four sergeants and not more than twenty (20) privates…
>
> That each member of said company shall be required to furnish himself with a suitable horse and pack animal, six-shooting pistol (army size), and all necessary accouterments and camp equipage, the same to be passed upon and approved by the enrolling officer before enlisted, and should any member fail to keep himself furnished as above required, then the officer in command shall be authorized and required to purchase the articles of which he may be deficient and charge the cost of same to the person for whom the same shall be provided; provided that all horses killed in action shall be replaced by the Territory, and the cost of horses so killed in action shall be determined by the captain.[18]

Whether or not Dave Allison learned of the Arizona Ranger manpower buildup and traveled from Roswell to Arizona Territory or whether he was personally recruited for the job is undetermined but, in either case, as previously documented, at Douglas, Arizona Territory on April 27, 1903, forty-two year old William Davis "Dave" Allison became an Arizona Ranger.

One anecdotal adventure of Dave Allison is quite interesting and, indeed, it proved humorously captivating enough to make a mark in Captain Thomas Rynning's somewhat overdrawn memoirs. According to the Captain, he and Dave slipped south across the international border on a star-filled Southwestern night in an effort to locate Sam Scott, a fugitive, who Rynning described as a "pretty slippery hombre."[19] Reportedly, on a tip from Red Seeley it was learned that Scott was hiding out at a ranch operated by a border liner owning a mammal moniker. Rynning wrote, "That rancher sure had a hell of a name to go to bed with: Pigg. He raised hogs, too. Dave (Allison) said he used one more *g* in his name than his pigs so's not to get their mail mixed up."[20] Approaching the ranch house the two lawmen split up, Allison riding to the rear of the abode to cut off any escape, Rynning to the front. Rynning almost stumbled onto Scott who was sleeping outside under the stars and utterly oblivious to his pending predicament. Surprised in his bedroll, Scott let out with a string of blue-streak epithets characterizing Southwestern lawmen and their parental lineage in common, and Arizona Rangers in particular. Responding to the noisy hubbub, "Dave come loping up when he heard Sam's opinion about John Laws in general, and told me to get his knife, that he always carried one. I'd already reached into the outlaw's bedding and got his gun, keeping him rolled up tight as bologna all the time. When he recognized our voices his oration become an education in cussing even for Arizona Rangers, but in spite of his unkind remarks we kept him hugged close to us like we was just wild with joy to meet up with him again, till we eased the Bowie out of his snug-fitting tarp."[21]

To the north, at Morenci, Arizona Territory, the troublesome rhetoric was much more serious. Located about six miles northwest of Clifton, just west of the border dividing New Mexico and Arizona Territories, Morenci could well lay claim to a crisply pleasant 4,838 ft. elevation, the waters of the San Francisco River on the east, and a complete envelopment by rutted mountains staunchly anchored by deposits of a seemingly inexhaustible supply of copper. Catching her name from a Detroit Copper Company executive's hometown, Morenci, Michigan, the company town could legitimately boast of mineral riches, starch-collared cigar smoking shareholders, pale faced middle-class mine managers, and a culturally mixed and racially diverse throng of underground hourly wage workers.[22]

From the very beginning, because of the relatively isolated location of the community, mine owners quickly recognized the unqualified obligation to furnish commissary to the attendant labor force—at substantial profit—of course. "Often the company lost money on the copper they shipped, but these losses were more than offset by the profits on the stores. Had it not been for the stores the enterprise could not have existed."[23] Gradually, however, due to entrepreneurial expansion of mining operations, and the incessant influx of a requisite labor force, over time independent merchants, retailers, and a smattering of "sporting men" capitalized on the financial opportunities offered by gratifying the appetites of hungry, thirsty, and lustful ore-humpers. Restaurants flourished, hospitable hotels were crammed plumb full, and chilly night air was delightfully permeated by rinky-dink tunes and ribald recitals spilling forth from bawdy whorehouses and saloons. At Morenci, Clifton, and nearby Metcalf, after working a ten hour day, many a fatigued miner imbibed and became bleary-eyed on an overdose of "Dago Red," but back East a different stimulant was gorging burning bellies and heating up the blood of everyday working men. A labor movement, calculatingly nudged by well-orchestrated union organizers, steadfastly committed sympathizers, and a fiercely loyal membership, was at hand. Arizona

Territory was not immune—an inoculation was in order. The territorial legislature measured the dose, filled the statutory syringe, injected the political needle, and painlessly delivered the stabilizing serum. Or so they thought!

The Twenty-second Territorial Legislature, the same body that had doubled the size of the Arizona Rangers in their lawmaking session of 1903, passed into law despite the objections of Governor Alexander Brodie, what would generally be characterized as the "eight hour law."[24] Simply put, the new statute dictated that "employment of working men in all underground mines or workings shall be on a basis of eight hours per day, except in cases of emergency where life or property is in eminent danger."[25] On June 1st the new regulation went into effect and mine owners immediately chopped two hours off the work day—likewise proportionately reducing wages. Disgruntlement swept through the near mutinous copper camps. Mine management, in an act of uncompromising good faith and undisguised magnanimous self-interest, offered to compensate the workforce with nine hours pay for eight hours work. Through their leadership, the labor force, comprised mainly of Mexicans, Mexican-Americans, and a sampling of working-class Europeans, flatly rejected the newly tendered wage structure proposal. From their perspective, hourly workers calculated that take home pay was being reduced by one-tenth.[26] Two days after the law went into effect, the underground miners walked off the job and were joined by the smelter-men; 3500 employees idled, the mines, mills and smelters tightly shut down.[27]

Several men can actually be credited with an active leadership role at the head of striking miners, "As the strike progressed, it became known the principal men in charge were Abram F. Salcido, president of a Mexican society, Frank Colombo, an Italian, and W. H. Laustenneau, a Rumanian."[28]

The latter, however, is the best known and most often mentioned of the strike leaders. William H. Laustenneau, by some reports was a blacksmith by trade and had worked his way across the Mexican border settling in the Morenci area about 1900—other renditions postulate the Rumanian immigrant had been sent to Arizona Territory as a labor organizer in the Spring of 1903 by the Chicago based Industrial Workers of the World Union.[29] Regardless, the brown-eyed Laustenneau, a father of two children, had previously suffered personal losses, the death of his wife, and the amputation of fingers from his left hand, thus his graphic nickname, "Three-Fingered Jack."[30] There is, however, unanimity in each and every account. "Three-Fingered Jack" Laustenneau was an orator of superb skill, an audacious agitator, and a mulish and dangerously defiant firebrand.

While the pay scale was the main point of contention, other critical issues were argued. "Three-Fingered Jack" prodded management and fervently whipped the disconcerted crowd with demands relating to company assessments for hospital and life insurance, and clearly cautioned mine owners not to increase the prices in company stores unless there was an across the board rise in the standard market prices. Unionism? "The Mexicans and Italians had their own local organization but were not members of the Western Federation of Miners. As a matter of fact, representatives from this union's headquarters in Denver urged moderation when the strikers threatened to blow up the railroad bridges and to loot the company stores."[31] Laustenneau wasn't taunting with impassioned cries of reticence and restraint!

William H. "Three-Fingered Jack" Laustenneau. Strike leader during the Morenci mining troubles. Courtesy, Yuma Territorial Prison State Park, Yuma, Arizona.

The trio of activists presided over smoldering, and sometimes frenzied meetings at an old lime pit which had been wedge-cut from a mountain looking down over Morenci. "Liquor flowed freely, and there was angry talk about looting the company stores, dynamiting area railroad bridges, and damaging the mine works."[32] Graham County Sheriff Jim Parks arrived on the scene with a few real deputies, and then deputized a peculiar posse of civilian store clerks and retailers, who one grizzled lawman was to later scoffingly characterize as "counter jumper deputies," an inefficient force which was outgunned and overwhelmed from inception.[33] Striking miners were emboldened and obstinately shepherded into lock-step formation, especially after being assured by Laustenneau that their actions had the unequivocal and sympathetic blessings of American President Theodore Roosevelt and the Mexican President, Porfirio Diaz.[34] What "Three-Fingered Jack" failed to do, though, is advise the milling masses that Arizona Rangers weren't in on the deal.

Not unexpectedly, powerfully connected mine owners turned to the Territorial Governor's Office, and bluntly demanded an instantaneous and forceful performance from Arizona Rangers. After all, "The Rangers' intercession on behalf of private individuals was a common occurrence. They had a history of closely working with employer groups, such as Arizona cattlemen associations, in order to preserve the interests of private enterprises."[35] The territorial chief executive was away on a trip back East, and the ticklish decision making process fell on Acting Governor Isaac T. Stoddard, who wired President Roosevelt requesting that federal troops be at once dispatched to Morenci.[36] Whether or not mine management, at least in the back of their minds, had intended on using the territorial police as "strike breakers" is undetermined but, assuredly, from Acting Governor Stoddard's perspective the threat was indeed genuine, and there was an unadulterated gamble that unless actions were quickly taken there could actually be loss of life and/or the malicious destruction of costly and difficult to replace mining machinery. Captain Rynning was ordered to the scene. On the *transitional frontier*, communication and mobility had been greatly improved from just a few years earlier and, in truth, utilizing telephone, telegraph, and spider-web railroad connections, it wasn't too long at all before Captain Rynning had rounded up his squadron of *transitional lawmen* and headed out for Morenci. Recently recruited Ranger Private W. D. "Dave" Allison was an integral part of the lineup. Those rangers not traveling with the headquarters command were ordered to proceed to Morenci with haste and unite with their compatriots. On the evening of June 7th, a Sunday, the Arizona Rangers disembarked the train at Morenci, carrying smokeless powder .30-.40 caliber Model 1895 Winchester rifles, Colt's .45 caliber single-action revolvers strapped to their sides, newly issued tin-stars pinned to their vest, and a hell-to-pop attitude under their stylishly hand-shaped hats.[37]

Photo of Arizona Rangers at Morenci. Most contemporary informants identified Ranger Dave Allison as fourth from left. Courtesy, Arizona Historical Society, Tucson, Arizona.

Bill O'Neal objectively disregards political correctness and rightly reflects the Arizona Ranger's racially prejudicial assessment of the strikers and their sympathizers when he quotes Ranger James H. "Bud" Bassett, "...mostly Mexicans, but a lot of Dagoes, Bohunks, and foreigners of different kinds—no whites at all."[38] Characteristic of the times, even the *Bisbee Daily Review* reported, "The strike is now composed almost entirely of Mexicans...Quite a number of Americans have left the camp. These men are taking no part with the Mexicans."[39] The newspaper writer went so far as to predict that the strike "will probably be the end of Mexican labor in the district."[40] Certainly though it wasn't necessarily a one sided state of affairs, as the very same journalist concisely reported that prominent strike leaders were haranguing and making use of harsh language concerning the "*gringos*."[41] The recently reinforced contingent of Arizona Rangers, as would be expected, were all "white," ready to go, and most probably psychologically incapable of accepting any "monkey-business" from a bunch of non-English speakers—not in the 1903 Southwest!

Morenci was clogged with belligerent miners, quarrelsome malcontents, loud-mouthed ruffians, profit minded pimps, card sharks, and a whole regiment of those nameless and shadowy misfits wanting to take stabs at stirring up trouble, all the while ingloriously draped in the brave anonymity of a crowd. One historian simply states, the Rangers "found themselves in a tight situation."[42] Another notes that most of the demonstrators were armed with "rifles, pistols, and knives."[43] "Dago Red" freely flowed, slurred speeches were inarticulately uttered, and passionate proposals to redress real and imagined wrongs, gradually gave way to an orgy of riotous behavior and drunkenness in the puke-puddled streets.[44] Captain Rynning stationed his ranger contingent, who themselves were certainly not Angels, throughout the town, and although the night didn't necessarily pass quietly—next morning the sun didn't shine on dead bodies lying in the mud, the blood, and the beer. Ranger Dave Allison's exact duty assignment for the night, as of this time, remains historically indeterminable. With confidence though, it can be faithfully reported that he was definitely a participating member of the Ranger platoon at Morenci, and accordingly, as would be expected, he performed "up to snuff" during an action in which all the lawmen acquitted themselves honorably.[45]

In truth the sun didn't shine at all. It was raining—at times quite hard—but while the drops fell to the ground the tensions rose upward. Strike leaders, from their lime-pit perch peeking down over Morenci, continued to harangue and agitate the crowd amid rumors that their ranks were soon to be reinforced by several hundred supporting miners from nearby Metcalf.[46] Reportedly with their forces strengthened, the miners were planning on advancing on Morenci and looting the huge Detroit Copper Company store.[47] Others, however, were inclined to acknowledge that the striking miner's true intentions were not exactly verifiable, but the diagnosis for an escalation of the discord and predictions of mischief and bloodshed were epidemic.[48] Taking to heart the age old axiom that in most instances the best defense is a good offense, Arizona Ranger Lieutenant Johnny Foster dispatched Rangers "Bud" Bassett and Henry Gray to head off the advancing Metcalf bunch, and in no uncertain terms advise them to return to their camps and homes. There was no collision of opposing forces, the unfaltering duo of lawmen sloshed up the road toward Metcalf, the disconcerted miners splashed toward their belligerent buddies by a different route, through Chase Creek Canyon.[49] Whether or not the advancing miners could hear "Three-Fingered Jack" berating mine management and pumping vitriol into the festering crowd is guesswork, probably not, because just overhead thunder rolled, and streaks of lighting danced along mountain ridges. Pelting rain plummeted from the electrically charged sky like "pitchforks."[50] Rangers and miners alike sought a parcel of dry ground as they watched Mother Nature turn day into night and put forth a gully washer, a real frog-strangler!

Scampering miners scrambled for high ground as frothing whitecaps swilled together forming a merciless wall of water eight feet high, ruthlessly cascading south through Chase Creek Canyon.[51] Telephone messages from the Longfellow Mine above had warned downstream residents to flee—get ahead of the churning and crashing currents—few heeded the warnings. "Then the storm broke loose in Clifton, the rain falling in sheets, as if spilled from a mighty reservoir, accompanied by hail as large as walnuts, propelled with force as if shot from a Gatling gun…The flood waters struck the upper end of the town with a crest of from six to eight feet, carrying houses, horses, wagons and human beings on to the Frisco river with a speed and fury indescribable…Houses were picked up and jammed against others only to break into a thousand pieces, carrying their helpless occupants for a few hundred feet, when they sank beneath the murky waters never to be seen alive again."[52] Abruptly the downpour ceased, the mats of hail begin to melt, howling winds seemed to take one last gasp and die, while the horrific thunderstorm trekked elsewhere. Fatalities? At least twenty—more by other accounts.[53] Many of the Mexican laborers lived in the hauntingly narrow confines of steeply banked Chase Creek Canyon. Since the principal flood damage lay along this watercourse, not only did they lose their homes, but also their spirit for any further unruly misbehavior and misadventure.

To their credit many drenched miners burrowed in the rubble looking for the injured, for survivors. The squadron of Arizona Rangers diligently patrolled the streets maintaining order and casting an ever watchful eye for any potential looters. Others, however, were not of benevolent nature. "Three-Fingered Jack" Laustenneau wrung himself out, shook like a teeth-gnashing cur, and without delay began nipping and growling once again. Several local deputies were captured, disarmed, and threatened within an inch of their lives at the Longfellow Mine. At the Detroit Copper Company Mill others had been disarmed, roughed up, and members of the mining management team had been threatened with violence.[54] Back at provisional Ranger headquarters in Morenci, Lieutenant Foster fed up with the rotten state of affairs opted for decisive action, best described by one of the participants, "Bud" Bassett:

> The principal leader of the strikers was a fellow called 'Mocho'—meaning 'crippled hand'—by the Mexicans. The Americans called him 'Three-fingered Jack.' He wasn't a Mexican. Some said he was an Austrian—other that he was a Roumanian—anyway, he was some kind of a Bohunk. He could talk English, and he was the head man of the strikers. Well, Johnny said to me, 'Bud, I guess it's up to us to get Mocho.' We'll try, I replied. So we

> started up the trail toward the pit, and half-way up saw a man coming down. We thought it was Mocho, and sure enough it was. 'Don't you fellows go any further,' he said, 'or my men will kill you. All I got to do is make a motion.' Then Foster and me threw our 30-40s down on him and Johnny said, 'and all I have to do is to pull trigger and you're a dead Mexican. Best thing for you is to come along with us.' He took Johnny at his word, and that was the wise thing to do...And when Mocho was locked up the backbone of the strike was broken.[55]

With "Three-Fingered Jack" wrapped up in the clutches of police custody, other Arizona Rangers, Dave Allison included, fanned out through Morenci, arrested a number of other strike leaders, and made systematic house to house searches, confiscating a wide assortment of weapons, "doubled-barreled guns, revolvers with four barrels...guns with brass barrels, and a lot of other kinds—all of foreign manufacture...some of them homemade."[56] By the time the Arizona National Guard, 230 strong, arrived in Morenci the turmoil, for the most part, was over. When U. S. Troops from Fort Grant in New Mexico Territory and from Fort Huachuca in southeastern Arizona reinforced the Territorial Guardsmen, the Rangers were dismissed.[57] Almost!

Prior to their departure from Morenci the entire company of Arizona Rangers, their trusty lever-action Winchesters in hand, lined up and were formally photographed by Rex Rice of the Phelps-Dodge Mercantile.[58] By most accounts Arizona Ranger Private W. D. "Dave" Allison is identified as the lawman standing fourth from the left. This unique photograph of stern faced, rifle-toting, badge-wearers has through the years become quite well-recognizable as one of the standard depiction's of *transitional lawmen* on the *transitional frontier*. Somewhat ironically, especially in light of previous commentary in this particular narrative, in 1962 the Winchester Arms Company used the photograph in a nationwide advertising campaign. The photograph was captioned "*19 Texas Rangers: only 18 Winchesters. Why?*" Arizonans howled in indignant disbelief and "pointed out these were Arizona Rangers, the arms company ruefully apologized and gave a banquet in Phoenix to atone for its error."[59]

In a packed Solomonville courtroom "Three-Fingered Jack" Laustenneau and seventeen of his shackled and seditious sidekicks were put on trial for their actions during the troubles at Morenci. Although actual testimony from a score of witnesses revealed that there had actually not been "unparalleled scenes of bloodshed and crime," most jurymen and spectators alike thought the defendants had damn well come too close. "Three-Fingered Jack" having been put up by his comrades to act as their legal counsel, was ineffectual in arguing the wayward strikers' case, especially when Mine Superintendent Alexander McLean testified that "heavily armed men surprised him in his office and gave him one minute to close down the works, and that the strike leader threatened to blow up the town with dynamite and to loot the ruins."[60] Laustenneau and nine of his partners were sentenced to two-year terms in the Territorial Prison at Yuma for inciting a riot.[61]

In truth, what were the quantifiable facts spilling forth from the fractious strife at Morenci? The miners trudged back to work, tunneling underground once again extracting costly copper, now courteously content to accept nine hours pay for eight hours work.[62] Owners and investors smiled, no unruly gang of foreign speaking rascals was going to disrupt their profitable pursuits, not for too long, not when they could promptly summon Arizona Rangers at their beck and call. "Three-Fingered Jack," thoroughly incorrigible, after a vicious but failed prison break, picked up an additional ten-years on his sentence, and died in prison.[63] Captain Thomas Rynning was gifted with a gold watch by mining company executives.[64] Arizona Ranger Private W. D. "Dave" Allison was promoted to Sergeant.[65] And the Territorial Chief Executive was handed Captain Tom Rynning's concise report about the fateful sequence of events, "Almost the entire month of June the company was at Morenci assisting the sheriff of Graham County in protecting property and preserving peace, disarming the strikers, and arresting the leaders of the riot."[66]

Ranger Sergeant Allison's promotion was later officially confirmed by Arizona Territorial Governor Alexander Brodie.[67] Surely Dave Allison was pleased with the new promotion, and undoubtedly he could put to good use the extra ten dollars tacked on to his monthly pay. He was now earning $110.00 per month, nothing to sneeze at on the Southwestern *transitional frontier*.[68]

There was no pay distinction between the four Ranger Sergeants of the Company, but Dave Allison was designated *first* Sergeant.[69] With the title went the headaches, and Dave Allison immersed himself in the sometimes suffocating quagmire of routine clerical duties relating to Arizona ranger recruitment, records, requisitions, responses, and reimbursements.

Giving unambiguous credence to the contention that journeyman cowboy and legit lawman Dave Allison was an accomplished hand with horses, and wasn't necessarily a teetotaler, is evidenced by the remarks of an old-timer who personally knew him during the attention-grabbing Arizona Territory days: "Allison had a well trained horse. He would ride the horse to town and leave him in front, while he went into a saloon. After awhile he would go to another saloon, and would whistle, and the horse would follow him down to the next place he stopped. Maybe he would spend the whole day in the saloons of the town, and there would be his horse in front of the saloon he was in."[70]

Certainly it wasn't all mundane headquarters drudgery. On one occasion, Captain Rynning and Dave found themselves on the trail of a "hard customer" who had callously murdered a school teacher.[71] Later the Captain was to describe the desperado as having his right arm shot off in a previous gunfight, but "he was poison with his left; could draw and shoot like a rattlesnake. And he was a killer clear through to his ornery backbone."[72] Reportedly the suspect had by the desert grapevine sent word to Cochise County Sheriff Albert (Del) Lewis, and any interested Rangers who might overhear, that he was afraid of no living man, that he was not to be trifled with in the slightest, that he would kill dead as hammers any officers who were foolishly hardheaded enough to sally forth and try to make him answer for the vicious killing.[73] First Sergeant Dave Allison and his Commander ignored the threats and skillfully stalked the bad-tempered *hombre* through the old stomping grounds of "Curly Bill" Brocius, in the vicinity of Galeyville, to an old rock cabin cut into the side of a picturesque mountain in southeastern Arizona's Chiricahua range.[74] Actually belonging to the Double Diamond Ranch, the obstreperous outlaw's stonework stronghold was a foreboding fortress with a single entrance, one way in—the same way out.[75] The ranking ranger recorded, "It didn't look extry good."[76]

Reconnaissance suggested to the lawmen that the "murdering old hellion" was indeed on the inside of the cabin, camped out, making himself at home as they could observe wisps of blue smoke coming from the chinked chimney. Rynning and Allison mulled over their wartime strategy. Laying protracted siege was not a practical option, not when there was other work to be done, other outlaws needing attention.[77] Dave Allison, experienced in such unbendable matters, knew there were but two viable choices, get the wily son-of-a-bitch or turn tail and slink back home empty-handed. In characteristic fashion he told his boss, "The only chance is for the two of us to jump in the door together and spread a bit as we go in. When he sees two he'll likely be so surprised he'll be rattled for half a second and not shoot till we've got him."[78] Rynning didn't question Allison's uncomplicated and straightforward logic.

Stealthily the pair of officers silently crept toward the solitary doorway, knowing full well that while doing so they were innocently exposed "sitting-ducks." Evidently the brutal renegade was napping for the lawmen made it to the narrow aperture of the solid rock fortification undetected. Harmoniously each lawman eared back the hammer of his Colt revolving six-shooter, nervously nodded to the other, and without weakness both "lammed in together."[79] On the inside, in dim flickering firelight the startled brigand furiously jerked his own weapon.[80] Having multiple targets to chose from, the battling bad guy hesitated for a split-second, an interval frozen in just enough time for Dave to slip a shot his way, hitting him in the leg "grazing the bone," and for Rynning to dispassionately shoot him through the "loose hide on his flank."[81] Falling as if thunderstruck, the wounded warrior crumpled to the cabin's tightly packed earthen floor in a heap, saying, "Goddamn it, I was so rattled when I seen two of you I didn't know which one to shoot first and you beat me to it."[82] Later, commenting about an audacious Dave Allison's overall *fearlessness*, the Ranger Captain remarked, "He was a grand party when it come to any kind of scrimmage."[83]

Clearly Ranger Sergeant Dave Allison made an exceptionally favorable impression on his Captain, and in turn, the Territorial Governor, Alexander Brodie. On October 26th, Dave Allison turned in his Sergeant's badge and was sworn in as the Ranger Company's Lieutenant.[84] Of the appointment a Nogales, Arizona Territory newspaperman wrote in the *Border Vidette*, "The new lieutenant has a long and good record as a peace officer in the territory, Texas and New Mexico. He was Sheriff of Midland County, Texas, for ten years. He was first sergeant of the Texas Rangers under the famous Captain Hughes for one enlistment of two years."[85] As previously documented, Dave Allison was known throughout the Southwest for his reputation, causing one author to comment that although Dave had "a deceptively angelic face" he was still "a noted gunman in his own right.[86] An additional factor, however, may have been factored into consideration for Dave Allison's promotion to Ranger Lieutenant. Simply stated, Dave Allison was older in years, had more hard-core and practical down in the trenches law enforcement experience than the majority of subordinate Arizona Rangers.

According to Rynning, one day he "grabbed Dave Allison" and headed out after fugitives, the previously mentioned Burt Alvord and Billy Stiles.[87] Suspecting that the outlaws were heading north out of Mexico, Rynning and Allison camped out in some cedar breaks near the only water source to be found for miles around. Hoping to ambush or apprehend the thirsty pirates, the lawmen staked-out the water tanks. Late in the afternoon, according to Rynning, Allison made his intention to kill a deer, for in their hurry to depart Douglas the man hunters had failed to fill their pockets or saddlebags with foodstuffs. At first, Rynning demurred, suggesting the shot might scare off their prey, but allegedly, after listening to Allison's belly growl for awhile, and his own hunger pains beginning to cramp his gut, the command decision was made—fire away! Allison killed a deer, and certainly Rynning didn't abstain from the meal, but next morning the lawmen found tracks five hundred yards away which indicated the outlaws *may* have heard the shot and bypassed the intended trap.[88] Years of practical day to day law enforcement know-how had long ago taught Dave Allison that, in most cases, in the Grand Scheme, it really wasn't necessary to miss a meal—or a nap. Sooner or later the fugitives would trip themselves up and slip into lawmen's snares. History in this case proved him very right, but that's another hair-raising and oft repeated adventurous Western story.

Hillary Loftis, aka Tom Ross, aka Charlie Gannon. He trekked on the opposite side of the legality line from Dave Allison. Courtesy, Panhandle-Plains Historical Museum. Canyon, Texas.

Meanwhile, over in that lonesome looking country around Hobbs, New Mexico Territory, just east of the Texas line in Gaines County, Hillary Loftis, operating under the alias Tom Ross, was back on the scene.

He had married Trixie Hardin, and by some accounts had more or less settled down, but unquestionably he was still a sought after Wilbarger County fugitive.[89] Learning of the possible whereabouts of Loftis, Sheriff Charles Tom, Martin County, Texas, and Company "B" Captain John H. Rogers, Texas Rangers, set off in an industrious search for Ross. They began rummaging around on the stark tabled Staked Plains. Developing intelligence that their quarry, at the time, was working at an out-of-the-way cow-camp on the Halff Ranch, the undaunted team of weathered lawmen persisted with their prudent pursuit.[90]

As one author rightly reports, the next chapter of this Llano Estacado event is "clouded in mythology," but nevertheless a quick recap is not out of place.[91] The determined pair of lawmen finally caught up with Loftis—actually it was the other way around—Loftis doubled-back on his trail, and let loose with his Winchester on the flabbergasted duo. Captain Rogers later explained to the Texas Adjutant General, John A. Hulen:

> In June, 1904, while scouting in the plains country near the line of New Mexico, I made an unsuccessful attempt to arrest Hill Loftis, alias Tom Ross; he ran out of shooting distance from me, thereby avoiding arrest. Later in the day he lay in wait and waylaid me, shooting my horse in the jaw, getting the drop on me with a big Winchester, while I had only a pistol. I was completely in his power; and it looked as if he would kill me in spite of all I could do or say. This party is an old time robber of a hard gang.[92]

In other, unsubstantiated versions, Loftis made the lawmen "eat the warrant for his arrest." Another adaptation simply declares the officers, shaking in their boots, unequivocally guaranteed that they would never ever—under any circumstances—try to arrest him again.[93] And these two didn't! Later, in a court action, when no witnesses could be located that *could* or *would* testify against Loftis, the ten-year old Wilbarger County robbery charge was officially dismissed, and the one-time fleeing fugitive was once again a liberated man, but as history indelibly records, he was nevermore to be too far removed from troubles with the law.[94] Arizona Ranger Lieutenant W. D. "Dave" Allison too was having his own brand trouble with the law—his boss.

Dave Allison's resignation from the Rangers was requested and tendered.[95] The hard-core factual material relating to William Davis

Allison's departure from the Arizona Rangers can be traced to but one account, Captain Rynning's remarks. "Dave had been one of my rangers, and whilst I had to let him go because he was always getting up to his neck in debt trying to break every faro bank and Monte game both sides of the line…"[96] Shades of Midland? Suffice to say, Captain Tom Rynning's disciplinary action may have been systematically applied and scrupulously warranted. Impartial analysis of the existent facts unmistakably points toward but one logical conclusion, that Dave Allison's termination from the Arizona Rangers was not voluntary.

ENDNOTES
Chapter 4. "A grand party in any kind of a scrimmage."

[1] W. D. Allison to Texas Adjutant General, December 22, 1902. Just what State of Texas property Dave Allison had in his possession is undetermined, but the correspondence clearly states, "...I have delivered to my Capt. All the state property in my possession. Some of which he has turned over to Capt. McDonald—and the rest is to be shipped in a car detained for Alice." Courtesy, Texas State Library and Archives Commission. Austin.
[2] *Territory of Arizona—Oath of Office—Arizona Rangers*, signed "Wm. D. Allison," April 17, 1903 and "Thos. H. Rynning," Captain Arizona Rangers. Courtesy, State of Arizona, Department of Library, Archives and Public Records, Phoenix. Additionally, *Service Records, Arizona Rangers*, copy courtesy Bill **O'Neal** author of *The Arizona Rangers*. Hereafter cited as **O'Neal**. A special note of thanks must be extended to **O'Neal**, who graciously made available a wealth of material gathered while preparing his definitive study of the Arizona Rangers. As would be presupposed, he possessed voluminous records on the Arizona Rangers in general, as well as a plethora of valuable biographic information on individual rangers, William Davis Allison included.
[3] **DeArment**, P. 12.
[4] *Territory of Arizona—Oath of Office—Arizona Rangers*. Courtesy, State of Arizona, Department of Library, Archives and Public Records, Phoenix. Also see, **O'Neal**, P. 44. And see, **Thrapp**, Volume I, P. 17. Unfortunately, **Thrapp** correctly identifies Allison's enlistment date, but is in error when he comments that Allison remained an Arizona Ranger up until the time the organization was disbanded.
[5] *Tombstone Daily Prospector*, April 4, 1923. Also see, *Tombstone Epitaph*, April 4, 1923. Apparently all the newspapers were just "picking up" a story as it appeared in the *Arizona Daily Star*.
[6] *Arizona Daily Star*, April 5, 1923.
[7] Correspondence to author (July 25, 2000) from Rose **Byrne**, Archivist, Arizona Historical Society, Tucson. "We did not find any information about a connection between Dunlap and William Allison."
[8] **O'Neal**, P. 1. To date this is the definitive study of the Arizona Rangers. *The Arizona Rangers*, edited by Joseph **Miller**, and hereafter cited as **Miller**, is basically a compilation of newspaper articles about the law enforcement organization. Numerous articles, of course, have been presented in magazines and historical journals, as well as chapters dedicated to the Arizona Rangers in books encompassing issues of a much broader scope. Several of which will be cited, but for a single source—knowledgeably researched— and pleasingly understandable—**O'Neal** is required and highly recommended.
[9] Ibid., P. 3. Quoting the remarks of Arizona Territorial Legislator Kean St. Charles of Mohave County. And see, **Winsor**, Mulford, "The Arizona Rangers," *Our Sheriff and Police Journal*, Vol. 31, No. 6. (1936), P. 50. Hereafter cited as **Winsor**. Also see, **Kelly**, George H., *Legislative History, Arizona, 1864-1912*. P. 212. "Among the recommendations made were the following: ...Authorizing the formation, at the pleasure of the Governor, a company of mounted rangers, comprising of a captain, sergeant, and twelve privates to patrol the frontier counties." Hereafter cited as **Kelly**.

[10] **Kelley**. P. 212.
[11] **O'Neal.** P. 4. And, *Arizona Territory Revised Statutes 1901*, Section 3216 and 3217. "Said men shall be furnished by the territory with the most effective and approved breech-loading cavalry arms, and for the purpose the governor is hereby authorized to contract in behalf of the territory for ten stands of arms, together with a full supply of ammunition, the same to be all of the same make and caliber, and each member of the company to be furnished with the arms to be used by him at the price the same shall cost the territory, which sum shall be retained out of the first money due him." Courtesy, State of Arizona Department of Library, Archives and Public Records, Phoenix.
[12] *Arizona Territory Revised Statutes 1901*, Section 3225, "Members of said company shall have full power to make arrests of criminals in any part of the territory, and upon the arrest of any criminal, shall deliver the same over to the nearest peace officer in the county where the crime is committed." Courtesy, State of Arizona Department of Library, Archives and Public Records, Phoenix.
[13] **Jensen**, Jody, "Birth of the Arizona Rangers, Outlaw Violence Spurred the Growth of the Rangers," *Old West*, Spring 1982., P. 30. Also see, **Winsor**, P. 50, "As has been said the cattle interest, aided and abetted by representatives of two other important industries—mine and railroad—was chiefly responsible for creation of this super-police force."
[14] *Report of Arizona Territorial Governor to Secretary of the Interior, 1903.* Of the Arizona Ranger personnel the Governor further declared "They are picked men enlisted from the hundreds of fearless cowboys of the Territory, who are skilled in riding, trailing, and shooting." Courtesy, State of Arizona Department of Library, Archives and Public Records. Phoenix.
[15] **Wagnoer**, Jay J., *Arizona Territory, 1863-1912, A Political History.* P. 383. The close association between the Arizona Rangers and the cattle industry is further confirmed by the author. "Working closely with the Livestock Sanitary Board and the Arizona Cattle Growers' Association, the Rangers attended roundups and served as livestock inspectors, especially along the border." Hereafter cited as **Wagnoer**.
[16] **Waltrip**, Lela and Rufus, "Top Man of the Fearless Thirteen," *True West*, November-December, 1970. P. 25. The authors report that one old-timer made a historic comparison of the initial thirteen Arizona Rangers, "No North West Mounted Police or Texas Rangers ever did more for civilization than this hard riding, straight shooting, fearless 'thirteen' of Arizona."
[17] **Wagoner**, P. 374.
[18] *Acts, Resolutions and Memorials 22nd, Legislative Assembly, Territory of Arizona, 1903*. Courtesy, State of Arizona Department of Library, Archives and Public Records. Phoenix.
[19] **Rynning**, P. 221.
[20] Ibid.
[21] Ibid., P. 222.
[22] **Barnes**, Will C., *Arizona Place Names.* P. 288. Morenci was first called Joys Camp and the Post Office was established in 1884. Hereafter cited as **Barnes**. Also see, **Park**, Joseph F., "The 1903 'Mexican Affair' at Clifton," *Journal of Arizona History*, 18:2 (Summer 1977), P. 119-148. Hereafter cited as **Park**.
[23] **Park**., P. 124. Quoting James Colquhoun, *The History of the Clifton-Morenci Mining District.* **Park** reports that butchering was done every other morning and that beef or mutton could be purchased at twelve and a half cents per pound.

[24] **Kelly**, P. 223. Governor Brodie believed, and with some justification, that a careful investigation should be initiated into what possible side effects might attach to a Territorial statute mandating private enterprises to regulate the number of hours worked on a particular shift, before any such law was enacted and enforced.

[25] Ibid., P. 225. Interestingly, and as direct example of the influence of private interest leverage on lawmakers, especially as it relates to law enforcement, the Twenty-second Legislature also exempted railroads from taxation for a period of ten years, and passed a special act providing for the appointment of "peace officers by railroad companies, such officers to serve on the railroad premises, the railroad company to be responsible, civilly for any abuse of authority by such officers." P. 226-227.

[26] **Park**., P. 142.

[27] Ibid. Also see, James H. "Bud" Bassett typescript. Hereafter cited as **Bassett**. Courtesy Bill **O'Neal**, Panaloa College, Carthage, Texas.

[28] Ibid. Eighty to ninety of the striking miners were either Mexican Nationals or Mexican-Americans.

[29] Ibid. Also see, **Macklin**, William F., "Labor Leader or Morenci Mine Martyr?," *Valley Growers Magazine*. n. d. Hereafter cited as **Macklin**. **O'Neal** reports, "There was a strong anarchistic element in the labor movement of that time, and a radical group based in Chicago dispatched agitator W. H. Laustenneau to the Clifton-Morenci-Metcalf district." P. 49.

[30] *Territorial Prison At Yuma, A. T., Description of Convict.*, Inmate No. 2029. Courtesy, Yuma Territorial Prison State Historic Park, Yuma.

[31] **Wagoner**, P. 386.

[32] **O'Neal**, P. 50.

[33] Ibid. Quoting **Bassett** typescript.

[34] **Trafzer**, Cliff and **George**, Steve, *Prison Centennial, 1876-1976*. P. 10. Hereafter cited as **Trafzer** and **George**.

[35] **Macklin**, P. 43.

[36] **Wagnoer**, P. 387. The Western Federation of Miners, based in Denver, condemned the Acting Governor for requesting U. S. Army assistance, and verbally charged him with being "guilty of treason to the principles of organized labor." By and large the Arizona public supported Stoddard's actions.

[37] **O'Neal**, P. 50. The author reports, "Telegraphs ordering Rangers to report to the crisis area were fired off to the seven scattered elsewhere around the territory." Also, when the Arizona Rangers were first organized they were not issued badges. In the reorganization of 1903 the law added, "The captain shall provide and issue to each Ranger a badge, uniform in size and shape, with the words 'Arizona Ranger' inscribed thereon in plain and legible letters, which badge shall be returned to the captain upon the said Ranger going out of service, the expense of which badge shall be paid for as part of the incidental expenses provided for." *Acts, Resolutions and Memorials, 22nd Legislative Assembly, Territory of Arizona, 1903*. Courtesy, State of Arizona, Department of Library, Archive and Public Records, Phoenix.

[38] Ibid. Quoting **Bassett** typescript.

[39] *Bisbee Daily Review*, June 5, 1903. Quoted by **Park**, P. 142-143.

[40] Ibid. Captain **Rynning** characterized the crowd. "But the camp was full of a mighty bad bunch of Mexican murderers and cattle thieves, fellows that didn't care any more about killing or getting killed than a bobcat would." P. 231.

[41] Ibid.
[42] **Miller**, Joseph, *Arizona, The Grand Canyon State.* P. 325. Hereafter cited as **Miller (II)**.
[43] **Park**, P. 143.
[44] **O'Neal**., P. 50.
[45] **Virgines**, George E., in a speech given to the Chicago Corral of the Westerners on September 27, 1983, and reprinted in *The Westerners Brand Book*, Volume XXXIX, March-April, 1982. P. 5. "A small force, including twenty-five Rangers, the local sheriff and a few deputies held the town against a mob of more than 3,000 strikers. With the cool efficiency that had become a Ranger trademark, they were able to preserve law and order and protect life and property until the territorial militia and the U. S. Army arrived." At Morenci, the contingent of Arizona Rangers had two group pictures taken. Dave Allison is identified and pictured in the photographs. And, a copy of one of the photographs was a part of his personal possessions at the time of his death in 1923.
[46] **Winsor**, P. 57. Metcalf was a copper camp on the branch railroad up Chase Creek, approximately eight miles northwest of Clifton, Arizona Territory. It was named after Robert B. Metcalf, an early day miner. See **Barnes**, P. 273. Also see, **Sherman**, James E. and Barbara H., *Ghost Towns of Arizona.* P. 96. "Before long (1882) the town of Metcalf had taken root and expanded into an extensive community. Four or five thousand people composed the population. Included in the town were a bank, school, hospital, dairy, pool hall, and movie theater...The depression years brought Metcalf's story to an end."
[47] Ibid.
[48] **Bassett**, P. 2. "There was talk of several hundred of the Metcalf strikers heading for Morenci, and of course nobody could tell what their intentions were or what they might take it into their heads to do." Courtesy, Bill **O'Neal**, Panola College, Carthage, Texas.
[49] **O'Neal**, P. 51. Chase Creek flows southeast and empties into the San Francisco River at Clifton, Arizona. See, **Barnes**, P. 88.
[50] **Bassett**, P. 2. "It was sure raining pitchforks at the time and maybe that dampened their spirits some." Courtesy, Bill **O'Neal**, Panola College, Carthage, Texas.
[51] **O'Neal**, P. 51.
[52] **Miller**, P. 72. "How anyone who was on the creek side of the town escaped is a miracle, but hundreds did escape, many of them being mangled and bruised from head to foot. Had this storm occurred in the night time the loss of life would have been appalling."
[53] **O'Neal**, P. 51. Of the flood **Park** reports, "Suddenly, two torrents of water converged on the junction of Chase Creek and the San Francisco River, formed a crest that ripped through the length of Clifton, destroyed nearly $100,000 in property and took a death toll of nearly fifty persons, according to later estimates. P. 143.
[54] Ibid., P. 52. **Winsor** says, "Reports that they intended to make themselves masters of the town continued to be circulated, accompanied by threats against the lives of mining company officers and department managers. A large force of armed strikers captured the Detroit Copper Company mill and disarmed the sheriff's deputies, who were guarding it." P. 57.
[55] **Bassett** typescript, P. 3-4. Courtesy Bill **O'Neal**, Panola College, Carthage, Texas. **Winsor** states, "With Laustenneau locked up the atmosphere cleared." P.

57. Also see, **Rynning**, P. 233. In this account the Captain takes personal credit for capturing "Three-Fingered Jack" Laustenneau, "Guess Mocho didn't think it mattered much if a couple of men rode up on a mule. I caught him a belt on the jaw with my fist and when he fell I stepped on his hand and got his six-shooter." Most historians award the arrest to Lt. Foster and Ranger Bassett.

[56] **O'Neal**, P. 52-53. Quoting **Bassett**. Also see, **Park**, P. 145, "…the strikers were disarmed, their houses were searched, and arrests were made."

[57] Ibid., P. 253. The Arizona National Guardsmen were under the command of Colonel James H. McClintock, Adjutant General of Arizona Territory.

[58] Ibid., P. 53. The author reports that only Arizona Ranger Jeff Kidder was not present for the photograph. To this day, accurately identifying each Arizona Ranger in the famous photograph is problematic. Dave Allison had a copy of this photograph, and he had Ranger Kidder marked on his copy, ninth from the right. Arizona Historical Society files indicate that several of the pictured individuals are identified differently by different informants.

[59] **Wagnoer**, P. 389.

[60] Ibid.

[61] **Macklin**, P. 44. Also see, *Territorial Prison at Yuma, A. T.—Description of Convict.* Inmate Number 2029. "Sentence: 2 yrs. And $2,000.00 fine from 10/24/1903. Crime: Riot." Courtesy, Yuma Territorial Prison Sate Historic Park, Yuma.

[62] **O'Neal**, P. 53.

[63] **Trafzer** and **George**, P. 11. "Ultimately, the agitator died in the prison hospital and the doctor there recorded that the cause of his death was neither mistreatment, privation, nor poor accommodations."

[64] **Winsor**, P. 57.

[65] *Territory of Arizona, Governor's Proclamation*, appointing William D. Allison to Sergeant in the Arizona Rangers, dated August 1, 1903, signed by Arizona Territorial Governor Alexander O. Brodie, October 6, 1903. Courtesy, State of Arizona, Department of Library, Archives and Public Records, Phoenix.

[66] *Report of the Governor of Arizona Territory to Secretary of Interior, 1903.* Contains Captain Rynning's annual report on activities of Arizona Rangers. Courtesy, State of Arizona, Department of Library, Archives and Public Records, Phoenix.

[67] *Governor's Proclamation*, as cited above.

[68] **O'Neal**, P. 43. And see, *Acts, Resolutions and Memorials, 22ND Legislative Assembly, Territory of Arizona,1903.* Courtesy, State of Arizona, Department of Library, Archives and Public Records, Phoenix. The 1903 pay raise dictated the following monthly salary schedule: Captain $175, Lieutenant $130, Sergeant $110, Private $100. Under the new organizational structure there was of course the one Captain, one Lieutenant, four Sergeants, and twenty privates.

[69] Ibid. P. 45. The author quotes a letter to a prospective Arizona Ranger recruit from Captain Rynning in which Allison is mentioned as "our first sergeant."

[70] Comments of old-timer Arcus Reddoch on Arizona Rangers he remembered. Typescript courtesy Bill **O'Neal**, Panola College, Carthage, Texas.

[71] **Rynning**, P. 275.

[72] Ibid.

[73] Ibid.

[74] **Spangenberger**, Phil. "Thomas H. Rynning, Adventurer With a Six-Gun," *Guns of the Gunfighters.* P. 31. Hereafter cited as **Spangenberger**. For

Chiricahua Mountains see **Barnes**, P. 92. Fore Galeyville see **Sherman** and **Sherman**, P. 58. The authors report that although Curly Bill and his bunch frequented the area, in its heyday "Galeyville was not made up exclusively of rustlers and outlaws. There were many hard-working miners and merchants. About four hundred people formed the town's population. Galeyville reported having eleven saloons, six merchandise stores, two hotels, two restaurants, two butcher shops, two blacksmith and wagon shops, three lumber yards, a dairy, a jeweler, lawyers, a notary public, an assayer, a justice of the peace, physicians, a shoemaker, a Wells Fargo office, and a short-lived newspaper." When Dave Allison and Rynning tramped through the area, however, Galeyville had for all practical purposes disappeared.

[75] **O'Neal**, Bill, *Encyclopedia of Western Gunfighters*. P. 272. Hereafter cited as **O'Neal (II)**. Remarks concerning ownership of the cabin are attributed to **Rynning**, P. 275.

[76] **Rynning**, P. 275.

[77] Ibid., P. 276.

[78] Ibid.

[79] Ibid.

[80] **O'Neal (II)**, P. 272. According to **Rynning**, "Sure enough, he got his gun out like a flash, but seeing two of us when we broke in he was rattled just long enough for us to shoot first…" P. 276.

[81] **Spangenberger**, P. 36.

[82] Ibid., P. 37. The author acknowledges he is taking the direct dialogue from **Rynning's** *Gun Notches*. **O'Neal (II)**, P. 272, reports that after being shot in the hip and the leg, the fugitive "promptly surrendered." No doubt!

[83] **Rynning**, P. 293.

[84] *Oath of Office* executed by William D. Allison upon promotion to the rank of Lieutenant. "I William D. Allison do solemnly swear that I will support the Constitution of the United States and the law of the Territory of Arizona; that I will true faith and allegiance bear to the same, and defend them against all enemies whatsoever, and that I will faithfully and impartially discharge the duties of the office of Lieutenant of The Arizona Rangers of Arizona according to the best of my ability, so help me God." Signed, "William D. Allison." Also see, *Muster Rolls*, Arizona Rangers. Courtesy, State of Arizona, Department of Library, Archives and Public Records, Phoenix.

[85] *Border Vidette*, November 7, 1903.

[86] **Bolling**, P. 11.

[87] **Rynning**, P. 240.

[88] Ibid., P. 241.

[89] **DeArment**, P. 15.

[90] **Fenton**, P. 19.

[91] Ibid. The author reports, "Yet memoirs of settlers who did not witness the event firsthand, basically agree on the important facts…"

[92] **Sterling**, P. 379. Quoting Rogers report to the Adjutant General.

[93] **DeArment**, P. 15. Rogers was thoroughly convinced that to have resisted Loftis in any fashion would have been akin to an act of suicide. History seems to concur with his assessment. Also see, Harvey **Harris** typescript. Courtesy Vicki **Jones**, Southwest Collections, Texas Tech University, Lubbock. And see, **Cox**, Mike, *Texas Ranger Tales II*, P. 143-144.

---

[94] Ibid. The author reports that Loftis was arrested in Gaines County for fighting, in Eddy County, New Mexico Territory for failure to pay a lawyer, and back again in Gaines County on an Assault charge. Other arrests were for carrying a pistol, and the more serious charge of robbery in Lea County, New Mexico. His brushes with the law, in one form or the other, remained rather constant.

[95] *Service Records, Territorial Arizona Rangers*. "Discharged Feb. 4, 1904. Resignation (At Request)." Courtesy, Bill **O'Neal**, Panola College, Carthage, Texas.

[96] **Rynning**, P. 293. The rest of the sentence is a compliment, "…he (Allison) was a grand party when it come to any kind of a scrimmage."

5

"a hard-boiled twister"

Truthfully, on the Southwestern *transitional frontier*, after leaving service with the Arizona Rangers, Dave Allison's name was not much tarnished. He quickly hired out his gun as Chief of Security and personal bodyguard for the vibrant frontier character and self-made mining mogul, "Colonel" William Cornell (Bill) Greene.[1]

William Cornell Greene. Wholly flamboyant frontier character, mining mogul and employer of Dave Allison. Courtesy, Arizona Historical Society, Tucson, Arizona.

Since the age of nineteen, the Wisconsin born Greene had ranged throughout the West, and had worked as a surveyor, teamster, farmer, cowhand, and even a greasy-fingered butcher, before he finally cast his lot in Arizona Territory during 1877.[2] Bestowing on himself, for promotional purposes, the unearned title of "Colonel," the ambitious Greene had hard-scrabble prospected in the vicinity of Prescott and Wickenberg, and then during September 1880, made the migration to thriving Tombstone with an ex-sheriff, territorial legislator, and politician extraordinaire, John Harris Behan.[3]

Later, during an 1897 dispute over an irrigation ditch, Greene's adversary, Jim Burnett, allegedly resorted to the use of dynamite. Unfortunately Greene's nine year-old daughter, Ella, and her playmate, Katie Corcoran, were drowned in the rushing and flooding aftermath at an area swimming hole. Greene resorted to revenge! On a Tombstone street Greene found Burnett and killed him slingshot dead.[4] The jury acquitted Greene "more on account of his colorful, dominant personality, than on account of the jury's belief that Burnett had really blown up the dam."[5] And accordingly, in later years Colonel Bill Greene never forgot the friends who had stood by him throughout the confounding high-profile legal difficulties, and thereafter he rewarded those steadfast supporters with lucrative jobs, grubstakes, and loans.[6]

By the time he hired Dave Allison, however, Colonel Bill Greene, who had always been attracted to Mexico and the Mexican people, was realistically the head honcho, a certifiable mining magnate, for an extensive copper extracting operation centered in the rugged and harshly isolated outreaches of the Mexican state of Sonora, at La Cananea, forty-five miles south of the American border.[7] The surrounding hills were remarkably rich in copper deposits, and by the year 1906 had attracted significant sums of United States minted coin, to the tune of $7,500,000 in the Cananea district alone.[8]

The booming Mexican mining economy was making astutely invested Americans rich. As president and general manager of the Cananea Consolidated Copper Company, Greene built a railroad from where the copper smelters were located, at the Mexican inhabited community of Ronquillo, to Naco, on the Arizona Territorial line. At La Mesa, the American residential community at the base of the Cananea Mountains, the "Colonel," at the stupendous cost for the time period, exceeding $50,000, constructed an elegant and pretentious thirty-four room personal residence.[9]

Herbert Brayer sets the northern Mexico stage: "In 1906, with copper selling on the domestic market at more than twenty-five cents per pound, the mines surrounding Cananea were working at capacity. American owned and financed, these employed between eight and nine thousand Mexicans and some twenty-three hundred American miners. The largest mine and the smelter, as well as most of the town were owned by the Cananea Consolidated Copper Company, a part of the Colonel W. C. Greene mining organization, then prominent in Arizona. The smelter copper was taken from Cananea to the United States by means of a narrow-gauge railroad which connected with the Southern Pacific railroad at Naco, Arizona. The railway and the unimproved wagon and automobile road from Naco were the only means of ingress and egress from this Mexican mining community."[10]

William C. Green, in automobile addressing the dour crowd while armed allies look on during the 1906 Cananea, Sonora, Mexico, mining strike and mutinous tumult. Library of Congress.

Border-country author Leon C. Metz presents supplementary details: "A narrow-gage railroad zigzagged twelve miles up the Cananea canyons, a track so elaborate in its engineering that admirers dubbed it 'the scenic line of the Southwest.' By 1906 the company's main transportation tunnel reached six thousand feet, hooking up with thirty-five miles of underground workings. A system of feeder belts, blast furnaces, crushing and sampling mills and concentrators kept the shafts humming."[11] Dave Allison had bulldogged on to a big operation.

Unquestionably though, the *transitional frontier* and the border country were volatile. A prominent Southwestern writer and historian said: "the old frontier was dying and a modern, if not yet civilized, age was dawning."[12] And as he correctly hypothesizes, the "borderland between the United States of America and the Republic of Mexico has never been a place for the fainthearted."[13] Unforgiving racial prejudice was ubiquitous, suspiciously wary governments parried for even the slightest political leverage, while an ever-expanding capitalist economy on the north side of the border blistered forth—across the line.

Continuing with his introductory assessment of the time and the place, Douglas Meed said: "The old giant, the lawmen, the desperado, the horse soldiers, the trail drivers, both Anglo and Mexican, rubbed shoulders with the softer, if craftier, businessmen, engineers, politicians and lawyers, who would, in a short time, eclipse them. But within the next two turbulent decades, hard men would still ride with gun in hand across this last frontier and blaze new legends before they vanished along with the untamed Indians and the buffalo…Whether Mexican or American they were a breed unto themselves. Their features etched by blowing sand, burning sun and bone-aching chill, their characters forged by an unforgiving and treacherous land, they were intensely individualistic, fiercely loyal, often belligerent and very, very dangerous."[14] Hard-steeled Dave Allison had dogmatically chiseled his way onto this unstable frontier stage, and into this conglomerate of colorful characters.

With thousands of scruffy bottom-tier miners, mostly Mexicans, and hundreds of imported shift bosses, mostly Americans, there was no shortage of saloons, dance halls, whorehouses, and a whole regiment of gamblers, pimps and prostitutes populating Ronquillo. One writer amplifies, "A regular riot of humanity swarmed in his (Greene's) mines of a day and fought, five and six deep, to reach their drinks at Frank Proctor's seventy-five-foot bar of a night. John Cameron, veteran of the works in its earliest stages, recalls that every night thugs hammered 'from one to three' drunks to death in the streets, usually with rocks, and robbed them. The Americans went in bunches for safety."[15] That Bill Greene hired personal bodyguards and a corps of gunmen is undisputed.[16] That he was a chance taker and gambler there is not doubt and, at least according to one report, he was predisposed to employ those of like ilk. Reportedly one employee, Allen Bernard, who was his sometimes go-between with Mexican government officials, could "gamble off a thousand dollars at a throw and put it down as expenses."[17] Colonel Bill Greene was not inclined to question personal morality, he had circulated far too long in the West. When the ostentatious Greene hired Dave Allison he bought the use of a gun. Allison was expected to "hang around" Cananea, serve as a disincentive for those contemplating wrongdoing, and if all else failed, to die valiantly fighting in efforts calculated to protect Green's life, family, and personal property.[18]

Of course, along with the barrooms, bordellos, and beer-gardens there were also the traditional company owned stores, shops, offices, and the smelting plant, all politely removed from La Mesa by the railroad bridge spanning across a profoundly unwelcoming arroyo.[19] Everyday life should have been idyllic; sadly, it wasn't.

Aside from the undercurrents of unspoiled ethnocentric viewpoints bubbling forth between divergent and ever competing cultures, disharmony in the Cananea Mining District could be boldly traced to several less than elusive dynamics. Near the front in grievances was the simple fact that American workers were paid in gold, Mexican laborers received their wages in silver *pesos*, a 50% discount by comparison.[20] Playing right into the hands of U. S. owned interests operating in Mexico was the Mexican government policy which regulated the earnings paid to its citizens, a dictate that capped the wages of non-agricultural workers, so as not to have too wide a disparity between peasants working on the farms and ranches and those more fortunate and geographically juxtaposed, who sans government intervention could pocket two or three times as much *dinero* as their agriculturally engaged brethren.[21] Labor union leaders back in the United States were indignantly appalled at the barefaced disparity between Mexican and Anglo working conditions, especially since the later "held virtually all the high paying positions."[22] Hints of unionism were gusting their way south of the border, handiwork of the United States based Western Federation of Miners.[23] Furthermore inflaming the exasperating economic discord was revolutionary agitation, intentionally aimed at Mexico's President Porfirio Diaz from an American breeding ground for south of the border rebels, St. Louis.[24] In comments relating to Mexican involvement deep in Mississippi Delta bowels, the *El Paso Herald* mentioned the strife was "revolutionary in character, fomented from headquarters in St. Louis, where a junta of revolutionists has been active for some time, several of whom were recently arrested for alleged libelous newspaper publications."[25] At Cananea, radical political and labor agitators were distributing by the ton revolutionary handbill after handbill, partisan newspaper after newspaper, in efforts to stir the fermenting pots of unionism.[26]

North of the international line, at Bisbee, Arizona Territory, on May 31, 1906, laughing off-duty Anglo miners guzzled beer and ate hot dogs while they enthusiastically rooted and gesticulated for their favorite baseball team. Several thousand cheered and shouted as the alternating tobacco-spitting squads, uniformed in homespun pin-stripped jerseys, took their respective turns wildly swinging the bat but, in the end, the Cananea crowd boarded the south bound train for the speedy trip home with downcast spirit, smiles erased from their sunburned faces. "In the best game seen in years," Bisbee had won, the score 5 to 4.[27]

Flamboyant Colonel Bill Green, on the other hand, wasn't the least interested in a harebrained competition counting balls and strikes. The strike he was being made aware of was more ominous—dangerously so. So much so, that he had an associate on the U. S. side, at Nogales, secure the messenger services of Jeff Milton, the noted Southwestern lawman and gunman, who for an equitable fee of $500 delivered to Greene a sack containing $50,000 cash, presumably to be used for munitions and more security.[28] Informants had been tipping Greene off to impending trouble, most probably to break out the very next day when Mexican miners were to walk off their jobs and demand fewer hours and higher wages. The "Colonel" was also cognizant that union agitators and Mexican revolutionaries where thumping out anti-American denouncements and guaranteeing rich reward for a triumphant insurrection; especially would-be rebels were reporting substantial piles of Cananea Consolidated Mining Company cash safely stashed behind the local bank's securely sealed vault door. Dynamite had already been stolen.[29] Clearheaded judgment was emotionally dumped. Viva the Revolution! Viva the Rebellion! Viva the Revolt! Viva!

The intrepid Colonel Bill Greene offers his personal insight:

> On the night of May 31, I was informed by a man who was working for the Cobre Grande that a Mexican working there had told him that trouble was going to start in Cananea on the morning of June 1st, at 5 o'clock; that a socialist club had held three meetings at midnight on May 30, at which a large number of agitators of socialistic tendencies were present; that agitators of the Western Federation had been through the mines inciting the

> Mexicans and that they had been furnishing money for the socialistic club at Cananea.
>
> He also gave us a couple of copies of the revolutionary circulars that had been widely distributed, together with a number of other details.
>
> While it looked ridiculous to me that a thing of this kind could be done, their program included dynamiting the bank, where it was reported that we had $1,000,000, breaking open the stores and getting fire arms and ammunition and with them starting a revolution against the Diaz government.
>
> Soon after I saw a Mexican whom I had confidence in and upon asking I found that he had heard the same rumors, he giving further detail that agitators had stolen, a few nights before, a few boxes of powder, which I knew to be the truth.[30]

Shrewd, calculating, and not drawn to overstatement, Bill Greene could well read the pictograph on the proverbial outhouse wall. Quickly, in the deep of night he summoned Dave Allison, instructing him to without delay began arranging for defensive repulsion of the anticipated onslaught, while he himself had a Pullman coach connected to an available locomotive and made a mad-dash for the U. S. boundary line.[31] At the Queen of the Copper Camps, Bisbee, the unflagging Greene woke up the company store manager, and impatiently purchased nearly one hundred rifles, a score of revolvers, and 5000 rounds of desperately needed ammunition.[32] One newspaper, the *El Paso Herald*, reported that "it was whispered that he (Greene) had taken a Gatling gun along with him to protect his magnificent mansion…"[33] Before the first rays of morning light, Greene was back at Cananea, and after "…a quick distribution of arms and ammunition, a lonely, fearful and outnumbered group of Americans, led by gunslinger Dave Allison, waited for the sun to come up on what promised to be a very dangerous day for them and their loved ones."[34] On the outside of the boss man's elegantly furnished colossal home, completely encircling the showy mansion was a stone wall approximately eighteen inches high. Inside the house frightened women and children were protectively placed. On the perimeter, behind the tiny wall, Dave Allison deployed the men folk in strategic defensive positions—the Alamo all over again some few no doubt mused. A time to stand!

The morning sun topped the Cananea Mountains for its habitual peek at hustling and bustling miners scampering about trying to make it to work before the 7:00 A. M. shift whistle beckoned. This day, Friday, June 1st, however, when the cock crowed, the Mexican miners gathered in protest. Quickly all mines in the Cananea District were shut down and toil at the huge smelter was forced to an unproductive standstill.[35] By noon, as many as 5,000 flag waving strikers had assembled at the main plaza and were making their demands known, while others among them urged an overthrow of the Diaz government, which had "sold out to the *gringos*."[36] Chanting crowds proclaimed "*Viva Mejico!*," others hollered "*Ocho Horas! Cinco Pesos!*" (Eight Hours, Five Pesos), but all, strikers and revolutionists alike, knew adjustments were soon to be made—one way or the other![37] At the mansion on the hill, and at selected positions throughout the mining company complex, "*gringos*" nervously counted cartridges while they fingered their six-shooters and Winchesters.

The gutsy Bill Greene unflinchingly addressed the swarming multitude declaring that he was paying higher wages than other mining companies in Mexico and that future fine-tuning of pay and workday concerns could only be amended upon consultation with their own governmental officials.[38] Backed up by Dave Allison and a squad of seasoned stalwarts, Greene stood firm assuring the milling crowd that he would treat them fairly, but they should not be "led astray by troublemakers."[39] Greene returned home.

In town though, as the afternoon summer sun grew measurably warmer, Fahrenheit frustrations rose appreciably. Sometime during the sizzling sideshow, someone noticed that not all Mexican citizens of the Cananea composites were participating in the high-pitched call for improved working conditions and for better local and national government. Their individual involvement was very much missed and logically deemed indispensable, that is, if any meaningful changes were to truly take place, and so it was reasoned that a march through town, and a general reinforcement of their ranks from *all* workers would appreciably legitimize their struggle for "justice and dignity."[40] The chaotic throng swept their dragnet through the settlements and businesses toward the Cananea Consolidated Copper Company owned lumberyards, which were "very extensive," and employed a large number of Mexicans.[41]

Forewarned by a panicked telephone call, George Metcalf, the lumberyard manager, made ready. According to one report, Metcalf was a "blunt man with a previous reputation for intransigence and stubbornness," but in probing historic reality it makes little noteworthy difference whether or not he was indeed a gregarious gentlemen or impolite scalawag, what does matter is that he was irrevocably unswerving in his defense of the lumberyard and himself..[42] As rebellious strikers advanced on the lumberyard to liberate Mexican employees, Metcalf ordered the yard gate be clamped shut, and a fire-hose nozzle aimed at the cheering and jeering crowd. With rifle in hand, he was unalterably determined to make his last stand. His admonitions to cease and desist were ignored, the high-pressure valve was turned, and infuriated miners were drenched by the dazzlingly aimed spray—some of them. Others, however, by now irreversibly enraged, quickly surrounded Metcalf and beat him to death with miner's candlesticks, the sharp pointed steel instruments they used in the mines.[43] Metcalf's brother, Will, also a lumberyard employee, rushed to George's defense, but he too was killed.[44] According to the *El Paso Daily Times*, the Metcalf brothers "shot nine Mexicans before they themselves fell."[45] Anglo snipers, perched on the rooftop of the lumberyard let loose with a volley, and three Mexicans tumbled to the ground—doorknob dead![46] Outraged, the now riotous horde set fire to the lumberyard office, and burned to death the two dead-eyed sharpshooters.[47] Smoke from the blazing conflagration could be seen for miles all around, but back on the ground, close to the choking and horrendous heat, the once discontent crowd had by now metamorphosed into an unruly and bitterly dangerous mob. Journalistically, the *El Paso Herald* sensationalized the violent story for its predominately American readership, "After George Metcalf and his brother Will had been killed, the body of George Metcalf was horribly mutilated…(and the Mexicans) stabbed the dead body repeatedly until it was one mass of wounds…they stabbed him in what must have been 100 places."[48]

"Shouting like Comanche Indians and cursing and drinking," the rabble was by most eyewitness accounts leaderless, although to be sure there were a few dominant personalities, those with impassioned agendas urging them on but, in truth, the mob was riotously far removed from any simple semblance of levelheaded restraint.[49] Colonel Greene, who had once again ventured out for a delicate inspection, quickly conferred with his General Manager, A. E. Dwight, and determined that his personal compliment of rough and ready warriors were spuriously outnumbered. He beat a hasty retreat back to the tenuously safe refuge of the mesa top mansion. "When he got there he ran inside, grabbed his rifle and rushed out to join Dave Allison and his men for a last-ditch defense of their wives and children."[50] Apprehensively the defenders well knew it was a case of "root-hog or die."

Methodically, Dave Allison and Bill Greene evaluated, and then made a few absolutely critical modifications to their precariously positioned defensive stratagem.[51] Dwight, who for the moment, had remained behind in Cananea hustling up a gaggle of American reinforcements was the target of an angry agitator's almost well-aimed pistol shot. The bullet creased Dwight's scalp, and he observably lurched under the zinging projectile's ricocheting flight. Plainly the General Manager was in a perilously hazardous situation. Dave Allison, Bill Greene, and a few more Caucasian combatants, guns in hand, boldly sprinted to Dwight's rescue. Four of the agitated Mexican insurgents surrounding supervisor Dwight, dependent on individual perspective, were either mercilessly murdered or justly gunned down.[52] Others were wounded, by some reports, as many as fifteen.[53] Quickly the American relief squad retreated to Greene's personal compound on the hill. Ducking for cover behind the low rock wall, defenders returned fire on the horrifying swarm, who by this time had burglarized hardware stores and pawn shops, illegally acquiring an arsenal of assorted shooting-irons, explosives, and were now industriously engaged in firing intolerant pistol and rifle bullets into the American occupied stronghold.[54]

Four Americans who had been cut off in their retreat to the Big House took shelter in a small adobe residence and made ready to sell their lives dearly—at the highest possible price. From the mini-fortress, and from the "Colonel's" protective enclave the harried Americans could readily observe billowing black smoke, regurgitated from the hungry inferno engulfing the lumberyard. Cautiously peering from their shielding adobe quarters the four trapped Americans watched as hundreds of weapon-carrying protesters charged the Big House. With the safety of the women and children uppermost in his mind, and judiciously aware there was nowhere to retreat, Dave Allison "ordered his men to hold their fire until the mob was within 70 yards of their scrawny stonewall. Then raising up, the defenders opened up with a rapid fire that cut down many and drove the rest of the attackers scrambling for cover."[55]

Utilizing sticks of the stolen dynamite, thoroughly exasperated insurgents fashioned primitive grenades and ineffectively hurled the explosive packages at the defensive breastworks in vain effort to dislodge bitterly determined adversaries. After dark the quartet of hungry and thirsty Americans in the adobe house resolutely opted to run the gauntlet and unite with their pinned-down comrades at the hilltop garrison. After shouting their plans to Dave Allison, who directed a blistering cover fire, the four Americans and two women, raced across ground littered with bodies "sprawled grotesquely on the grounds in front of the Big House."[56] The withering barrage released by Dave Allison and his platoon proved effectual, and after the 100 yard mad-dash the panting sprinters collapsed behind the welcoming wall.[57] Inside the manor house, American wives hurriedly fed and furnished steaming coffee to the recently arrived reinforcements. The fatigued men were then furnished cigarettes. Dave Allison brought them up to speed, telling them "the supply of cartridges would run out by morning. After that…well, help had better come pretty damn quick."[58]

While Dave Allison was supervising ground level defenses, others, those above his pay-grade, were frantically pleading for that "damn quick" help. American Counsel at Cananea, Dr. William J. Galbraith, who was also one of Greene's mining company employees, frantically wired the State Department, "Aid from the United States is absolutely essential."[59] Bill Greene himself anxiously telephoned Walter Douglas, general manager of the Copper Queen Company at Bisbee, pleading for immediate assistance—before it was too late.[60] Douglas, in turn, contacted Dave Allison's old boss with the Arizona Rangers, Captain Thomas Rynning. Rynning and Greene conferred over a telephone line, which by some oversight the mutineers had failed to cut. Reportedly, after explaining to Rynning just what had happened, Greene exclaimed, "Hell is popping here, and every American's life is in danger."[61] In another version Greene pled:

> For God's sake, Tom, get a few hundred armed men together and burn the railroad track up getting here before we're all wiped out. Dave Allison's got a few good men at my house in Mesa holding out against big odds, but they're rushing us steady and we can't stick it out a lot longer.[62]

Realizing the state of affairs was dangerously deteriorating, Colonel Greene also telegraphed the Governor of Sonora at Hermosillo, Rafael Izabal. The Governor, over 200 miles distant from the seat of the trouble, dispatched troops under the leadership of General Luis Torres, notified the Mexican government, and according to the *El Paso Herald* of June 2nd took a most astonishing step.

> The state department also (in addition to Galbraith's messages) received a direct application from the governor

> of the state of Sonora, Mexico, for help from the American side, a most extraordinary occurrence. This direct appeal was the subject of hasty consultations today between the secretary of state, chief of staff, Brig. Gen. Bell, and the law officers of the war department, inasmuch as a question of right of the United States to send troops into a friendly state is in doubt.

Desperate cries for immediate help even reached the desk of President Theodore Roosevelt at Washington, D. C.[63] The border country, both north and south, and at the very highest levels of two national governments was in a state of legitimately alarmed turmoil. American troops were dispatched to Naco, and placed on standby status. Mexican President Diaz ordered the much-feared Russian born Colonel Emilio Kosterlitzky and his unforgiving band of hard-ridin' *Rurales* to advance on Cananea. Douglas Meed wrote: "What had started out in the morning as a strike, by noon had turned into a riot; by later afternoon it had become a battle, and as night fell, it looked as if there might be a war between Mexico and the United States."[64]

Arizona Ranger Captain Tom Rynning, third from left, and the Mexican Rurales' icily-nerved commander, Emilio Kosterlitzky, fourth from left, on white horse. Courtesy, Arizona Historical Society, Tucson, Arizona.

While predictably mistrustful governments wrestled with questions of diplomatic import, a toughened, unsentimental, no nonsense swarm of Southwesterners scurried into action. At El Paso, the "Drummers' Special No. 3" was delayed an hour and a half while over 100 rifles and thousands of rounds of ammunition were anxiously collected from the local hardware store and rushed to the train station. The resident newspaper reporter unsurprisingly jumped into the hysteria when he inked about the "seriousness of the situation" and the "buzz of excitement."[65] The munitions were hastily loaded into a boxcar and the locomotive chugged out of Union Station, destined for Bisbee.[66] Unmistakably though, it wasn't merely a quartermaster operation, rushing needed supplies to the front. Bisbee was utterly overrun as horse backers on jaded mounts rushed to town, and goggle wearing volunteers peered through the steam seeping from over-heated radiators, as they too raced at break-neck-speed to do battle. In short order, more than 500 civilians were parading Bisbee streets, later as the crowd continued to grow, as many as 2000 hard-edged border liners were clamoring to cross the international boundary, rush to Cananea, kill Mexicans—save the day.[67] Farsightedly, realizing a looming disaster could erupt anytime, the Bisbee Mayor wisely ordered City Marshal Michael J. "Biddy" Doyle to suspended the sale of liquor and shut down the barrooms.[68]

Arizona Ranger Captain Rynning and Walter Douglas put out the impassioned call for an invasion force of toughened volunteers, and had little trouble in recruiting a sufficient regiment of armed men itching for a fight. For the most part the mishmash militia was comprised of leathery-faced cowboys, legit lawmen, physically robust copper miners, and a whole bucketful of Spanish American War veterans. Rynning himself described the recruits as a "wild bunch" and knew they had plenty of fight in them, but was rightly disturbed that if not the utmost care was taken the boys would go "surging across the line to clean up on the Mexicans."[69] While the keenly eager enlisted ranks were busily engaged in depleting Bisbee merchants' inventory of bullets and bowie knifes, the hierarchy, Rynning and Douglas, worried logistically with putting together railroad transport for the troops, most of which were in varying stages of slowly sobering up.[70]

Several, a squadron of about fifteen, (twenty-four by other reports) may not yet have purged whiskey from their blood streams but, for sure, they were impatient and not in the least bent toward common sense or self-discipline. Recklessly they saddled their horses and departed for the Mexican border. At the line, Edward Buchner, a soldier for the day, but a

Y. M. C. A. physical director the rest of the time, sallied forth to do battle. Attempting to cross into Mexico, he "became embroiled with the Mexican border guards…and received a bullet wound in the arm during the fight and one Mexican officer was wounded."[71] Tensions were understandably ratcheted up another notch.

As the clock neared the midnight hour, a trainload of Cananea refugees arrived at Bisbee. When the tales of gruesome excesses were coaxed from panic-stricken wives and crying children, the explosively charged atmosphere almost ignited into a hysterically unrestrained ten-mile march toward the border.[72] Realizing that there still remained at least 65 women and 27 youngsters in harm's way at Cananea, only served to heighten their sense of urgency.[73] The Captain knew the time factor was critical, evidenced by his praise of the man he had earlier fired: "If we could get through right quick there was a chance Dave Allison would hold them long enough."[74] Quickly loading his hand-picked "expeditionary force" of approximately three hundred fighters onto a waiting train, Rynning departed Bisbee, headed south, destination Naco, the squatty adobe structured Southwestern burg which exactly straddled the international line.

At Naco, efforts were undertaken to sculpt the bit-chomping volunteers into at least reasonable replication of a formal military command.[75] Officers were appointed, men were divided into four distinguishable companies, and 22 crack-shots were expressly assigned to a separate sharpshooter squadron.[76] Hurriedly the small army was assembled and maneuvers began, the drilling designed more to accomplish proper maintenance of discipline than to give meaningful training to a military force.

Without resorting to specific citations of the bushel-basket full of telegrams tapped out hysterically, suffice to say, the Mexican government was afraid their country was about to be invaded, and too, the United States government was afraid that Mexico was about to be invaded. Captain Rynning, still an employee for the Territory of Arizona was wading in delicate waters. Depending upon which version is accepted, he either did not receive, or chose not to accept, any orders contrary to his sense of duty. He simply saw the Cananea incident in humanitarian terms, no doubt sprinkled with a degree of racial prejudice. He, himself declared:

> Bill Greene and Dave Allison and a few more of our *amigos* were putting up a one-sided fight down there in the Cananea Mountains to protect the women and children

> from a mob gone loco with race hatred. They needed us bad. A soldier is always supposed to do the right thing in a pinch and I was going to do it, governors or no governors.[77]

Arriving at the border by train, finally, were Sonora Governor Izabal and Mexican General Torres. Painfully mindful of the pickle he was in, Iazbal knew if he allowed armed invaders into his country, in all probability, he would be executed upon orders from Mexico City. Conversely, if he failed to act shrewdly more Americans, and more of his own citizens, would be killed. Placing all his hopes on Colonel Kosterlitzky, who even with the most tortuous time spent in the saddle was still hours away from the turbulence at Cananea, would prove ill advised and impractical, especially knowing that poised just across the border were fiery-eyed *gringos* critically primed to "kick ass and take names."[78] Ambassadors and attachés could diplomatically debate forever, on the damn bloody ground something needing doing—right then!

Captain Rynning, upon consultation with Governor Izabal came up with the solution. Curtly he dispatched a telegram to Arizona Territorial Governor Joseph H. Kibbey at Phoenix requesting an immediate leave of absence, forthrightly knowing he was not going to dilly-dally around and wait for some slowly twisted mealy-mouth worded bureaucratic answer. With complicity from the Governor of Sonora and the Mexican General, Rynning ordered his men to cross the international boundary as individual *tourists*, not as an organized armed force. On the Mexican side of the border, Governor Izabal swore in Tom Rynning as a Colonel in the Mexican Army. Colonel Rynning then asked the Bisbee bunch to join the Mexican Army and offer an oath that they would pledge to obey orders from the Sonora governor. Historian Meed politely summarizes the minutiae, "Governor Izabal made a speech thanking them for their services in putting down a dangerous insurrection and with national pride and diplomatic niceties assuaged, the men boarded the train on the Mexican side of the line."[79] A scribe for the *El Paso Daily Times* offered the obvious: "No one seems to know or care upon what authority Americans are invading Mexico in armed bands."[80]

In a political dither, and probably justifiably so, Arizona Governor Kibbey instructed:

> Volunteers going into Mexico do so at the risk of divesting themselves of their American citizenship and

> protection as such while there. I cannot permit an officer or man in the territorial service to go into Mexico at this time. Use every precaution to preserve order on our side of the line.[81]

Pitching governmental red-tape and naiveté into to the trash heap would be the expected course had the message even reached rank-and-file members of the Bisbee battalion, which of course, it didn't. Independently minded cowboys frequently resisted hard and fast orders from their very own bosses out on the open range, and certainly in this instance, the Governor in far away Phoenix was impotent. The lawmen and ex-officers in the crowd, as clearly illustrated by events, were deftly skilled at skirting the fine lines of statutes and legal procedures, having long ago learned to maneuver around legislative legalize and over man-made hurdles. Of the veteran *Rough Riders*, hell, they were just ready to roar and rip. Tom Rynning knew he was riding a runaway horse and, with a smidgen of luck, he could manage just enough pressure on the figurative reins to prevent the headlong tumble over a precarious cliff.[82] Wisely, Tom Rynning had loaded the troop train and, at last, had most of the rambunctious ramblers all together, in one place, and under a reasonable measure of quasi-military control.

The race was on! At Cananea, conscious that reinforcements had been requested, but absolutely unsure of their accomplishment, the besieged Americans couldn't have cared less about diplomatic dogma or shrewd schemes. They were under intense sniper fire, dead bodies lay before them, and "Allison's men were down to a few bullets each and surrender was out of the question."[83] They knew just as George Armstrong Custer's doomed men must have known, there was no chance to parlay—no negotiations—once the position was overrun it would be war to the knife, hideous mutilation would follow, without mercy. Dave Allison rallied his men the best he could, knowing once he and the other protectors were down, who knew what unspeakable outrages would befall the ill-fated women and children huddled at the Big House.[84] Surely, at least during these deathly trying circumstances, Dave Allison was the man for the job.[85]

The relief train made the mad dash across Sonoran desert flats, and not a minute too soon. Upon his arrival, Mexican Colonel Thomas Rynning disembarked into the muddle and found the scene to be absolutely "boiling."[86] At the site of Greene's mesa top mansion is where he determined that gunfire was most severe, but thankfully, the fortifications were being well generaled by his old Arizona law enforcement comrade:

> Dave Allison and his handful of hard-boiled twisters was lying behind an eighteen-inch high stone wall that run round the house. They were outnumbered fifty to one, but cool as if they'd only been bucking faro. Every time the Mexicans rushed, the Americans would lie dead till the mob was just across the road from the wall, and then they'd cut down on them with the kind of shooting that makes every bullet do its business. The killing at this point had been the heaviest in the district.[87]

Arrival of the Bisbee brigade, coupled with the fact that many of the insurgents were completely fatigued, brought about a table-turning end to the wretched state of affairs. Rynning deployed his sharpshooters on the adjacent hillsides, offering them a murderous field of fire. Others he used to augment Dave Allison's haggard platoon, and the rest were dispatched to reconnoiter, systematically searching out and destroying a number of squinty-eyed snipers. Although at last quietness draped the copper camp, the undercurrents of unsettled grievances and dissatisfaction rumbled through the Mexican multitudes. It was a tenuous cease-fire.[88]

Standing in an automobile, teetering back and forth to catch his balance like some gawking sightseer, the sassy Colonel William Cornell Greene, accompanied by Governor Izabal, addressed the milling masses, a crowd estimated at several thousand.[89] As the throng swarmed around Green's car, American volunteers and Dave Allison's crew of salty gunslingers stood ready to unleash a hail of rifle fire at the very first hostile move intended for Greene or the Governor.[90]

Izabal and Colonel Greene spoke to the protesters, the Governor demanding a cessation to the indiscriminate and unprovoked violence, the Colonel expounding on his financial predicament, which fortunately was captured by a traveling newspaperman with the *Bisbee Daily Review*, who was an actual eyewitness on the scene, and herewith his story is quoted in part:

> Then Col. Greene spoke. His language was Spanish, and he was followed closely. He stood bareheaded and unarmed, facing a crowd of at least three thousand Mexicans, men, women, and children, whom he knew would not be in sympathy with his remarks, but with a

> smile on his face, and perfect control of his words and actions, he began:
>
> "You Mexican people all know me, I have been a poor man myself. Some of you were my friends then, and all of you know that I have acted always honestly and fairly with you. When I have been able to pay you $3.50 for your work, I have gladly paid it. But a man cannot pay more than he makes. I cannot pay you five dollars at this time. The revenue from the mines would not permit it. I have tramped over these hills for a long time. I have spent millions of dollars in building up here among you the most thriving mining camp in Mexico. I have always been fair and candid with you, and I ask you to do the same by me."
>
> Col. Greene spoke in earnest. He went into the operations of the company from its inception. During his remarks the correspondent of the *Review* mixed with the crowd. He listened to the remarks made by the rank and file present. Often they ridiculed certain statements made by Col. Greene. But the meat of the coconut, and the bone of contentions, was contained in the remark of a Mexican laborer to another, who said, 'Yes, all that is true, but why don't the company pay the Mexicans the same wages they pay the Americans?'[91]

As Greene was addressing the dissatisfied, it was noticed that an uneasiness, a restlessness, was venomously fluttering through the group. "Immediately no less than five hundred rifles were trained on the square. The crowd scampered like rats, but fortunately not a single shot was fired at this time."[92] Greene and the Governor, their worried public speaking engagement finished, continued their gloomy inspection tour, accessing the monetary damage, counting corpses in varying stages of decomposition, and ended by conferring with the local Mexican constabulary before returning to the Big House for an extended palaver.[93]

In the afternoon, not content with suffering a failed attempt at overthrowing Mexican President Diaz's decidedly dictatorial regime, hard-core insurrectionary captains once again ordered sniper fire directed toward patrolling American sentinels at the Big House. Three Anglos were killed; however, it was an uneven swap. Rapidly, Winchesters and Colts muzzles barked back, and a dozen Mexican rebels were killed.[94] Mexicans coming near the Big House were admonished to halt, at long distance, "if the command did not suffice, more effective means were used."[95] For the most part, however, the Bisbee Volunteers, under military orders of Governor Izabal, were by now confined to the train that had brought them.[96] And much to their credit, "no American volunteer broke his pledge of obedience."[97]

Chafing under the collar of restraint, no doubt the American contingent of fighting men looked on with an envious eye when late in the evening they espied Colonel Kosterlitzky and his seventy-five ferocious *Rurales* kicking up dust and galloping into town after suffering a grueling twenty-hour horseback trip from their company headquarters at Magdalena, sixty miles distant.[98] Immediately, as if the curtain had dropped on the last act, indiscriminate sniping abruptly ceased as word swiftly spread that the elite and notoriously ruthless para-military squadron had slid to a hoof-tracking stop in their mutinous midst. Of Kosterlitzky's reputation, a reporter with the *El Paso Herald* who was covering the rousing story penned, "The Mexicans are in deadly fear of Kosterlitzky, even his own soldiers share this fear, and they will do all that he tells them. The peons almost tremble at the mention of his name."[99] Almost before he managed to dismount, Kosterlitzky declared marital-law, and unhesitatingly instructed everyone within hearing distance to spread the word, Mexicans were to get to their houses. Americans were to get to their houses. Bisbee Volunteers were to remain at the depot. After dark, which it nearly was, anyone found on the street, regardless of nationality was to be summarily shot. Kosterlitzky, who has been described as "cold and inevitable as death," was a man of his word.[100] A hush fell on the town. Later, in the company of Colonel Bill Greene, Kosterlitzky vigilantly patrolled the streets assuring everyone that by damn the disorder was over.[101]

By 10:00 P. M. Governor Izabal graciously thanked the Bisbee Volunteers for their service, said farewell to his short-tenured Colonel in the Mexican Army, Tom Rynning, and bid the Arizona delegation adieu. The train by a quarter to midnight was back at Naco, where thirsty soldiers hastily jumped from boxcars and raced through green painted swinging doors—it was time to drink and relive the gloriously bloody escapade with thrilling stories, even though in truth, few of them ever fired a shot.[102]

With the departure of American volunteer forces, Kosterlitzky had his men round up suspected strike leaders and revolutionary agitators. Later, some were fortunate to last long enough to enjoy a few balmy years in a tropical prison; others wished they had. Twenty-two of the suspected traitors were marched in a column toward the railroad station on the outskirts of town. The prisoners never completed the jaunt. A *Rurale*, corn shuck cigarette dangling from his cracked sun-burnt lips, when asked, simply replied "they got away"—and devilishly smiled—"but just a little way."[103] Others were "jerked to Jesus" under the stout limb of a nearby tree. Although the numbers vary between an even dozen and as many as 150, the executed weren't counting—they were just dead! Quickly, surviving native townsmen were offered three viable choices; be drafted into the army to fight hostile Yaqui Indians whose farmlands were being condemned as "national wastelands," and then auctioned off to subsidize Mexican railroad expansion; return to work in the copper mines and dutifully proclaim they were most proud to be once again drawing honest pay for honest work; or put a blindfold over their tearful brown eyes and momentarily stand before a blood- splattered and bullet-chipped adobe wall.[104] Most went back to work. A few fled to the hills. Peace, at last, was restored to Cananea.

There is no scorecard for the number of Mexican rioters that fell before Dave Allison's guns. All we know is that he stood his ground and fired away, effectively. Dave Allison, unlike a few of the better known and highly publicized Western gunmen, had no need to embellish on his own story in contrived efforts to capture profit and fame. Grassroots historian and writer, Joyce Means, succinctly asks, "Who knows how many fights he (Allison) participated in while helping protect Col. Greene during the Cananea riots in Mexico...?"[105]

Surely after the Cananea turmoil was over Dave Allison could have had lifetime tenure on free-wheeling Bill Greene's hefty payroll, but he opted out of the lucrative labors. For whatever reasons and, pure guesswork will by necessity have to do, Dave Allison left Mexico and sought once again to make his fortune in the good ole U. S. A.—*maybe* at Lena's persuasive prodding.

ENDNOTES
Chapter 5. "A hard boiled twister"

[1] **Meed**, Douglas V., *Bloody Border: Riots, Battles and Adventures Along the Turbulent U. S.—Mexican Borderlands*. P. 5. The author, acknowledging that William Davis Allison is in the employ of Greene simply makes reference to "gunslinger Dave Allison." Hereafter cited as **Meed**. Also see, **DeArment**, P. 12. "Allison left the Arizona Rangers in the spring of 1904 and went to work for mining magnate William C. Greene as chief of security and personal bodyguard. And see, **O'Neal**, Bill, "The Cananea Riots of 1906," *Real West*, August 1984. "Dave Allison, a former Texas Ranger, Texas sheriff, and lieutenant of Arizona Rangers, had been hired by Greene as a security man, and he organized the American defenses, forting up at Greene's massive mansion." P. 36.
[2] **O'Neal**, P. 98.
[3] **Young**, P. 55.
[4] **Bailey & Chaput**, Vol. I, P. 50. And see, **Young**, P. 55. Also see, **Sonnichsen**, C. L., "Col. W. C. Greene and the Cobre Grande Copper Company," *Journal of Arizona History*, 12: 2 (Summer 1971) P. 74. Hereafter cited as **Sonnichsen (II)**. And see, **Haley (II)**, P. 322.
[5] **Haley (II)**, P. 322. And see, **Chesley**, P. 33. "Greene had a dam on the river, which they blowed up, and these little girls were bathing there. Burnett didn't do it himself but had it done." Also see, **Traywick**, Ben T., "Copper King of Cananea," *Golden West*, November 1970. "The investigation proved that he did not blow up Greene's dam. The Chinese, who were not familiar with the use of explosives, were the ones who destroyed the dam." P. 17.
[6] Ibid., P. 323. According to the author, Jeff Milton asserts that "Bill Greene never forgot a friend." Also see, **Breakenridge**, William M., *Helldorado, Bringing the Law to the Mesquite*. P. 205., "Greene was acquitted. He soon after got possession of the copper mines in Cananea, Mexico, and made an immense fortune, and everyone who had stood by him during his trouble was handsomely rewarded by him." **Bailey & Chaput** report, "Greene had friends by the legion and there was no way any court in the county or Territory would have convicted him." Vol. I, P. 50.
[7] **Brayer**, Herbert O., "The Cananea Incident," *New Mexico Historical Review*, Volume XIII (October 1938). P. 388. Hereafter cited as **Brayer**.
[8] Ibid.
[9] **O'Neal**, P. 98.
[10] **Brayer**, P. 388.
[11] **Metz**, Leon C., *Border, The U. S.—Mexico Line*. P. 188. Hereafter cited as **Metz (II)**.
[12] **Meed**, P. xi.
[13] Ibid.
[14] Ibid, P. xii. The author clearly marks the sociological/economic distinctions between the two facing cultures. "On the American side, while prosperity was by no means evenly spread, there was the leavening of the political democracy and an ever-enduring dream of a better tomorrow…In Mexico, suffering the political and social repressions of a rude and selfish dictatorship, the few became rich, while the many were mired in perpetual poverty."
[15] **Haley (II)**, P. 359.

[16] Ibid., P. 323. "He hired personal bodyguards and gunmen, spent his money lavishly, bought a splendid house in the capital of Hermosillo for entertainment of public officials, became a close friend of President Diaz, and wielded influence in Mexico where it counted." Also see, **Meed** P. 4., "Greene attempted to add Jeff Milton…to his stable of gunfighter, which already included Dave Allison…"
[17] Ibid. And see, **Chesley**, P. 33, "And Scott White, who went to work for Bill, used to get twelve thousand dollars a year and all expenses…" **Breakenridge** also states that Greene was a lover of fine horses.
[18] **Meed**., P. 4. Allegedly Greene attempted to hire noted frontier gunman and lawman, Jeff Milton, and accordingly told him, "All you have to do in Cananea is hang around." It is *surmised* that since Dave Allison was also a gunfighter with a renowned Southwestern reputation, that he too was told much the same thing, although there is not paper documentation to the supposition.
[19] **O'Neal**, P. 98.
[20] Ibid., P. 99.
[21] **Brayer**, P. 389. The author reports, "The purpose of this curious enactment was aptly, though maliciously, stated by Antonio I. Villareal, secretary of the Liberal Party junta at St. Louis who said, …*Colonel Greene was willing to pay the Mexican laborers wages as good as those paid American, but the Mexican Governor and his clique saw danger in this. It would mean that the Mexican peasant would leave the farm, where the Mexican employer pays from twenty-five to fifty cents a day, and see employment in the mines, where he could get two or three times as much salary…The low salary in the mines is the result of official influence brought to bear on the American mine owners, Mexican officials have used their official power—their friendship with Diaz—as a means of keeping the wage standard down to the minimum.*"
[22] **Metz (II)**. P. 189.
[23] **Meed**, P. 29.
[24] *El Paso Herald*, June 4, 1906. Other north of the border hotbeds for Mexican revolutionaries were Los Angeles, California and Toronto, Canada. See, **Ball**. P. 228.
[25] *El Paso Herald,* June 4, 1906.
[26] **O'Neal**, P. 99.
[27] **Brayer**, P. 389. Quoting the *Bisbee Daily Review*, May 31, 1906.
[28] **Meed**, P. 4. Also see, **Haley (II)**, P. 360. "Proctor brought the money to his room in an old tow sack and threw it down on his bed. Jeff tied it on his saddle and after dark set out on a good horses, at a lively gait. He changed mounts at one of Greene's haciendas on the way and rode into Cananea about day."
[29] Ibid., P. 5.
[30] **Brayer**, P. 395. Quoting *Douglas Daily Dispatch*, June 19, 1906.
[31] **Meed**, P. 5. Green rushed first from Cananea to Naco, Arizona Territory, then to the Cochise County mining community of Bisbee.
[32] Ibid.
[33] *El Paso Herald*, June 4, 1906.
[34] **Meed**, P. 5., Also see, **O'Neal**, P. 99. "William D. 'Dave' Allison, a former Texas Ranger, Texas sheriff, and lieutenant of the Arizona Rangers, had been hired by Greene as a security man, and he organized the American defense, forting up at Greene's massive mansion."
[35] **Brayer**, P. 395. The author states that the first mine to shutdown was the Oversight, quickly followed by the Capote and Veta Grande.

[36] **O'Neal**, P. 99.
[37] Ibid., for "*Viva Mejico!* " **Meed**, P. 5, for "*Ocho horas! Cinco pesos!*"
[38] **Brayer**, P. 395. Also see, **Meed**, P. 6. "He (Greene) pointed out that it was the Mexican government that was pressing him to reduce their wages and that he was bound by Mexican law." Also see, *Douglas Dispatch*, June 2, 1906.
[39] **Meed**, P. 6. And see, Tanner, Karen H. and John D., *Last of the Old Time Outlaws, The George West Musgrave Story.* The authors place the well-known outlaw George Musgrave and his brothers on Greene's payroll during strife. P. 172
[40] Ibid.
[41] **O'Neal**, P. 99. **Brayer**, P. 397. And, *El Paso Herald*, June 6, 1906.
[42] **Meed**, P. 6.
[43] **Brayer**, P. 396.
[44] Ibid. According to the author, George Metcalf's brother, Will, "before he had gone a dozen paces, fell dead, pierced by a dozen bullets."
[45] *El Paso Daily Times*, June 2, 1906.
[46] **Meed**., P. 8.
[47] Ibid.
[48] *El Paso Herald*, June 6, 1906.
[49] **Meed**, P. 8.
[50] Ibid. Unquestionably the author places Dave Allison in charge of the defensive forces, as does **DeArment**, P. 12, "…Allison and his guards held off repeated attacks by Mexican miners on Green's house at Mesa."
[51] Ibid., P. 9.
[52] Ibid. It should be noted that the author does not specifically credit Dave Allison with killing any of the crowd surrounding Dwight. He simply records, "While Greene and Allison were setting up defenses around his home, General Manager Dwight was still trying to bring order out of chaos in the main street of Cananea…As he (Dwight) staggered back, Greene, leading a handful of Americans running down the street to his rescue, opened fire. Four leaders of the mob fell stricken…Greene, Dwight and the rest of the men retreated hastily to the Big House." The *El Paso Herald*, June 6, 1906 reported, "It was here that the first serious fight occurred and that a number of the Mexican rioters were shot."
[53] **Brayer**. P. 398. Also see, *El Paso Herald*, June 2, 1906 which reported, "Following the killings (Metcalfs), the Americans attacked the Mexicans and killed and wounded about 50, according to some reports. According to other reports Mexicans attacked the Americans and Mexican officers fired into the Mexican mob."
[54] **Meed**. P. 10.
[55] Ibid. According to at least one report, there were as many as one thousand riotous adversaries making the assault on the American's defensive position.
[56] Ibid., P. 11.
[57] Ibid.
[58] Ibid. Also see, **Metz (II)**, P. 191. The author disputes the use of explosives by the rioters, "Rumor had it that the miners possessed dynamite and firearms, and although this proved false, the managers could hardly be blamed for their fears."
[59] *El Paso Herald,* June 2, 1906.
[60] **Brayer**, P. 398. Walter Douglas was the son of Dr. James Douglas, a Canadian who built the Phelps Dodge empire. He had a "passion of anonymity," but he proved to be one of the real Arizona powerhouses, and when he retired in

---

1930, he was chairman of the board of the Southern Pacific Railroad, in addition to being president of Phelps Dodge. See, **Sheridan**, P. 161-186.

[61] Ibid., P. 399.

[62] **Meed**, P. 14.

[63] **Rynning**, P. 292.

[64] **Meed**, P. 13.

[65] *El Paso Herald*, June 2, 1906. **Miller**, P. 118, Quoting the *Douglas Dispatch* of June 2, 1906, places the number of rifles sent from El Paso at 1000.

[66] Ibid. "Owing to a misunderstanding of orders, last night's train had left the yard and started for Bisbee without the shipment of arms, when the order was given for the train to return to the station and wait for the guns."

[67] Ibid. And see, **Winsor**, P. 57. "Although this trouble occurred in a foreign country, when Colonel W. C. Greene, principal owner of the property, with large interest and influence in Arizona, wired to Bisbee for succor, the response was instantaneous."

[68] **Meed**. P. 14. Also see, *Bisbee Daily Review*, June 2, 1906, as quoted by **Brayer**. "Fully two thousand people were huddled in the plaza, excitedly discussing the news and anxiously awaiting the latest details from the scene of terror…Already men, drunk with excitement, were beginning to show the effect of drink…Mayor Caven issued an edict that all saloons be closed and this was promptly done." In their biographical sketch of "Biddy" Doyle, **Bailey & Chaput** note that he was a Constable and Deputy U. S. Marshal at Bisbee, and make no reference to him being Chief of Police. Vol. I, P. 101.

[69] **Rynning**, P. 291. Clearly the Captain knew, because of the disposition of many of his troops, that he was literally playing with diplomatic fire. He said if his little army crossed the border improperly supervised, that "There'd have been an open season for Mexicans and there's no doubt there'd have been another war with Mexico. It was up to some of us to get the boys soothed down a little."

[70] **Brayer**, P. 400. Quoting the *Douglas Daily Dispatch*, "…very soon all the arms in the Copper Queen were at their disposal. Several pawn brokers trebled their money on rusty old shooting irons, and a little army was percolating through the streets." Although usually not reported in today's climate of political correctness, **Rynning** turned down two men wanting to enlist simply because they were black, "But the two-ex dragoons were Negroes and I was afraid of mixing breeds in that kind of a jam." See, **Rynning**, P. 292.

[71] Ibid., P. 401. And see, *El Paso Daily Times*, June 2, 1906.

[72] Ibid., P. 400. And see, *El Paso Daily Times*, as cited. Clearly we cannot establish with documents or primary sources that Dave Allison's wife, Lena, and their daughter, Hazel, were in Cananea at the time of the riot, but *probability* would indicate they were, and were quite *possibly* on the refugee train carrying Greene's family, "The family of Colonel Greene arrived here (Bisbee) this afternoon but the Colonel remained with his property."

[73] *El Paso Herald*, June 2, 1906.

[74] **Rynning**, P. 293.

[75] Ibid., P. 296. "…we got the boys lined up in a rough-and-tumble formation so we could control them…"

[76] *El Paso Herald*, June 4, 1906.

[77] **Rynning**, P. 296. According to **Rynning**, he had his friend, B. A. Packard, simply to hold any telegrams from anyone—"and keep them till I got back from Mexico."
[78] **Meed**, P. 15.
[79] Ibid., P. 16. Also see, **Wagnoer**, P. 392. "The Governor (Izabal) was agreeable and, in order to avoid international complications, asked the Americans to cross the line as an unorganized mob."
[80] *El Paso Daily Times*, June 2, 1906.
[81] Ibid., June 3, 1906.
[82] **Miller**, P. 123. Quoting the *Douglas Dispatch*, June 2, 1906, "This struck terror into the very hearts of all, and it was hard to keep the men from rushing across the line in a forced march to Cananea."
[83] **Meed**, P. 16.
[84] Ibid. Accordingly, one of the defenders advised Colonel Greene, "we'll be washed up by noon."
[85] Ibid., P. 30.
[86] **Rynning**, P. 301. Also see, **Spanenberger**, P. 37. "The force moved by Mexican troop train down to the mining district and arrived on the scene during one of the assaults on the barricaded Americans."
[87] Ibid.
[88] **Meed**, P. 18.
[89] **Brayer**, P. 405. Quoting the *Bisbee Daily Review*.
[90] Ibid., "Around the square occupied by the important company buildings American guards were stationed with rifles trained on the crowd. The front porch of the company store was bristling with fighting men." **Meed** reports, "Cradling their rifles, with their fingers on the triggers, the men peered down on the crowd swarming around the Colonel's automobile." P. 18.
[91] Ibid.
[92] Ibid. Melodramatically, and by some accounts falsely reported, by others it was told as the gospel truth, either way **Rynning** glossed up the story saying, "The car stopped in front of the bank and Bill stood up and begun haranguing the mob in Mexican. He told them he'd always been their friend, had given them the biggest wages paid in Mexico. Just then several Mexicans yelled, 'Kill the Gringos!' and one jerked his gun. Bill beat him to the draw and the fellow fell dead almost across my feet, and Bill went ahead with his talk without letting that incident interrupt the flow of his conversation." P. 302.
[93] Ibid.
[94] **Meed**, P. 20. **Brayer**, P. 407 identifies the three dead Americans as, Cananea railroad employee, Conrad Kubler; bartender Bert Ruth; and Cananea Consolidated Copper Company mining employee, Bert Lockey.
[95] **Brayer**, P. 408. Quoting the *Bisbee Daily Review*.
[96] Ibid.
[97] Ibid.
[98] **Meed**, P. 21.
[99] *El Paso Herald*, June 6, 1906.
[100] **Meed**, P. 22. Reportedly, Kosterlitzky was under orders in regards to dealing with the lawless, "Catch in the act; kill on the spot."
[101] **Brayer**, P. 408-409.
[102] Ibid. "Not a shot was fired by them, and not a shot was fired at them…"
[103] **Meed**, P. 24.

---

[104] Ibid., P. 27. Also see, **Metz (II)**, "When the brutality of taking possession ended, the Yaquis were either dead, in flight, or sold into plantation slavery in the hemp fields of Yucatan." P. 186.
[105] **Means**, P. 87.

6

"Things doing in police circles."

Once again Dave Allison took up residence at Midland, a move which seems to imply that assorted allegations questioning his probity and his past bookkeeping difficulties were either somewhat exaggerated, or politically fabricated, or forgiven, or forgotten. Regardless of any fault-finding rumors, categorically loyal Lena Allison didn't believe a single derogatory word defaming her husband, as evidenced when she unequivocally avowed, "I am positive that Mr. Allison was never short in his accounts, as Sheriff of Midland County, and all of his old-time friends will substantiate this statement."[1] Whether or not she was correct, or was simply blindsided by unconditional love and devotion is not known. After a short-lived six-month re-acquaintance with old friends in the cow business and once again becoming a permanent player in Midland's upper echelon social circles, "the better citizens again persuaded Dave to run for sheriff…"[2]

Without resorting to a hopeless stab at counting specific votes in selected precincts, the fiercely rousing race, suffice to say, was a campaign where one of the contestants "electioneered" assiduously against Dave Allison, and for all practical purposes refrained from slinging any political mud whatsoever at the other candidate, cowboy W. M. "Bob" Beverly. When it was all said and done, Bob Beverly was declared the undisputed victor, and even he later acknowledged that verbal fisticuffs between the other two rivals, well, it guaranteed his bite from the political plum.[3] Bob Beverly was named the new Midland County Sheriff. Irrefutably, Dave Allison did have a great many influential friends throughout the whole of Midland County, but for this fastidious West Texas election cycle—just not enough.[4] Maybe some of em' hadn't forgiven—or forgotten!

With not much tying him down at Midland, Dave Allison assented to Lena's urgings to relocate. Her father, Robert, was once again suffering a setback. He was in poor health and without doubt having his only daughter near would add to his physical and psychological comfort and, besides, there was plenty of hard work to be done around the house or out from town on his cattle ranches. Dave and Lena moved to Roswell.[5]

Located in Chaves County on the Rio Hondo near its junction with the Pecos River in southeastern New Mexico Territory, Roswell too, like so many Southwestern communities, especially after the turn of the century, was growing as a crossroads Mecca and commercial headquarters for vast grassland ranching empires and as a center for the irrigated farming operations.[6] Like Midland, Chaves County was Dave Allison's kind of country, cow-country. To the east lay the vast Llano Estacado, to the west Sacramento and Capitan Mountains cast their timbered shadows on flat rangeland floors. Located in the nation's most important artesian basin, Roswell developed into New Mexico's fourth largest city.[7] With a healthy mixture of Hispanics and Anglos all bustling about eking out a living, a sleepy little adobe village Roswell was no more. Dave's father-in-law's house at 700 N. Lea was located in what the Hispanic working-class Christened the *Barrio de los Ricos*, the neighborhood of the rich.[8]

Robert and Lucy Johnston, Dave Allison's in-laws. Roswell, New Mexico. Courtesy, Linda Weiler, Roswell, New Mexico

The physical residence may have indeed been lavish for the time period, but sadly, all too soon, a wreath was respectfully displayed on the front door. On February 21, 1909, Dave's father-in-law passed away.[9] Aside from the natural and anticipated bereavement, Robert W. Johnston's death was to have a profound affect on the marriage of Dave and Lena Allison. Nothing suggesting martial disharmony, but rather periods of long and lonesome separation while Dave followed his law enforcement destiny and Lena dutifully cared for her aging mother, Lucy. Neither Dave or Lena were the kind of person that would willingly shirk responsibility. Roswell would be the couple's permanent home base, although there were many more notable Southwestern adventures for Dave Allison elsewhere.

Lena Allison and her mother, Lucy Johnston, at "the house" Roswell, New Mexico. Courtesy, Linda Weiler, Roswell, New Mexico.

Normally historic narratives and biographies are best put down in chronological order. In the majority of instances it's less confusing than bouncing about and skipping back and forth between years, however, in this case, a slight digression will prove indispensable in precisely telling the Roswell segment of Dave Allison's compelling story.

At Alum Bridge, West Virginia on February 3, 1880, Roy Woofter first saw the light of day and his life story, although cut precipitately short, played significantly in the biographic study at hand.[10] About the time Dave

Allison signed on with the Arizona Rangers in 1903, twenty-three year old Roy Woofter migrated to south central Iowa and settled at Albia, Monroe County, where, according to several reports, for a time he served as a thoroughly trustworthy and highly proficient police officer, as did his brother, Homer.[11] Unfortunately, for whatever undisclosed medical reasons, Roy, after just a three year stopover in the Hawkeye State and seeking healthful rejuvenation, packed his valise and shuffled toward the setting sun and into the Southwest, ultimately establishing a permanent mailing address at Roswell.[12] At the outset, Roy Woofter found seasonal work on a nearby Pecos Valley farm. Also, shortly after his inauspicious arrival in the Roswell area, the gallantly handsome and devoutly religious Western young man determined three things, two of which were pleasing.

On left, Roy Woofter, Roswell, New Mexico Chief of Police with his brother, Homer. Roy was viciously gunned down and the position was filled by no nonsense Dave Allison. Courtesy, Sarah Hindman, Albia, Iowa.

First, the temperately dry Roswell climate, as so many others had previously discovered, was delightful and utterly invigorating. Secondly, Roy Woofter made his lifelong career choice. He successfully applied for and was accepted as a brand new patrolman with the Roswell Police Department.[13] Roy knew he had found a home at agreeably sunny Roswell, now too he had a legitimate job—a honorable profession. Life for Roy Woofter was on the upswing, and there is little doubt that he and his blushing bride of one year, the former Miss Margaret Forsyth, could now be reasonably expected to begin laying plans for starting a family.[14] Third, and to his dismay, he came to the uncomfortable realization that internally, just beneath the surface from fussy examination, the city of Roswell and municipal government was the scene of an utterly chaotic and absolutely repugnant political mess. A piously righteous kind of moralistic war was being unceremoniously and uncompromisingly waged between two obstinately single-minded factions, a case that could well meet the criteria for being legally styled—*Wets vs. Drys*.

Generally known for being an officer who was intrepidly "faithful, fearless and courageous in the discharge of his duty," Roy Woofter, a member in good standing at the First Methodist Church, was also dedicated to wholesome rehabilitative practices and was actively urging construction of an Industrial Home for wayward boys.[15] After conferring with New Mexico Territory Supreme Court Chief Justice William H. Pope about the matter Roy Woofter publicly commented:

> I am certainly in favor of establishing a home in New Mexico for incorrigible boys, between the ages of eight and eighteen years. A real home: one as near as possible under the circumstances to a family home, located on a nice big farm with strict discipline. In this home let there be a school course, the same as our public school; let there be various work shops. Here the incorrigibles may be taught best suited to their life work. It will be most beneficial to each one when they leave the home…The very purpose of this proposed Industrial Home would be to keep boys from becoming criminals; to do this there must not be the environment and association with other criminals. There are several boys in Roswell who should be in a home of this kind. I also know some in the reform school at Springer, who could have been saved from the brand of a criminal, had there been an Industrial Home in

> the territory we could have stopped them when the first started out in their reckless career.[16]

Roswell Chief of Police Roy Woofter, next to wagon driver, after a whiskey raid. Courtesy, Sarah Hindman, Albia, Iowa.

Patrolman Roy Woofter was soon to capture the local spotlight on a matter more in line with traditional thoughts of police work. In a politically controversial circumstance, the Chief of Police (actually the title was City Marshal) was ordered to make a raid on one of the rooms at the Central Hotel, a suspected gambling operation. Chief of Police Champion refused, and after conferring with Roswell City Attorney Bowers, Mayor Richardson commissioned Roy Woofter to get the job done, so there could be no "tipping off," as was alleged to have happened on past occasions. Taking another patrolman in tow, Roy "swooped down" on the gambling game while it was in progress and identified the thoroughly dismayed participants, of which; two were leading Roswell physicians; one a prominent real estate man; another a well-known cattleman; and sorrowfully, one of Chaves County Sheriff Charles L. Ballard's very own deputies was snagged in the clandestine game. Needless to say, the raid was the "topic of conversation on the streets" the next day.[17]

The long and the short of it resulted in Chief Champion stepping down, and Roy Woofter being appointed to the position of Roswell Chief of Police in his place, an act which elicited one newspaper editor to cautiously comment that generally people had considerable faith in Woofter, "unless the job spoils him." Somewhat wryly that same print journalist further remarked about the necessary steps requisite in having a top notch police department, "...it is simply a matter of getting the right men, of using the same principle as is used in every private business. If the appointees are not wholly satisfactory, fire them every Saturday night until a bunch is gotten that is worthwhile...It is all poppy-cock to say that such a force cannot be gotten."[18]

At Roswell a definite reform movement was underway. At the April, 1910, city election, besides getting a new Mayor, Dr. George T. Veal, the son-in-law of Southwestern livestock tycoon C. C. Slaughter, and one of the authoritative powerhouses in the Texas and Southwestern Cattle Raisers Association, the citizens of Roswell voted their city dry—no alcohol—no excuses![19]

That being the case, it's reasonable to guess bourbon whiskey cut with branch water wasn't being served at the reception following Hazel Allison's July 31, 1910, Roswell wedding. Whatever Dave Allison thought or had to say about the bridegroom will have to go unrecorded, most probably there was a trace of mist in his eyes and a lump in his throat when he welcomed John Cummins into the family. *Fearless* men love their daughters too. Dave and Lena had been forewarned they wouldn't be seeing too much of their beloved girl child. John Cummins wasn't a cowboy, no, he was a U. S. Civil Servant, a lock-master in the Panama Canal Zone, and for the next thirty years, that place was home for Hazel, although she did manage occasional trips back to the Land of Enchantment and joyful reunions with her mother and daddy.[20] Hazel may have been on her way to tropical Panama, but Dave Allison was still situated in cow-country New Mexico and Roswell was still dry.

Perhaps a few drinking and gambling men tagged Chief Roy Woofter a hardhearted zealot on a moral crusade, others no doubt praised him for a job well done, trying to rid Roswell of sinful evils and fermented drink. An examination of old newspaper clippings does indeed suggest the Police Chief was a busy man. On one occasion he arrested Jim McNiece, caught in the act of selling whiskey, on another he arrested a man named Meyerscough for "receiving a flask of whiskey." Another man obviously befuddled, reeking with liquor on his sour smelling breath, stepped off the train at the local depot and declared he was "looking for Jesus," naturally sardonic members of the "spit and whittle club" told him he had plainly gotten off in the wrong town, however, shortly thereafter Chief Woofter had a spot reserved for him—it wasn't at church. Arresting drunks and bootleggers wasn't necessarily benign and routine every time. Once while the Chief was making an arrest the cantankerous drunk pulled a secreted knife, and in a hard fought scuffle Woofter was stabbed, yet still he managed the unruly prisoner's trip to the jailhouse. Thankfully, Woofter's wounds were not life threatening. And, if the report is indeed accurate, Chief Woofter's philosophy about drinking in public, even at Christmas time, was an overstatement in simplicity, "Stay at home. If your people don't want you at home with booze in you, we certainly don't want you on the streets." [21]

No doubt even a few of the area preacher's eyebrows were raised when it was announced that Chief Roy Woofter had filed a complaint against the Eastern Railway Company of New Mexico for "knowingly bringing into the city from another town within the territory a certain quantity of intoxicating liquors."[22]

The "Whisky War," as the newspaper dubbed it, was seemingly spiraling out of control, rational thinking forsaken. Chief Woofter raided D. R. Patrick's confectionery store and seized a "quantity of intoxicants." Doug Wilson, a former saloonkeeper, appeared on the scene claiming the illicit liquor actually belonged to him, and forthwith through courthouse machinations reclaimed the amber colored contraband. Chief Roy Woofter, who refused to release the whiskey, was arrested by Chaves County Constable Fred Behringer. In turn, Behringer and his attorney, Charles Gilberts, were arrested for "interfering with an officer," but the ludicrous goings-on were far from cessation. Once again Chief Woofter, this time along with Mayor Veal and a deputy sheriff, were arrested and charged with "malicious prosecution." As the newspaperman deprecatingly concluded, "Intense bitterness prevails."[23]

As would be expected, although somewhat embarrassingly, Mayor Veal and Chief Woofter were released and ultimately came clear of any criminal charges, after a preliminary hearing which many thought was a "travesty on justice."[24] Of the whole sorted whiskey affair the *Roswell Daily Record* offered analysis, "One of the arguments in the late campaign used by the 'wets' was that prohibition could not be made to stick in Roswell. And now that it is sticking the same crowd is out yelling for help because it does stick."[25]

And for sure, that boy from far away West Virginia, that young man who had read about wild and woolly law enforcement out in the blustery and brassy Southwest was doing his part to make prohibition "stick." On May 26, 1911, Chief of Police Roy Woofter went before the Roswell Police Judge and signed an affidavit charging J. O. "Jim" Lynch with violations of the city's liquor ordinances. He obtained an arrest warrant and a search warrant for Lynch's residence, 100 N. Richardson Avenue.[26] The next day, late in the afternoon, in the company of Roswell patrolmen Ed and Henry Carmichael, Chief Woofter located and arrested Jim Lynch. Advising the defendant that officers had a warrant to search his residence, the quartet proceeded to Lynch's dwelling. Inside the house, Lynch verbally chastened the officers, telling them they could not search his "private" room, while doing so the suspect forcefully bolted from the lawmen's grasp and locked himself in the bedroom. After failed attempts to kick in the door, Woofter and Henry went to the outside seeking another avenue for dislodging their target. Without warning a horrendous boom echoed throughout the neighborhood, Roy Woofter doubled over in disbelief, a large caliber rifle ball had blasted through his abdomen and zipped out his back, near the hipbone.[27]

Without delay the two Carmichael brothers moved Woofter to an adjacent house, summoned a doctor, and anxiously waited. The Chief of Police never lost consciousness through the excruciatingly painful ordeal, and after a doctor arrived on the scene Woofter was later moved by ambulance to St. Mary's Hospital.[28] Frantically, at the emergency room four physicians meticulously tried to repair the gut-busting damage, and with guarded optimism closed the gaping wounds.[29] Pumped full of strychnine, adrenaline, and morphine, Roy Woofter was rolled from ER and placed in a hospital room where he was given an enema of doubly strong coffee and saline solutions were injected "under the skin" during the course of dutiful nurse's Herculean efforts directed at saving his slowly ebbing life.[30] Fighting for life throughout the night, Woofter told a bystander, "Pray for the man who shot me; I am praying for him."[31] Near daybreak on Saturday, May 28th, Roswell's thirty-one year old Chief of Police passed to the other side.[32]

Without incident Jim Lynch had been taken into custody by Chaves County Sheriff deputies Jim Johnson and Clarence Young fifteen minutes after the shooting, and two years later, at Carlsbad, New Mexico, he would be convicted of murder.[33] After a reverent memorial service in Roswell, the young bereaved widow Woofter and her deceased husband returned to Albia, Iowa, where Roy's body was serenely and lovingly interred. At

Roswell though, it was anything but peaceful. The two factions, "Wets" and "Drys" battled royally, the latter loudly demanding that all betting dens, bawdy houses and bootlegging sites be forcefully shut down, the former, well, at least a few of em' were making threats against the very lives of Mayor Veal and the Carmichael brothers.[34] Mayor Veal was livid, and at a special town meeting in Roswell's Armory he harangued, blistering Justice of the Peace M. W. Witt for coddling criminals, and furthermore angrily declaring unmitigated war on the city's known liquor traffickers, "…officers know all about bootleggers in this city; who they are, where they are…and who has gone into them…these fellows must quit or get out of the City by Tuesday morning or they will be arrested and taken before the court and not before Judge Witt to be turned loose, but before Judge Pope, where they will get even-handed justice."[35] The incredible breakdown in civility and decorum of municipal government affairs was drawing critical. Indubitably, Roswell's wheels were fast coming off.

Whether Mayor Veal was already acquainted with Dave Allison is undetermined, but circumstantial evidence more than suggests his cattle baron father-in-law, C. C. Slaughter, was, and so the call went out. Roswell, in the throes of tumultuous times needed a well-seasoned and competent Chief of Police. Accordingly, since he was "one of the better known peace officers of the Southwest" and "because of his reputation as a brave and efficient officer," Mayor Veal appointed no-nonsense William Davis Allison as Woofter's replacement, a fact unequivocally noted in Cecil Bonney's *Looking Over My Shoulder, Seventy-five Years in the Pecos Valley*.[36] The Texas and Southwestern Cattle Raisers Association no doubt approved.[37]

Chief of Police William Davis "Dave" Allison, jumped into the new assignment full bore. One particular story provides evidence to that point, and additionally highlights the fact overwhelmed *transitional lawmen* were continually having to deal with the racing advances of developing technology. Ingeniously clever criminals were even adept at harnessing the kilowatt. Under the headline, "Things Doing In Police Circles," the *Roswell Daily Record* posted a story which is hereafter reported in full, with emphasis added to the last paragraph:

> Theodore Dieffenbacher, Better known as "Diffy," who, for sometime past has been rooming above the Morrison Bros.' Store on Main street, on Sunday morning at the early hour of four, had his place raided by Marshal

Allison and his colleague, Dan Kirkpatrick. "Diffy" had a complete gambling apartment, so the officers declare, in every respect. The main entrance was through room No. 7 and from there the guests were led thru two rooms to where stood the tables on which hard-earned cash, "Like the ship in the night," was seen but once and then no more. He had the entrance so wired that upon anyone stepping up to the door they stepped upon two pieces of tin concealed under a mat and so fixed that a small weight brought in contact and thus rang a buzzer in the gaming room. It is thought that in this way frequent visitors could make themselves known by certain signals.

It looked as if fate wished to give him a small chance, for when Mr. Allison, who for some time had been waiting diligently for the guests to make their exit, casually changed his position, he placed his hand on the mat and thus set off the alarm. "Diffy" came to the door and was immediately covered by a revolver and commanded to show them the room. Upon seeing that it was the Marshal he exclaimed: "My God, Dave, you have broken my heart!"

Although it was against his desire, he did as directed, and those found at the table were Lon Holland, Sam Mitchell, Marcus Jones and V. W. Cranor. They all gave bond and were released from custody until this morning at 9 o'clock, when they were arraigned and pleaded guilty. The court imposed a fine of $50 and costs. Mr. Dieffenbacher was arraigned alone. He made the same plea and was given the same fine. Immediately after the sentence he said to have exclaimed:

"I'll have to start another game to get, I guess," referring to the money with which to pay his fine.

After the hearing at Justice M. W. Witt's court, Marshal Allison, Fire Chief Whiteman, Fire Captain Dan Kirpatrick, George Williams, City Electrician Henry Selleck, and several reporters, went to examine the rooms in order to determine whether or not "Diffy" was keeping within the city ordinance in wiring his premises. "Diffy" was much peeved that his place should thus be shown to so many, and especially to reporters, and refused entrance

> to any but city officials. From the roof of the Sheridan building entrance could easily be obtained to the gambling place and in order that he might be protected from any such intrusion, "Diffy" had his window screens charged with 110 volts of electricity. A shock of this voltage might possibly prove serious to some persons. All current will be ordered cut off the entire second floor of the building until Mr. "Diffy" sees fit to do away with his electrical contrivances...
>
> *The Roswell police force under the guidance of Chief Allison, is doing itself proud and the fearlessness and fidelity to duty of the officers is becoming more apparent every day.*[38]

Shortly after taking office, Chief of Police Dave Allison submitted his end of the month report for June 1911, which included the following breakdown of arrests: Violations of ordinances, 7; drunks, 3; assault, 1; breaking pound, 1; Abusive language, 1; Bicycle ordinance, 1. Convicted 13; dismissed, 1. Additionally four more arrests were made for felonies, but the specific crimes were not identified. Aside from peace keeping duties, Chief Allison also reported his officers had served 57 notices "for widening sidewalks" during the month.[39]

Unmistakably, from the very beginning after taking office, Chief of Police Dave Allison was single-minded in his approach to dealing with lawbreakers, and to the indifferent spectator it might have looked as if, like his committed predecessor, that he was on a moralistic religious crusade—which he wasn't. Dave Allison wasn't, at least until he arrived at Roswell, a teetotaler, but he knew, and made sure everyone else knew—he would not be buffaloed—it was a new day in Roswell! He was going to get Roswell whipped back into shape, a clean point that the *Roswell Daily Record* wryly made note of, "Violators of the law are being brought to book in Roswell...While bootlegging was going on gambling was also carried on in violation of the territorial law but the new city marshal of Roswell is enforcing the law against gambling...What is being done in Roswell simply goes to show that the laws can be enforced if there is a disposition on the part of the officers to do so."[40] Dave Allison had the disposition to do so.

Short the concocted melodrama occasionally embroidered into breathtaking Western chronicles, facts reveal, even if the reader wants to ignore them, that much of the time—police work—well, it's just ordinary and routine most of the time. Surely, the justly *fearless* Dave Allison would have much preferred duty around the chuck wagons, talking shop about "Goddamn cow-thieves." No doubt as a *transitional lawman* on the *transitional frontier* he might too have been discomfited to even admit to those chapped-faced buckaroos that back in the city, back in Roswell town, he had issued all his policemen stop watches so the patrolmen could arrest those automobile aficionados who were "in the habit of 'scorching' within the city…"[41] Chief Dave Allison had calculated that a car traveling the city ordinance ordained ten miles per hour speed limit, must not go more than 14 feet per second—"scorchers" beware![42]

He was also trying to snag Kyle Fox, who definitely wasn't a "Goddamn cow-thief," but who had "skipped with all the aviation funds, owing the aviators and many others."[43] The Southwestern frontier was spinning in transition.

As the year was winding down, events too were swirling at the Catholic Club. Donning fantasy robes of judicial authority, one group of young ladies served on the bench of a "kangaroo court," others, imaginary truncheons in hand, fanned out through the waltzing multitudes and arrested partying merrymakers for such violations "as being pretty, for coming in wearing their hats, for talking, for laughing…" and one was unsympathetically hauled before the bar of justice for just being plain ugly.[44] The finale, however, was when "City Marshal Allison and some of his policemen were brought before the 'court' and fined for carrying concealed weapons. The fines were 25c apiece and over $9 was gleaned in this way for the church fund."[45]

Monotony or not there was still work to be done. An inspection of just a sampling from the *Police Judge's Docket Book* discloses the wide breadth of violation and code enforcement demanded of an active police force, such as: A. C. Holland, Gambling; Tom Preston, Vagrancy; Sam Stewart, Using Vulgar & Indecent Language; Charley Brady, Carrying a Deadly Weapon; A. P. Yarborough, Drunk; Tom Preston, Drunk & Disorderly; J. D. Kirpatrick, Fighting; Joe McGain, Riding Bicycle on Sidewalk; Dr. C. F. Beeson, Riding Automobile Without Lights; L. B. Craig, Shooting in the City Without Permission; C. W. Johnson, Riding a Bicycle at Night Without a Light; J. E. Ray, Driving an Automobile at Night Without a Light; T. L. Wilson, Selling Whiskey: J. H. Ochsner, Exceeding Speed Limit; John Doe, Chenanan, Indecent Exposure of Person; Harry Hutchison, Fast Driving; And repetitively the lists goes on.[46]

The work went on, day after day, night after night, but somehow it was different than when the Veal administration was inaugurated, or a little later when Dave Allison picked up the reins as Police Chief. Certainly there was crime, violations of city ordinances, youthful waywardness, and the ever escalating number of sputtering motorists darting down streets startling swayback nags hitched to the vegetable carts and milk wagons. The good news, however, was that citizens weren't killing the police and the police weren't gunning down Roswell city dwellers, although from time to time no doubt an occasional head was necessarily thumped. To be sure there were a fair share of hooligans and harlots, but Chief Dave Allison had pretty much shaped the law enforcement future for Roswell. Certainly he wasn't a "town-tamer," but then in truth, Wyatt Earp wasn't either. Dave Allison simply got the job done, during trying times and amid public controversy.

And that hullabaloo about drinking whiskey and guzzling beer was far from over. A newspaper editorialized:

> What argument is made in favor of a return to the saloons? Is it that as much liquor is sold now as was sold when we had saloons? It would be a reflection upon your intelligence to suppose that any of you give weight to that argument. The liquor interests would not spend their money as freely as they do to prevent the closing of saloons if more liquor were sold under the present system than would be sold through the saloons. The brewery is not a charitable institution. It is not run out of consideration for the public. It does not want the saloon as an education institution, it does not offer it as a moral center. It wants it as a means of selling liquor, and until the breweries become the champions of prohibition we need not pay any attention to the argument that more liquor is sold without saloons than with them.[47]

With the situation much improved over just two years earlier, Mayor George Veal opted not to seek re-election and correspondingly, according to political patronage protocol, the new mayor would be allowed to pick his own man for Police Chief. Mayor Veal and Chief Allison were subsequently replaced by W. M. Atkinson and Tobe Stewart, respectively.[48] The out-going mayor wished his replacement "smooth sailing" and the incoming city executive publicly pledged to maintain an uncompromisingly strong prohibitionist stance.[49]

While Dave Allison had been winding down his administrative business as Chief of Police he received a letter from E. R. Bryan, a staff member with the First National Bank at Midland. The bank in Seminole, Gains County, Texas had been robbed, and Bryan, dissatisfied with the actions of local officers, inquired of Dave Allison, "Can you catch these robbers? If so how much will it take to get you to catch and convict them. Please answer at once and mark your letter personal."[50]

Dave Allison and wife, Lena. Courtesy, Pat Treadwell, Tahoka, Texas.

The fact that William Davis Allison's sleuthing services were being asked for from Midland seems indicative of at least two conclusions: Dave was still managing to maintain his reputation as a lawman and tenacious man hunter; and since the request for assistance was coming from the upper economic strata at Midland, it gives rise to speculation as to accusations of any wrongdoing on his part while sheriff. Just maybe the insinuations had been a bit overblown and somewhat politically motivated. Unquestionably, while sheriff at Midland something happened to muck up the works, but from the best evidence thus far developed, dispassionately it seems downright dishonesty was not a contributor to the squalid mess. To banker Bryan's request, Dave Allison in part replied.

> You doubtless remember the information I gave you in November 1910. You also can recall that in years gone by I have never undertaken to guarantee the conviction of any defendant. If, however, you or the Seminole National Bank will send me $500.00 as expense money solely, and then you or it guarantee to pay me $500 each for a Grand Jury indictment against the robbers, be they two or more, I shall undertake to apprehend and convict them.[51]

Historically speaking there is a paucity of proof in establishing just how much time and effort Dave Allison expended chasing after the Seminole bank robbers. Probably not too much. W. D. Allison had sobering troubles of his own to contend with, right in Roswell. The Chaves County Grand Jury indicted him for having accepted and for offering a bribe. He "was placed under arrest by the sheriff and later released on a bond of $2000."[52]

The whole commotion had started a few weeks earlier. Battling over rangeland rights, a mini-war was festering between cowmen and sheep men. Allegedly, cowmen had distributed poison over the pastures, a concoction which cattle were immune to but not sheep. Sheep men hired lawyer Hiram M. Dow to assist in prosecuting the guilty parties, if and when they were ever apprehended. The District Attorney fully recognizing the investigative expertise of Dave Allison, hired him as a special detective, sent him to investigate the abhorrent crime, and forthwith make a report back to the prosecuting attorneys.[53]

Separating a little wheat from the chaff, Chaves County cowmen Jeff White and Dick Harper were indicted for having "exposed poisonous substances." Some people were saying Dave Allison had accepted a bribe of $500 to make a false report in the matter, and unquestionably, as everyone was well aware, the former Chief of Police was favorably and closely allied with Southwestern cattlemen and their economic interests. Dave Allison didn't shear sheep—ever! Compounding Allison's miserable predicament, which he himself created, the local District Attorney, K. K. Scott, was claiming that Dave attempted to bribe him to suppress the evidence and withhold information from the Grand Jury regarding the sheep poisoning case and "to keep and protect them (White and Harper) from punishment."[54] Things weren't prefiguring too well for *fearless* Dave Allison.

The case, on December 10th, 1913, went to trial. The gist of the allegation from the prosecution's perspective was that while standing on the sidewalk near the Joyce-Pruit store, Dave Allison in a conversation with District Attorney Scott offered a bribe to have certain witness not testify against White and Harper.[55]

After hearing others offer evidence, Dave Allison took the witness stand in his own behalf. Under oath Dave testified that he in fact did tell the prosecutor, "there would be a piece of money in it…but said he did it for the purpose of finding out whether or not Scott 'was fixed' with reference to the case as had been reported to him, and not for the purpose of bribing the district attorney."[56] Using today's criminal justice jargon, Dave Allison was working a "sting operation," at least so he claimed. The jury was indeed in a legitimate quandary, whose testimony should they weigh most important; after all, it was unmistakably a case of "take my word for it." There was no reason to suspect District Attorney Scott was not telling the truth, and if Dave Allison was utilizing a ruse to further justice, should he be shamefully spirited away to the penitentiary? For awhile the jury hung—deliberations in doubt. However, after rethinking, rearguing, and reviewing evidence an exasperated jury voted to acquit Dave Allison—not guilty![57]

Possibly the indictment and contentious trial were significant factors; but nevertheless, as always, William Davis Allison was a much sought after troubleshooter, and so, with Lena's affectionate blessings he packed his duffel and headed out, "Gone to Texas."

ENDNOTES
Chapter 6. "Things doing in police circles"

[1] Letter from Lena Allison to Dayton Moses, Attorney for the Texas and Southwestern Cattle Raisers Association. Dated April 16, 1923. Courtesy, Pat **Treadwell**, Tahoka, Texas.
[2] Ibid.
[3] Transcript, Bob Beverly to J. Evetts **Haley**, June 27, 1946. Courtesy, The Nita Stewart Haley Memorial Library and The J. Evetts Haley History Center, Midland. And, list of *Sheriffs of Midland County*. Courtesy, Gary **Painter**, Midland County Sheriff, Midland. W. M. "Bob" Beverly was born on May 5, 1872 at Ringgold, Georgia and later moved to Texas with his family, first settling at Denton, and later at Waco. For the greater part of his life Beverly cowboyed, but did from time to time effectively pull stints as a Western law enforcement officer. Beverly died on April 16, 1958, and is buried at Lubbock, Texas. For additional information on this uniquely interesting individual see, **Haley**, P. 2-6.
[4] Ibid.
[5] **Weiler** and **Treadwell**. Both family members, one from Dave Allison's genealogical side of the family, and one from Lena's branch of the family tree, concur that the couple moved to Roswell due to the poor health of Robert Johnston, Lena's father.
[6] **Julyan**. P. 303-304.
[7] Ibid.
[8] Ibid. According to the author, the other of Roswell's distinctly named neighborhoods were: *Chihuahita*, little Chihuahua; *El Alto*, "the heights"; *La Gara*, "the rag," where the poor people hung out their ragged laundry; and *Zaragosa*, the name of a south of the border city.
[9] **Weiler**. The exact cause of Robert W. Johnston's death is not known, but it was from natural causes, not accident, suicide, or homicide.
[10] For much of the information on the life of Roy Woofter the author is pleasantly indebted to relatives Carol **Marlin**, Albia, Iowa. Graciously she has furnished family papers, letters, newspaper clippings (some of which are unidentified by heading and date), hospital records, and several photographs. The wealth of treasure provided by Ms. **Marlin** will hereafter be cited as **Marlin.** Also, Albia relative Sarah **Hindman's** help proved invaluable.
[11] **Halvorson**, John. Typescript, "Roswell's First Police Officer Killed In The Line of Duty". P. 1. Courtesy, Commander Richard **Lucero**, Roswell Police Department Archives, Roswell. Hereafter cited as **Halvorson**.
[12] **Marlin**. And, from an unidentified obituary for Roy Woofter.
[13] Ibid.
[14] Ibid.
[15] *Roswell Tribune*, n. d., courtesy **Marlin**.
[16] Ibid.
[17] *Roswell Daily Record*, October 1, 1909.
[18] Ibid, n. d., courtesy **Marlin**.
[19] **Halvorson**, P. 1. Also, **Marlin** unidentified newspaper clipping, Woofter's obituary. And, personal correspondence to the author, dated July 31, 2000, from distinguished educator, writer, and City Historian for Roswell, Elvis E. **Fleming**,

---

who advised that George T. Veal served as Mayor of Roswell for one two year term, April 1910 to April 1912.

[20] **Weiler**. Family genealogical papers. And clipping from the *Roswell Daily Record.* n. d. Hazel and John Cummins returned to Roswell after his retirement from the U. S. Civil Service. Hazel too remained in Roswell at the family residence, 700 N. Lea Avenue, until her death from natural causes at the age of 83. The couple had no children.

[21] Assorted unidentified newspaper clippings, courtesy **Marlin**.

[22] Ibid.

[23] Ibid. In another clipping it was reported, "After a trial that exhibited a travesty of justice, Mayor Veal and Chief Marshal Woofter were held to appear before the Grand Jury, by R. D. Bell's court on Tuesday. This will not harm prohibition in the least."

[24] **Marlin**, unidentified newspaper clipping, n. d.

[25] *Roswell Daily Record*, September 1, 1910.

[26] The City of Roswell, *Police Judge's Docket*. P. 487. Courtesy, Commander Richard D. **Lucero**, Roswell Police Department, Roswell. Also see, **Halvorson**, P. 1. And see, *Roswell Daily Record*, October 14, 1913, "The next witness called was M. W. Witt, who testified that he issued the warrant and delivered it to Roy Woofter, commanding him to arrest Jim Lynch and to search his house for liquors."

[27] **Halvorson**. P. 2. Also see, *Roswell Daily Record*, May 27, 1911. The wound was described in this manner, "It was found that the bullet, an immense army ball, had entered about an inch above and a little to the side of the naval, passed through the stomach and bowels and out at the left side of the back at the point known as the hipbone, mashing off some of the bone and taking the pieces out with it. Internal bleeding was very free, especially at the wound in the stomach. A large amount of the intestines had passed out at the hole at the back when the first examination was made at the hospital." Roy Woofter was killed by a bullet from a .45-70 caliber rifle, "The shell picked up by Deputy Johnson shows that the ball was what is known as the U. S. A. ball, which weighs 405 grains and is made of soft lead."

[28] Ibid. And see, typescript of Roy Woofter's obituary, n. d., courtesy **Marlin**.

[29] Ibid.

[30] *Clinical Record*, "Roy Woofter," St. Mary's Hospital Patient Records, Roswell, New Mexico. Courtesy, **Marlin**.

[31] **Marlin**. Obituary.

[32] **Halvorson**, P. 2. And see, *Roswell Daily Record*, May 27,1911.

[33] Ibid. Some newspaper accounts indicate the trial for Woofter's murder was held in Clovis, New Mexico on a change of venue, or at least the sentencing.

[34] Ibid.

[35] Ibid.

[36] **Bonney**, Cecil. *Looking Over My Shoulder, Seventy-five Years in the Pecos Valley*. P. 157, n. 1. Hereafter cited as **Bonney**.

[37] *The Cattleman*, Vol. IX, No. 11 (May 1923) P. 13-14.

[38] *Roswell Daily Record*, July 3, 1911. The same newspaper story goes on to point out that Marshal Dave Allison, on the same day, served warrants on four individuals charging them with vagrancy.

[39] Ibid., July 8, 1911.

[40] Ibid., July 10, 1911.

---

[41] Ibid., September 20,1911.

[42] Ibid. He also determined that in areas where the Roswell posted speed limit was 15 miles per hour, that an automobile should not travel in excess of 22 feet per second. Also see, *Roswell Daily Record*, February 2, 1912. Of the problem of "speeding machines" Chief Dave Allison said, "There are too many people in this city who think that the city ordinances were made for mere sport and nothing else, but I have decided that there shall be no more leniency. I do not think that we have been lenient with anyone to any extent, but we have not been in a position to take over all those who are disregarding the city laws. There is no reason why the autoist should exceed the speed limit, and I don't propose to stand for it."

[43] Ibid. October 9, 1911. Chief Dave Allison sent telegrams to Amarillo, Texas and Carlsbad, New Mexico Territory in efforts to apprehend Kyle Fox.

[44] Ibid., December 12, 1911.

[45] Ibid.

[46] *Police Judge's Docket Book I*, P. 487-592 and *Police Judge's Docket Book II*, P. 1-157. Courtesy, Richard **Lucero**, Commander, Roswell Police Department, Roswell. Also see, *Roswell Daily Record,* February 8, 1912, for a public year-end report by Chief of Police Dave Allison.

[47] *Roswell Daily Record*, July 10, 1911.

[48] Ibid. April 16, 1912 and April 19, 1912. And correspondence to the author from Elvis **Fleming**, Roswell, as cited.

[49] Ibid. The headline of the April 19th edition clarified, "New Mayor and Councilmen Declare They Will Not Repeal Prohibition Ordinance but Stand By Their Pledges and Enforce It to the Letter. Veal Wishes New Officers Smoother Sailing."

[50] Letter from E. R. Bryan, First National Bank, Midland, Texas to W. D. Allison, Roswell, New Mexico, dated February 23, 1912. Courtesy, **Treadwell.**

[51] Letter from W. D. Allison, Roswell, New Mexico to E. R. Bryan, Midland, Texas, dated February 27, 1912. Courtesy, **Treadwell**.

[52] *Roswell Daily Record*, Nov. 5, 1913. And see, *Cost and Bond Docket Book, The State of New Mexico vs. William D. Allison.* Courtesy, Chaves County Clerk, Roswell, New Mexico and **Weiler**.

[53] Ibid. And see, State of New Mexico, Fifth Judicial District, County of Chaves, *Indictment* of William D. Allison. Copy Courtesy, **Treadwell**.

[54] *Indictment* as cited above.

[55] *Roswell Daily Record*, December 15, 1913. And see, Indictment.

[56] Ibid.

[57] Ibid., Also see, *Cost and Bond Book* entry, "The verdict—not guilty."

7

"There come the sheriffs and I must get ready for them"

Dave Allison migrated to far West Texas alighting at Sierra Blanca, not as a hobo or some lonesome itinerant cowboy, but once again, at the request of a special interest group—the cowmen of El Paso County, and its sister to the east, Culberson County.[1] One writer unequivocally, although erroneously, reports "Allison had been hired as a gunfighter by the Love brothers and brought to Sierra Blanca to deal with squatters who would settle on the vast landholdings claimed by the ranchers."[2] It sounds melodramatic to be sure and, make no mistake, the Love brother's cattle operations were one of the prominent ranching ventures in the neighborhood, but a surviving member of the Love family reports there was no "squatter" mess demanding the murderous services of "gunfighters." There *was* somewhat of an endemic predicament concerning stolen livestock in the Sierra Blanca country.[3] In large part, this was due to its lying along the Rio Grande, coupled with the fact Mexican bandits and insurrections habitually haunted the desolate and sparsely populated region, making the area particularly prone to cattle thieving incursions. And there were also a bundle of "Goddamn cow-thieves" of the blue-eyed variety.

For want of better terminology, William Davis "Dave" Allison, although exceptionally handy with a Colt's six-shooter, was not contemporarily considered a gunfighter in the stereotypical Hollywood mold. Dave Allison was a lawman. As historian Larry Ball characterizes, a *subscription deputy* was an official law enforcement position, but one wherein the lawman's salary was paid by citizen pledges or from special interest coffers.[4] At Sierra Blanca, Dave Allison had been recruited to do a job, paid by the stockmen of the two counties "to keep down lawlessness" in the vicinity.[5] To give him official authority, a *subscription deputy* of sorts, William Davis Allison carried an El Paso County deputy Constable's commission.[6]

Cattlemen were upset. An incident along the border had sorrowfully captured the attention of area ranchers.

On the night of February 9, 1913, U. S. Mounted Customs Inspectors Joe Sitter and Jack Howard, accompanied by Texas and Southwestern Cattle Raisers Association Inspector Ad Harvick executed an arrest warrant for Chico Cano, charging him with the theft of cattle. Unbeknownst to the officers when they departed the little Rio Grande River village of Pilares with their prisoner the next morning, plans for a ambush and rescue were already in the works. When about a mile and a half from Pilares a torrent of rifle fire unrelentingly pelted the small posse. Joe Sitter was slightly injured, Ad Harvick suffered a more serious bullet wound, and most unfortunately, Jack Howard was killed outright. After the initial shocking surprise evaporated, lawmen Sitter and Harvick scampered behind boulders and returned a blistering rifle fire. Chico Cano just scampered. The assassins had accomplished their mission and gave up the ground.[7]

And, just a month later, the ranches of Lawrence Haley and Lee Hancock were raided by Mexican bandits, causing a local newspaper editor to comment the malicious marauders were "...bad men and are armed to the teeth..."[8] Big Bend area law enforcers and cowmen were enraged—the bull was seeing red!

That same year, another tragic West Texas affair shattered any chances for a truce between cattlemen and cow-thieves. A tragedy that in part caused them to seek out *fearless* Dave Allison, agreeing to "chip in" and pay his salary.

El Paso County Deputy Sheriff William Henry Garlick and Texas Ranger Scott Russell had been "instrumental in running down a number of cattle thieves..."[9] West Texas cattlemen were pleased with the efforts of the two committed lawmen, especially when it was announced that the pair had successfully arrested members of the "Guadarrama clan."[10] However, unlike area cowmen, friends and relatives of the Guadarrama family were not cheering the two gendarme's efforts—in fact—threats were being made. And, as the *El Paso Morning Times* reported, both Garlick and Russell had been "making it warm" for the gang of cattle thieves, and Juan Guadarrama had personally challenged the officers to enter his domain at their own peril.[11] Undaunted, the plucky Southwestern lawmen ignored the threats made on their lives.[12]

On June 23, 1913, while on casual, but routine patrol at El Paso, in the "Mexican settlement near the El Paso smelter," the pair of officers momentarily exchanged pleasantries with Sergeant J. H. Sirks of Troop C,

Thirteenth Cavalry, U. S. Army. After biding the sergeant adieu, Deputy Garlick and Ranger Russell entered the *Eje del Barrio Libre* grocery store and meat market, where reputably it was alleged stolen livestock was sometimes surreptitiously butchered. The enterprise was owned by the Guadarrama family. Whether the action was designed forevermore to show the Guadarramas' they held absolutely no fear regarding threats, or whether the decision to cross the threshold into the store was calculated as a taunting insult will never be known. Jaun Guadarrama, was already forewarned, having told a compadre, "There come the sheriffs and I must get ready for them."[13]

El Paso County Deputy Sheriff William H. Garlick, killed in the line of duty while serving on a transitional frontier. Courtesy, Button and Marvin Garlick, Van Horn, Texas.

Once inside the grocery, the lawmen purchased some tobacco. Russell calmly rolled a cigarette, but while doing so noticed the inferior and rotten character of the tobacco, and so commented. Russell's complaint about the second-rate product were the last words he spoke. Maria Guadarrama, Juan's mother, who had slipped up behind the officers, savagely struck them in the head with a pick handle, or by other reports, a meat-clever, in any event, the ferocious blows caused both of the officers to crumple to the grimy floor.[14] Simultaneously, Juan Guadarrama opened up with his revolvers on the two prostrate lawmen. Deputy Garlick was struck, "One bullet went through the thigh, through the liver, and shattered a rib on the right side. Striking the rib it ranged downward, lodging in the spine. Another bullet entered his head back of the left ear and ranged downward, giving the impression he had been shot while lying on the floor."[15] Texas Ranger Russell "was shot below the right arm. The bullet passed through the shoulder and pierced the brain."[16] Both officers lay dead on the floor.[17] In an ironically wicked twist of fate, or maybe it was just the Blind Mistress of Justice at work, during the frenzied melee Juan Guadarrama also shot and killed his own mother.[18]

Texas Ranger Grover Scott Russell, far right, murdered at El Paso, Texas. Courtesy, Grady Russell, Incirlik, Turkey.

Hearing what he determined to be nine shots, Sergeant Sirks ran back to the store, entered and observed both officers lying in puddles of their own blood. In response to Sirk's question, "Who killed Garlick?" Juan Guadarrama replied, "I, did." Quickly the non-commissioned officer sounded the alarm, and Lt. Prince, who was nearby, ordered a detachment of soldiers to surround the grocery to prevent anyone from coming or going. Upon arrival of civil officers, Juan, Jesus, David, Sabino and Adolph Guadarrama, as well as T. Echeverria, Pablo Ramos, Manuel Ochoa, and Levio Dominguea were arrested and placed in the El Paso County Jail.[19] All of the arrested parties, to the man, were "considered dangerous characters."[20]

As would naturally be expected the local law enforcement community was incensed at the wanton killings. Cattlemen's blood was boiling, but in this instance they chose "not to take the law into their own hands, but they intend to take care of themselves should a crisis come."[21]

Deputy W. H. Garlick, and Ranger Scott Russell in the local press were praised as being brave and efficient officers. The honest part of El Paso was in mourning; for the underworld it was business as usual!

The remains of Capt. John R. Hughes's twenty-two year old ranger private, Scott Russell, were shipped to his home for burial at Stephenville, Erath County, Texas, where his father was the city fire marshal. Deputy William H. Garlick, was survived by his pregnant wife, and five children. His body was returned to Valentine, Jeff Davis County, Texas, for internment.[22] One of deputy Garlick's sons, Fred, vowed to avenge his father's death, not through some revengeful murder in the dead of night, but by carrying on the law enforcement tradition. Five years later, Fred Garlick, at the age of twenty-one, enlisted in the Texas Rangers and had a distinguished career, dedicatedly serving his community with assignments throughout West Texas.[23]

During most of his life W. D. "Dave" Allison had never been too far removed from the cow business, cattlemen and cowboys; and by this time, one of his strongest supporters, "Lish" Estes, was involved in ranching operations in the mountains south of Van Horn in Culberson County, Texas.[24] As well, Dave Allison was an "Association man"—one sympathetic to their way of life. In need of a range detective, the call from cattlemen went out to Dave Allison.

When Dave Allison detrained at Sierra Blanca he once again found himself on the *transitional frontier*. Right there in Sierra Blanca were two hotels, the Palace and the Klondike, restaurants, livery stables, mercantile stores, a school, and the inevitable saloons associated with frontier cattle towns.[25] There were telephones, although not everyone had one, and several auspicious citizens in the *transitional* neighborhood already possessed what most people were scrimping and saving for, an automobile. For the majority though, it wasn't a new Ford, but rather a reliable saddle horse or a buckboard. Sierra Blanca was, in her own way, striving to stay abreast with modern technology, but yet still, Sierra Blanca was a cowtown, with railroad stock pens available for public utilization, and the town's manmade dirt watering tank still in use as integral ingredients in the community's overall economic well-being. Of Sierra Blanca and her people a letter writer penned, "This is the funniest place I have ever been. It is supposed to be very tough and at least half the men wear boots and spurs and carry guns…I would not miss this for the world. I guess there are few places like it left."[26] Because of the Southern Pacific Railroad connecting with the Texas & Pacific Railroad, and afterward, due to the Southern Pacific angling southeast to eventually connect with the Galveston, Harrisburg and San Antonio Railroad in Brewster County, the settlement of Sierra Blanca flourished as a central shipping point for West Texas and Mexican cattle.[27]

Sierra Blanca stalwarts. Celebrated cowboy preacher L. R. Milican, front row, third from left, he performed Dave and Lena's wedding ceremony at Midland. Fourth from left, Tom D. Love, former Borden County, Texas, sheriff and the man who captured the legendary Oklahoma hellion, William Tuttle "Bill" Cook. Courtesy, Bill Love, Sierra Blanca, Texas.

However, just a hop, skip, and a jump from town, an uncongenial geography abruptly dominated the landscape. To the west and southwest meandered the Rio Grande River. Almost directly south, and then running southeasterly from Sierra Blanca between the purple hued Eagle Mountains and the boundary defining river was Red Light Draw, skipping straight past the mountain entrance to Frenchman's Canyon and then dancing on beyond the well-worn cutoff down to the old Indian Hot Springs. To the north lay the Territory of New Mexico, and to the northwest the historic Salt Lakes and ruggedly captivating Guadalupe Mountains.[28] For the most part, since the subjugation of the Apache, the Sierra Blanca country had remained austerely under-populated. Not that people didn't traipse back and forth over the area south of Sierra Blanca, for they did—there were plenty of revolutionaries, smugglers, bandits, and "Goddamn cow-thieves." Honest ranchers and cowboys, yes, there were even a few of them too!

One author postulates, because of its location, Sierra Blanca was a kind of neutral zone and escaped much of the conflict connected with the Mexican Revolution which had begun in 1910, especially because of the profit to be made trading with Mexican bandits and intransigent rebels. Carrying his analysis one step farther the writer declares, "Many west Texas ranches were stocked with cattle from Mexico that could be had at bargain basement prices in midnight trades for horses or arms and ammunition."[29]

A dodgy scalawag with an entrepreneurial spirit and a diminished allegiance to legality could very well become a financial "fat cat" by illicitly making clandestine deals with Mexican insurgents for munitions of war, especially after 1912, when the U. S. Government placed an embargo on all arms shipments to Mexico.[30] In fact, the same year Dave Allison started his range detective duties in the Sierra Blanca country, American troops, during April 1914, occupied the Mexican port city of Vera Cruz in an effort to thwart arms shipments from Germany to Mexico.[31] At the time, in World War I Europe, causalities were polluting hedgerows and blood-soaked trenches with a nauseating burnt stench from the deceased doughboys and the Kaiser's spike-helmeted soldiers. German intelligence agents, because the United States was furnishing indispensable war supplies to her European Allies, calculated, and not necessarily imprecisely, that continued turmoil on the Mexican border would in some measure divert American attention from across the Atlantic to its southern border, and might actually retard the United States from entering the European Theater with her own military invasion forces.[32] Additionally,

"A friendly government in Mexico could give Germany a base of operations in the Western Hemisphere, if and when they needed one..."[33] Chaotic conditions, reoccurring revolutions, wholesale banditry, and merciless adobe walled executions had been part of the norm along the Mexican border for years. Dave Allison wasn't expected to negotiate a cease fire and bring peaceful settlement to international hostilities, not by a long-shot. Dave Allison was simply hired to do what he was always hired to do—maintain some degree of territorial tranquility and terminate the activities of "Goddamn cow-thieves," Mexican or American.

If William Davis Allison was tough, so was Horace L. Roberson. H. L. Roberson, like Allison, was an ex-Texas Ranger and a former Inspector for the Texas and Southwestern Cattle Raisers Association.[34] According to his Ranger enlistment papers Roberson had been born at Staple's Store, Guadalupe County—down South Texas way in 1875.[35] Early in life Roberson had mastered self-restraint, and unlike so many others in his West Texas cow-country fraternity, he had opted not to swig liquor, smoke cigarettes, chew tobacco, dip snuff, or drink coffee.[36] The light brown-haired Roberson stood a little over six-foot tall, was all man—and all mean—at least according to several reports.[37] And, just like the older Dave Allison, H. L. Roberson had started out cowboying, but he had taken a hiatus from horseback employment and served a stint with the United States Army in the Philippines before returning to ranch work in Texas. Later, after service with the Texas Rangers, Roberson upon the advice of Captain John Hughes who counseled the advantage of accepting the higher paying job, resigned and took over as foreman for the million acre T O Ranch near Pilares.[38]

Owned by the Nelson Morris Cattle Company of Chicago, Illinois, the T O Ranch was running fourteen thousand head of cattle in the heartland of Mexican insurgence and rebellion, an area that was also quite familiar to borderland rogues who irrespective of political stripe or nationality were profiting and pilfering from the T O herd.[39] Reportedly, Roberson's working instructions from ranch management were short and sweet—put together a damn tough crew and hold the fort.[40] He did just that! Already with a reputation for having killed several men, as reflected in the *El Paso Herald* which reported, "He was tried for the alleged killing of a Mexican at Ysleta and another at Marfa, and came clear each time...," Roberson successfully recruited several *pistoleros* and hard-bitten Southwestern cowhands of like ilk.[41]

Firing Brown Paschal, the former foreman of the T O, and husband of Sierra Blanca's Palace Hotel owner, then replacing him with Horace

Roberson didn't set too well with everybody, especially a few of the pioneering town folk.[42] Roberson, because of personality, reputation, and circumstances had his disapproving critics. Some may have justifiably feared he might derail the lucrative gravy train, others, no doubt just didn't like him. Historically speaking, however, at the time he enjoyed steadfast support from the law enforcement community in general and from such notables in particular as Ranger Captain Hughes, the legendary Texas Ranger, Frank Hamer, and of course the Texas and Southwestern Cattle Raisers Association leadership.[43]

Resolute lawmen. Horace L. Roberson, back row, second from left, the man who killed Foot Boykin at Sierra Blanca and later became a Field Inspector for the Texas and Southwestern Cattle Raisers Association. Frank Hamer, one of the legendary lawmen who participated in the killing of the notorious outlaws Bonnie and Clyde, middle row, fourth from left. Dave Allison, front, center. Courtesy, Pat Treadwell, Tahoka, Texas.

Regardless, everyone was appalled when they learned Roberson and his whole squad of T O cowboys had been captured by Antonio Reyes, one of Pancho Villa's captains, and taken to Ojinaga, just across the murky Rio Grande from Presidio, Texas. Executions were expected. Graham "Bush"

Barnett, one of Roberson's men, and himself a killer of record, had earlier managed to get away and sound the alarm on the American side of the river.[44] After two days the captors received a telegram signed by Villa himself, demanding the forthwith release of the understandably nervous prisoners. Why? By particular unsubstantiated accounts the T O crew were released because, at Juarez, someone cleverly forged Pancho Villa's signature to the telegram; others, however, Roberson's supporters for the most part, claim he and his men were released because of one warrior's admiration for another; some suggest a ransom was paid; and lastly, and probably the most believable, Roberson and crowd were turned loose due to United States diplomatic and political pressure brought against Villa. Either way, Roberson and the T O cowboys, once they got the chance, hightailed it back across the twisting Rio Grande to the good ole U. S. A. Safe on American soil, according to West Texas chronicler Joyce Means, although there is not documentation, Roberson went on a killing spree and brutally murdered, Febronio Calanche and Rodrigo Barragan in their sleep, and then later gunned down an unarmed Sixto Quintana.[45]

Roberson with a sure enough hard-as-nails reputation wasn't in the slightest deterred from re-entering Mexico and tending to T O business. In the Bosque Bonito area, south of Sierra Blanca along the Rio Grande, rancher Dick Love in consultation with Roberson, deduced that some of his cows were running together with T O cattle. Plans were made to gather the beeves, cajole them to Sierra Blanca and sort the herd accordingly.[46]

After several days were spent picking their way across a tortuous rock strewn trail, the herd was finally watered at the Sierra Blanca public tank and then craftily hazed into the publicly accessible stock pens.[47] The next morning, January 16, 1915, part of the cattle were to be driven north of Sierra Blanca to Henry Foote Boykin's pasture, but that's when the dispute erupted.

When Roberson, who was horseback, arrived at the corrals he found Foote Boykin already there, "checking the brands on the cattle." Roberson ordered Boykin to get out of the pen. Boykin refused, and Roberson rode around a wing of the plank corral and confronted Boykin directly. Words became heated. Scorching expletives were hurled back and forth, and Roberson struck Boykin with a knotted lariat rope. Boykin jerked the rope from Roberson's hand and threw it into the pen. Refusing Roberson's demand to retrieve the rope, a bystander picked up the catch-rope, handed it to Roberson, who according to a variety of reports immediately thrashed Boykin with it once more. Regardless, Boykin rushed at the mounted Roberson, some say with an open pocket knife, others say not, but his movement caused Roberson's bay horse to rear and suddenly spin away from pedestrian Boykin. At that exact abrupt instant Roberson trying to maintain his precarious seat in the slick-forked saddle, yanked his .45 Colt six-shooter, agitatedly thumbed the hammer back and heedlessly jerked the trigger, popping a cap back over his shoulder at Boykin—he missed. Sadly though, the bullet found a mark, Walt Sitter, the son of U. S. Mounted Customs Inspector Joe Sitter. At the time, not realizing what he had just done, Roberson finally managed to get his gyrating cow-pony under some semblance of tolerable control, and soon thereafter, within seconds, forthwith shot Boykin four times, once dead center through the heart.[48] Boykin died on the spot. Roberson galloped out of town at breakneck speed, while nineteen year old Walt Sitter was being moved to the Palace Hotel, but soon, he too, just like Foote Boykin, expired.[49]

Although versions vary in minor detail, all concur that Constable W. D. "Dave" Allison, leading a posse, eventually arrested Roberson who had more or less turned himself in to rancher George Love, claiming he had killed Boykin in self-defense and protesting that the shooting of Walt Sitter was the result of a horrible accident. After taking custody of the prisoner, Allison flagged down the first westbound train, and instructed Baylus Newton (B. N.) Love and Charley Smith, George Love's father-in-law, to escort prisoner Horace L. Roberson to the Texas Ranger encampment at Ysleta, just below El Paso, which they did.[50]

Later, at El Paso, Roberson was indicted for the killing of Boykin; however, in a series of trials, convictions, appeals, new trials, new appeals, and years, Roberson came clear on the Boykin murder charge.[51] Not everyone was pleased. Little could they have known it then, but Roberson and Dave Allison would later, years later, play leading roles in the other's biographical sagas.

There was another border liner who was about to enter into the adventurous life story of Dave Allison. His name was Pascual Orozco, Jr., the muleteer from the Mexican state of Chihuahua, who, while Dave Allison had been circulating throughout the American Southwest in various badge-wearing assignments, had been writing his own chapter in the struggle for power, prestige, and *pesos* in the Mexican Revolution. In due course he unquestionably reserved an inimitable place in the history books. To fully understand the Dave Allison narrative, an abbreviated backward glance at part of Pascual Orozco's life is obligatory, for the pair, Orozco and Allison, from individual career choices were irreversibly locked onto a collision track.

Pascual Orozco, Jr., as has been previously noted was a "*conductor de metales*, the owner of an outfit which transported precious metals—mostly silver—by mule back from the mines deep in the mountains to the state capital at Cd. Chihuahua."[52] Standing over six-feet tall, with light complexion and reddish brown hair, the mustachioed "Pascualito" was known for his superb horsemanship, his astonishing marksmanship, and a fiery, almost unquenchable revolutionary spirit.[53] When the Mexican Revolution began in 1910, Pascaul Orozco, Jr. was already reasonably prosperous, although still young in years.[54] Pascual Orozco, Jr., partly by birthright, but mainly through hard work, and by some accounts ruthlessness, had either maintained or improved upon his semi-privileged status, for unlike the majority of native born Mexicans who were dirt poor peasants and irretrievably tethered to worn out land and wretched poverty, Orozco was not. To be sure, Pascual was financially secure, but "Pascualito" craved more.

When Francisco Madero hollered it was time for a governmental overthrow to oust General Porfirio Diaz's three decades of dictatorial control and firmly replace it with democracy, Pascual Orozco, Jr., on November 19, 1910, pronounced his steadfast support.[55] Though, as one historian and writer points out, Pascual's motive, at least initially, was cleverly calculated and designed for Orozco's personal and financial advantage—some business competition was very soon to be spared preferential treatment from the Diaz government.[56]

Garnering the position of Military Chieftain in the District of Guerrero, Chihuahua, and after effectively recruiting a regiment of case-hardened vaqueros, tough-muscled miners, and leathery-faced muleteers, Orozco without delay attacked, and literally overran Minaca, Chihuahua.[57] After seizing Minaca, the revolutionary forces with fixated imprecision maneuvered an about-face, retraced their steps, returned to San Isidro, Orozco's hometown, which almost with a sigh of anguished and thankful relief fell before the fêted rebels on November 21st.[58] The next day, Orozco assaulted Ciudad Guerrero. Lacking artillery, the revolutionary forces were rebuffed, but the insurgents laid siege to the town. To the rescue of the besieged came Federal relief forces commanded by General Juan Navarro—their clattering and clanging movements, however, were detected. Orozco attacked the Federal forces at Pedernales, completely routing the advance guard and capturing a significant quantity of desperately desirable supplies. Pascual Orozco, Jr., after the successful campaign against Navarro's column returned to Ciudad Guerrero which fell before the rebels on December 4, 1910.[59]

After the fall of Ciudad Guerrero, Orozco "issued a manifesto to the nation in which he dedicated himself and his men to the Madero cause and called for the complete overthrow of the Diaz government. Orozco's manifesto was the first *formal* document issued by the revolutionary forces actively fighting against the federal army and Mexican police."[60]

Journalistically, it would be difficult to improve on Douglas Meed's description of Orozco's army: "His troops were not much to look at on parade. Wearing the rough clothes of the cowboy they sported tall peaked sombreros with huge rolled brims and high leather boots with ferocious spurs. They were armed with lever-action Winchester or Marlin carbines or bolt-action Mausers. They strapped two bandoliers of cartridges across their chest and another around their middles. Many carried Colt 'Thumbusters,' .45-caliber revolvers in a belt holster. For real up close work many had machetes. Drilled they were not; formidable fighters they were."[61]

At the *Canon de Mal Paso*, on January 2, 1911, much of Pascual Orozco's actual history implicitly took on legendary proportion. And, indeed, the event was real—and it was the kind of heady stuff legends were made of. Working in consort with other rebel leaders, Orozco deftly orchestrated an ambush on a train carrying Federal troops under command of Colonel Martin Luis Guzman. Deep in Bad Pass Canyon the railroad track was obstructed. Once the slow moving troop train had entered the canyon the wooden bridges the train had crossed over were torched. The stymied locomotive engineer could not advance, nor could he reverse. From their elevated positions, strategically placed along both canyon walls, revolutionary sharpshooters opened a horrific fire directed at the unprotected and unsuspecting Federal soldiers below. Fish in a barrel—almost! Later, with close range head-shots and vicious arcs from razor-edged machetes, Orozco's rebels alleviated their wounded adversary's tortuous and miserable suffering. One thousand Federal troops died that day. In a calculated move to endear himself to his own troops and, at the same time, as an effectual publicity stunt designed to instill fear into Federal loyalists, Pascual Orozco, Jr. slyly ordered the deceased soldiers be stripped of their bullet-tattered uniforms, and the clothing collected for a return freight train bound for Mexico City—sardonic souvenirs for Mexican President Diaz. Tauntingly, Pascual Orozco Jr. pinned a personal note to the blood soaked cargo, "Here are your wrappings. Send me some more tamales."[62]

Maybe not in the whole of Mexico, but in the state of Chihuahua, Orozco's daring exploits were transformed in mythical proportion. If folklore is to be believed and, there isn't reason in this case to doubt it, of Pascual Orozco, Jr. songs were written, sexy senoritas swooned, and little Mexican boys emulated in their play, "Pascualito."[63]

Emboldened by his success, on January 7, 1911, Orozco attacked a Federal freight train on the Kansas City, Mexico, & Orient Railroad carrying valuable supplies. With just over fifty nifty rebels, he "fought a pitched battle, subdued the guards, and unloaded the provisions."[64] The train, with empty boxcars, was allowed to proceed. With his confidence bolstered, and his army well-supplied, at least for a time, Orozco initiated his cat and mouse game of masked troop movement, misinformation and deception. Expecting him to march on the State Capital at Chihuahua, Mexican government officials were completely taken off guard when instead, Orozco with 1500 men marched on Ciudad Juarez, just across the Rio Grande, from El Paso.[65] Unfortunately for Orozco, Ciudad Juarez was reinforced by Federal forces, and the insurrectionary leader cautiously abandoned his assault on the city—for the moment.

Later, however, with reinforcements and a newly united Revolutionary Army, Pascual Orozco, Jr. and Pancho Villa, working in conjunction (although they despised each other) were successful in seizing the Northwestern and the Mexican Central Railroad. At last, Ciudad Juarez was cutoff from the rest of Mexico. During the siege Pascual Orozco, Jr. was promoted by Madero to Brigadier General.[66] Ultimately though, Madero feared an all out assault on Ciudad Juarez and fierce fighting right at the American border might just slop over, killing or injuring United States citizens, generating an irreparable international incident. Therefore, after all the blustery conversations, diplomatic shenanigans, military positioning, and careful planning, he opted to withdraw from the field. "Orozco and his men were not so fearful of the nearness of the American border."[67] Orozco and Villa did what they came to do! Once the attack was underway, Madero was, in truth, incapable and downright helpless, unquestionably lacking any measure of effective military control whatsoever. From the American side of the Rio Grande it was a spectacle. As many as 15,000 voyeuristic onlookers nibbled on zesty tamales and sucked down buckets of ice-cold beer while they tapped their feet in cadence with the rat-a-tat-tat of bullet belching machine guns. Indeed, as one historian skillfully characterizes, "…it was one peach of a show," but as could well have been predicted some members of the spectator squadron zigged when they should have zagged—stray bullets connected with nineteen of them—five died.[68] After two days of intense urban guerrilla warfare it ended. On the afternoon of May 10th, rebel forces took control of Ciudad Juarez—the Federal garrison had surrendered.[69]

Pascual Orozco, Jr. and Pancho Villa wanted to stand Juan Navarro, the vanquished leader of the Federal forces in front of a firing squad. Madero demurred. The next day, May 11th, Madero named his provisional government cabinet. For Minister of War he did not choose Orozco. "Pascualito" was furious, and according to at least some reports had to be physically restrained from shooting men who were publicly defending Madero's personnel selections, and many thought Madero himself was in imminent danger.[70] Tempers cooled—for the time being. The fall of Ciudad Juarez broke the back of Mexican dictator Diaz. On May 25th, he resigned from office and went into European exile.[71]

Unquestionably, in telling the Dave Allison story it will not be possible to elaborate on all the intricate machinations and back-room conspiracies copiously linked with the Mexican Revolution. It will be sufficient to report the Revolution was far from over, and Pascual Orozco, Jr., for whatever reason was not personally imbued with a strong sense of personal and party loyalty; some were even calling him the "Judas of Chihuahua."[72] Allegations of bribery, egotistical egregiousness, unbridled ambitiousness, a politically poisoned philosophy, or just plain petty peevishness with the new Mexican *Presidente*, are in the final analysis moot. On March 3, 1912, Pascual Orozco, Jr. revolted.[73] For the next three years Orozco conveniently changed mounts, declaring support first for one faction, then the other.

Illustrative of the shifting times and the fact that Dave Allison, General Pascual Orozco, Jr. and all other wide-ranging Southwestern players were acting out their rousing stories on a *transitional frontier* can be historically ensnared by examination of just one truth. While down on the parched ground, Dave Allison was forking a western stock saddle, riding hell-bent-for-leather leading posses after "Goddamn cow-thieves," and while Pascual Orozco, Jr. was splashing back and forth through Rio Grande's swirling currents, and fighting for whichever splinter group suited him at the time—overhead a war too was raging.

For it was during the Mexican Revolutionary period that the Douglas Flying Club rigged up an airplane, armed it with five-gallon lard pails filled with "dynamite, scrap metal and chunks of concrete" and Christened the flying war-machine the "Douglas Bomber." On May 8, 1913, Charles Ford, indeed a heroic pilot, flew across the international line on a bombing run, destroying a section of crucial Mexican railroad track—*maybe*! And as celebrated Southwest writer Leon Metz explains, the worth of the air assault cannot be found in the success or failure of the mission, but rather by noting it was "the first hostile flight ever to originate from United States soil."[74] On another occasion, two American mercenaries, Dean Ivan Lamb and Phil Radar, each working for opposing Mexican Revolutionary bosses, in a dogfight over Naco, Arizona, "blazed away with six shooters at 12 o'clock high for twenty minutes with no damage done."[75] Had he seen the show, frontier lawman Dave Allison would have cringed in flabbergasted disbelief. Out West, well, times were a changin'.

Carrying on the tradition. Jim Bingham, a certified Peace Officer and current West Texas lawman, a deputy sheriff for Lynn County, Texas, examines a set of his great-great uncle Dave Allison's silver inlaid spurs. Courtesy, Pat Treadwell, Tahoka, Texas.

Little could he have known it then, but when the decision in Washington, D. C. was made to place an embargo on arms shipments to Mexico, the future of Pascual Orozco, Jr. hung in the political balance. Orozco could not competently re-supply his beleaguered insurgents with arms and ammunition, and consequently, his "rebellion was characterized throughout by great hostility towards the United States and towards its citizens who resided within territory held by the rebels."[76] As his revolutionary fortunes dawdled, and his "spiteful reprisals against foreigners, particularly United States nationals" increased, Pascual Orozco, Jr. evolved into a sometimes bandit and arms smuggler operating between Ojinaga, just across the border from Presidio, and El Paso.[77] At least one author forthrightly reports that Orozco, south of Sierra Blanca, seized and for a while firmly held onto the gargantuan T O Ranch—twice![78]

At the Mexican Capital in yet another brutal change in national leadership, Victoriano Huerta seized power. Pascual Orozco, Jr. jumped once again—onto the bandwagon—becoming a Brigadier General in the Federal Army.[79] As fate would have it though, Huerta himself, not too long thereafter was forced to flee Mexico and take up transitory residence in Spain. Orozco, once again deposed of meaningful power in Mexico, fled to the United States. At Los Angles "he tried to recruit men and supplies for the Huerta cause," however he skipped away from the City of Angles just ahead of an arrest warrant issued in his name for violations of American neutrality laws—a fugitive.[80] Wanted by his old nemesis in Mexico, Pancho Villa, and sought by U. S. authorities, Orozco slipped and slithered back and forth across the international line, and on one occasion managed to snake it all the way to New York City in a not too secret conspiracy to acquire arms and cash for a triumphant Huerta return.[81]

While in Spain, Huerta met with German secret agents, who as previously noted, were selfishly offering financial backing just to keep the Mexican pot brewing and American eyes focused on the smoldering coals.[82] During April, 1915, Huerta arrived in New York, German deutchmarks in his pockets, intrigue in his head, and lies on his tongue. To an eager beaver-press corps, Huerta berated rumors about returning to Mexico and regaining power, stating that he was only on American soil for a sightseeing vacation, but as author Meed pithily noted, "It has never been recorded that anyone, anywhere, believed him."[83]

Under constant surveillance by U. S. agents, it came as little surprise to anyone when Huerta, on June 24, 1915, started on a trip to San Francisco, but diverted to a southern route and the train stopped at Newman, New Mexico, just twenty miles north of El Paso, and indeed few were surprised at the coincidental seizure of 14 machine guns, 500 Mauser bolt-action rifles, and 100,000 rounds of ammunition from an El Paso warehouse leased to a Mexican exile.[84] Nor was it too much of a bombshell when it was discovered that there to meet Huerta at the depot, during the wee hours of the morning, was none other than United State's fugitive from justice, Pascual Orozco, Jr.[85] Orozco was straightforwardly placed under an ample military guard.

Boarding the train at the Newman station, U. S. Government representatives located Huerta and proclaimed, "We have 100 soldiers outside; we want you to accompany us. If you will do so peaceably, there shall be no trouble; but if not we will have to serve warrants on you." Huerta replied, "I am at you orders."[86]

Zachary Cobb, Customs Inspector in El Paso reported the incident to the United States Secretary of State:

> Last night I learned through railroad of Huerta's plans to leave train at Newman station, twenty miles north of El Paso. With Beckman (U. S. Justice Agent), District Clerk, two Deputy Marshals, and Col. G. H. Morgan, accompanied by twenty-five soldiers that he brought to prevent disorder or any attempt to interfere, we went to Newman Station this morning and found Orozco and Huerta's son-in-law awaiting train. We had prepared to use warrants if necessary but found it unnecessary. Beckman invited Orozco and Huerta to accompany us to federal building without arrest which they did. Without display we have treated them with consideration and proper courtesy.[87]

At the El Paso Federal Building, Huerta and Orozco were formally arrested and charged with conspiracy to violate United States neutrality laws. News quickly spread amongst the Mexican community and large crowds amassed around the Federal Building, some no doubt clamoring for the defendant's release, others of a different political persuasion possibly plotting assassination. El Paso Mayor, Tom Lea, realizing the potential for serious civil disorder and needless bloodshed, shrewdly suggested and respectfully requested the notorious defendants be officially escorted to the nearby military installation, Fort Bliss, for further legal proceedings. The Mayor's wishes were honored. Upon a hearing before a U. S. Commissioner, Huerta was released on a $15,000 bail bond, while Orozco's bond was set at $7,500, but because of their past revolutionary movements and due to Mexico being just across the Rio Grande river, both defendants were ordered to remain under house arrests, guarded by U. S. Department of Justice Agents.[88] Guarded, but not for long!

The Spanish-language edition of the *El Paso Morning Times* of July 4, 1915, told the story:

> The most sensational event of yesterday was the flight of Pascual Orozco. It is not known if he has crossed the international line yet. Six guards, three from the Department of Justice and three from the military garrison, were watching Orozco's house with firm orders to employ all means to prevent him from escaping. Neither the exact hour nor the exact means of his escape are known yet…It was at dawn when the guards discovered that they were watching an empty house…When the house was examined…it was noted that a window was open. Since about ten yards from the window there is a patch of high grass, it is supposed that Orozco jumped from the window and hid in the grass. It is also supposed that…after having walked a short distance…an automobile was waiting for him.[89]

Pascual Orozco's younger sister vividly recounts the remarkable development, first-hand: "We were thrilled to see my brother but pained by the circumstances. One July afternoon as the rest of the family enjoyed a *siesta* in the basement, I happened to go up the stairs to the kitchen for a glass of water. Pascual was donning his black hat, his well-known trademark. I quietly asked him where he was going, but he put his finger to his lips, signaling me to hush. I did so. I was seized with fear. He was calm and deliberate. The soldier out back had been drinking beer and dozed off. Pascual silently opened the door. He stepped gingerly over the guard. He took long, slow strides toward the alley. Pascual looked one way, then the other, made up his mind instantly, pulled the brim of his hat down slightly over his forehead, and strode away…"[90]

ENDNOTES
Chapter 7. "There come the sheriffs and I must get ready for them"

[1] *Report to Collector of Customs* of U. S. Mounted Customs Inspector Herff A. Carnes, September 1, 1915. Hereafter cited as **Carnes**. Courtesy Milton O. Gustafson, Ph. D., National Archives, College Park, Maryland. Culberson County was originally a part of El Paso County, but was officially separated and recognized as an independent county on January 5, 1912. And see, *History of Van Horn and Culberson County Texas*, by Rosa Lee **Wylie**. P. 13.
[2] **Bolling**, P. 12
[3] Interview with Bill **Love**, Sierra Blanca, Texas, March 14, 2001. Mr. **Love** is the son of Baylus Prince Love and the grandson of Baylus Newton (B. N.) Love who was commonly referred to as "Judge" Love, but who in point of fact was not a Judge. B. N. Love was one of several sons of Tom D. Love, the first Sheriff of Borden County in West Texas, and the lawman responsible for the capture of the notorious Oklahoma *mal hombre*, William Tuttle "Bill" Cook. See, **Alexander**, Bob, "an outlaw tripped up by Love," *NOLA Quarterly*, Vol. 26, No. 3, (July-September 2002). Tom Love also was one of the pioneer personalities commissioned to organize Hudspeth County when it was carved from El Paso County in 1917. When Dave Allison went to Sierra Blanca it was still a part of El Paso County.
[4] **Ball(S)**, P. 32-33. "When the sheriff found it impossible or inexpedient to commission a deputy for communities that desired one, a temporary alternative was possible in the form of a subscription deputy…That businesses, such as mining or cattle companies, desired resident deputy sheriffs was not uncommon. These organizations often lay in remote locales and kept large sums of money or valuable ores that enticed would-be bandits. Such companies offered to pay the wages of a deputy sheriff outright or requested that employees be commissioned, presumably at no extra pay."
[5] **Carnes**.
[6] Ibid.
[7] **Bruce**, Leona. *Banister Was There*, P. 158. The author reports that one of the killers was Lino Baiza, and since the slain Jack Howard was a U. S. Government employee, the suspect was later indicted for the murder by both Federal and State grand juries. Hereafter cited as **Bruce**. **Bolling** claims Cano was arrested for stealing horses. P. 8. And further asserts that Cano had been selling the Love brothers stolen cattle at the price of five dollars a head, an allegation which he makes without documentation or reference to any citation. Furthermore, **Bolling** rationalizes the ambush and killing because, "It was a rarity at the time if a Mexican prisoner ever made it to jail, usually being shot while 'attempting to escape.' Fearing that Chico Cano would be killed by the lawmen, his brother, Manuel, and two others set up an ambush on the mountain trail to rescue him." Frequently in print, Joe Sitter is identified as "Sitters" but an examination of his Texas Ranger Oath of Office, and other documents reflect that he signed his name "Joseph Sitter." Courtesy, Texas Ranger Hall of Fame & Museum, Waco.
[8] **Tyler**, P. 162.
[9] *El Paso Morning Times*, June 24, 1913. El Paso County deputy sheriff William Henry Garlick, on another occasion working in conjunction with Texas Rangers, was commended for his actions in a clash with Mexican rebels along the border, a

skirmish mentioned in a letter from Texas Governor O. B. Colquitt to Texas Ranger Captain John Hughes. See, **Martin**. P. 198-199. And see, *El Paso Herald*, June 24, 1913. "What is believed to have originated the plot of the Mexicans to exterminate the officers dates back to January 29, when rangers C. H. Webster and Charley Moore, now deputy United States marshals, and deputy sheriff Garlick encountered a band of rebels on the island. At that time Webster killed one of the band. Moore and Garlick encountered a band of 30 rebels and a fight ensued. The report was that one of the rebels turned up at the smelter later and reported that Garlick and Moore had killed two of the squad, one of whom was is that the Mexicans sympathizing with the rebel cause, and knowing of the activity of the officers planned to kill 11 of the them."

[10] *El Paso Morning Times*, June 25, 1913.

[11] *El Paso Morning Times*, June 24, 1913.

[12] Interview with Marvin **Garlick**, grandson of William Henry (W. H.) Garlick, and son of Texas Ranger Fred Garlick, at Van Horn, Texas on March 14, 2001.

[13] *El Paso Morning Times*, June 25, 1913.

[14] Ibid. Also interview with Button **Garlick**, great-grandson of William Henry Garlick, at Van Horn, Texas, on March 14, 2001, who advised family folklore has always maintained that Maria Guadarrama used a heavy meat clever to bludgeon his great-grandfather and Texas Ranger Scott Russell. According to reports in the June 24, 1913 edition of the *El Paso Herald* Deputy Sheriff Garlick held an arrest warrant for one of the Guadarrama boys and that was the reason he entered the grocery.

[15] Ibid.

[16] Ibid.

[17] Ibid. And see, *Death Certificate*, No. 12986, for William H. Garlick, El Paso County—Texas Department of Health, Bureau of Vital Statistics, Austin. Date of death June 23, 1913, cause of death, "Gunshot Wound-Murdered," occupation of deceased, "Deputy Sheriff." Dr. F. W. Lynch examined the deceased and determined that both men had been struck on the head with some blunt instrument as well as being shot.

[18] *El Paso Morning Times*, June 24, 1913.

[19] Ibid.

[20] Ibid.

[21] Ibid. "The shooting created much excitement yesterday, especially among the cattlemen in El Paso."

[22] *El Paso Morning Times,* June 25, 1913.

[23] *Warrant of Authority and Descriptive List*, W. F. **Garlick**, April 17, 1918. Also see, *Enlistment, Oath of Service, and Description Ranger Force*, Fred Garlick, April 20, 1918. Copies courtesy Marvin **Garlick**, Gazelle, California. After a mistrial, due to a hung jury, and a subsequent jury trial, Juan Guadarrama was sentenced to five years in prison for his part in the deaths of Garlick and Russell. Cases against the other defendants were dismissed. See, *El Paso Herald*, June 18, 1915. For closer inspection of the murders of Garlick and Russell, see, **Alexander**, Bob, "Hell Paso," *NOLA Quarterly*, Volume 23, No. 2, (April-June 2002).

[24] **Kerber**, P. 79. Article contributed by Nancy **McKinley**, the granddaughter of "Lish" Estes.

[25] **Means**, P. 146. An article by **Bolling**.

---

[26] **Blumenson**, Martin., *The Patton Papers, 1885-1940.* P. 298. Quoting an October 20, 1915 letter from George S. Patton Jr. to his wife, Beatrice. Hereafter cited as **Blumenson**.
[27] **Means**, P. 147.
[28] Hudspeth County Map, Texas Department of Transportation, Planning and Programming Division. Austin, Texas.
[29] **Bolling**, P. 3
[30] **Christiansen**, Paige. "Pascual Orozco: Chihuahua Rebel, Episodes in the Mexican Revolution, 1910-1915," *New Mexico Historical Review*, XXVI (April 1961). P. 112. Hereafter cited as **Christiansen**.
[31] **Meed**, P. 43.
[32] Ibid.
[33] **Meyer**, P. 125. The author concludes the German reasoning was sound, and that, "If United States arms and ammunition could be diverted from the Allies, because of the threat of a hostile government to the south, it would be an added benefit."
[34] **Means**, P. 66.
[35] *Descriptive List*, *Oath of Office* for H. L. Roberson dated October 11, 1911, signed by Captain John R. Hughes. Also see, *Descriptive List* dated April 11, 1914 and *Descriptive List* dated May 8, 1916. Courtesy of the Texas Ranger Hall of Fame and Museum Archives, Waco.
[36] *St. Louis Post-Dispatch*, July 22, 1923.
[37] Ibid. Both **Means** and **Bolling**, as well as others, characterize Roberson as having a poisonously dangerous and violent disposition. Others, however, disagree.
[38] **Means**, P. 66-67. And see, *El Paso Morning Times*, December 3, 1915. "Roberson testified that On September 1 he began his duties as foreman of the T and O ranch on the Mexico side of the river. His assigned duties were to take charge of branding of calves and other cattle. He stated there had been cattle theft and raids."
[39] Ibid.
[40] Ibid., P. 74. The author, in her notes, comments, "After reading the accusations against Roberson and those against some of his men, I agreed with Mance Bomar, 'The Nelson Morris Cattle Company went out and hired the toughest men they could find.'"
[41] *El Paso Herald*, April 5, 1923. And see, **Means**, P. 66-67. Also see, *El Paso Morning Times*, December 3, 1915. "Roberson said he had been an officer since 1911 and up to the time he became foreman of the T and O ranch. He testified he had been indicted twice on a charge of murder but had been acquitted in both cases."
[42] *El Paso Morning Times*, December 2 & 3, 1915. Some thought that Roberson acceptance of the T O foreman's position "caused Paschal and others to loose their jobs." Also see, **Bolling**, P. 7.
[43] Comments concerning Roberson's reputation with Captain Hughes and the Texas and Southwestern Cattle Raisers Association will be cited in endnote at chapter dealing with Roberson's death. For reference by Frank Hamer see, *"I'm Frank Hamer," The Life of a Texas Peace Officer* by H. Gordon **Frost** and John H. **Jenkins**. P. 68. "A friend of the Hamer's, H. L. Roberson, saw what happened and called Frank. As Hamer himself later related, Roberson 'informed me that my brother was liable to be killed.'"

[44] **Means**, P. 67. The author reports that Barnett killed three Mexicans on T. M Stormy's ranch. Also see, **Skiles**, Jack., *Judge Roy Bean Country*, for an account of Graham Barnett killing Will Babb on December 8, 1913, at Langtry, Texas. P. 176-178. Graham Barnett indeed had a reputation as a hard-case killer, but it did not prohibit his later service as a Texas Ranger. Barnett's time, however, ran out when he was machine-gunned to death at Rankin, Texas on December 6, 1931. Courtesy, Texas Ranger Hall of Fame and Museum. Waco.

[45] Ibid., P. 71.

[46] Ibid., P. 72.

[47] Ibid. The author states the corrals were owned by the Texas and Pacific Stockyards at Sierra Blanca.

[48] **Bolling**, P. 149-150. Also see, *El Paso Morning Times*, December 2, 3, 4, 5, 1915. And see **Means**, P. 72. And, author's interview with Henry Foote Boykin, Jr., the deceased's son, September 12, 2002. Foote Boydin, Jr. was three years old when Roberson killed his father at Sierra Blanca.

[49] **Means**, P. 72. The author states Walt Sitter died in the presence of his girlfriend, Johnnie Philomel Cox. Most considered the killing of Walt Sitter an unfortunate accident, indicating in part, that at least some few must have thought Roberson justified in killing Boykin. And see, *El Paso Morning Times*, December 3, 1915.

[50] **Bolling**, P. 150. And see, **Means**, P. 72. Texas Ranger Pat Craighead testified that Roberson boarded the train and "was looking for someone to arrest him as he wanted to give up." See, *El Paso Morning Times*, December 3, 1915. The two versions are not necessarily inconsistent. B. N. Love and Charley Smith were only there to make sure Roberson surrendered to someone with legal authority. Very likely they were present when Roberson voluntarily turned himself over to Craighead for subsequent delivery to the Texas Ranger camp.

[51] *El Paso Herald*, April 5, 1923. Also see, **DeArment**. P. 13.

[52] **Blanco**, Serafina Orozco viuda de. "My Recollections of the Orozco Family and the Mexican Revolution of 1910." *Password*, Vol. 25.1(Spr. 1980). P. 12. Hereafter cited as **Blanco**.

[53] Ibid. Also see, **Meed**, P. 34-35. "In a time of boisterous machismo, he was calm and soft-spoken but beneath an unassuming air there was an aura of determination and strength. With his aquiline face, sharp, chiseled nose, light brown hair, fair complexion and rangy build, he had the look of a Conquistador. His enemies, and there were many, agreed that he had the hard ambition and the cold ruthlessness of those Spanish Grandees that he so closely resembled." Michael **Meyer**, Orozco's biographer, adds, "In his element—talking to a group of peons, leading guerrillas into battle, or reasoning with a company of malcontent soldiers—Orozco was at his best and demonstrated complete mastery of the situation. In an unfamiliar or undesired environment, his composure often left him and he would force himself to wrestle with his inadequacies." P. 17.

[54] **Meed**, P. 35.

[55] **Christiansen**, P. 97.

[56] **Meed**, P. 36.

[57] **Metz**, Leon C., Notes from unpublished manuscript for upcoming volume on the history of the Mexican Revolution. Hereafter cited as **Metz (III)**. Also see, **Meed**, P. 36. "…he (Orozco) took to the field in a series of savage raids and ambushes against forces loyal to the Diaz government."

[58] **Christiansen**, P. 100.

[59] Ibid. And see, **Metz (II)**, who declared this, the attack on Navarro's forces, Orozco's first real victory.
[60] Ibid., P. 101.
[61] **Meed**, P. 36.
[62] **Meyer**, P. 23-24.
[63] **Meed**, P. 37.
[64] **Meyer**, P. 24.
[65] Ibid.
[66] Ibid., P. 29
[67] **Christiansen**, P. 106.
[68] **Meed**, P. 40. The author suggests that some of the shots in the direction of the American crowd may not have necessarily been "stray."
[69] **Christiansen**, P. 106.
[70] Ibid., P. 107. For Minister of War, Madero selected Venustiano Carranza.
[71] Ibid.
[72] **Meed**, P. 40
[73] Ibid. **Christiansen** simply reports, "The wealth and power he (Orozco) had anticipated as his reward for service in the revolution never materialized to a degree acceptable to him." P. 108
[74] **Metz (II)**, P. 215. The author reports that to add stability to the "bombs," fins were soldered on by a local Douglas, Arizona, tinsmith. For practice targets, old bed sheets were pinned to the ground to simulate railroad tracks.
[75] Ibid.
[76] **Christiansen**, P. 112.
[77] Ibid., P. 115. And, **Metz (III)**, "Along with his other talents, he (Orozco) evolved into an arms smuggler working out of El Paso."
[78] **Means**, P. 67.
[79] **Meed**, P. 41.
[80] **Christiansen**, P. 117.
[81] Ibid., P. 118. And see, **Meed**, P. 43, "American authorities wanted to jail him (Orozco) for neutrality law violations; Villa just wanted to cut off his head."
[82] **Meed**, P. 43.
[83] Ibid., P. 44. The author reports that as a result of Huerta's not too secret deal with the Germans, that $1,000,000 was placed at his disposal and promised him the delivery of 10,000 Mauser rifles. **Meyer** sets the figure at $895,000 and states the total German commitment to Huerta was in the neighborhood of $12,000,000. P. 127.
[84] *El Paso Herald*, June 28, 1915. For information on other related arrests and another weapons seizure, see, *El Paso Herald*, June 30,1915, "A shipment of 346 rifles and 46,000 rounds of ammunition was located in the Mexican quarter Tuesday night, according to a report received by the police. It is believed that the ammunition had been bought by agents of the Huerta junta here and was to have been used in the new revolution."
[85] Ibid. By some accounts Orozco was waiting for Huerta in an automobile, however, according to the *El Paso Herald*, "Arriving at Newman at sunrise, the officials found their surmised confirmed when they noticed Gen. Pascual Orozco behind some shrubbery near the railroad. Col. Morgan immediately ordered that soldiers be placed on each road leading into the station, with instructions that they were to keep close guard over 'Pascual' until United States officials took a hand."
[86] Ibid.

---

[87] **Meyer**, P. 129. Citing, *Papers Relating to Foreign Relations of the United States—1915.*
[88] Ibid., P. 130. Also see, **Blanco**, P. 15. And see, *El Paso Herald*, June 28, 1915.
[89] *El Paso Morning Times*, Spanish-language edition, July 4, 1915 taken from **Meyer**, P. 130.
[90] **Blanco**, P. 15.

8

"We all dismounted and began firing."

William Davis Allison had little time to worry about where some escaped Mexican politico was hiding. In that cantankerously lonesome Sierra Blanca country and over near Van Horn, thirty-five miles to the east, in Culberson County, there was more than plenty of work to go around for lively West Texas lawmen.

And, just as surely, it can be safely reported Dave Allison was stunned when apprised of a ghastly news report emanating from around Valentine, Jeff Davis County, just south of Sierra Blanca. Once again border country lawmen were gunned down. That warily U. S. Mounted Customs Inspector, Joe Sitter, who had "killed several Mexican outlaws on the border," was once again patrolling the ageless Rio Grande.[1] On May 23, 1915, Sitter commanded a small squadron of strong-minded and steadfast borderland officers. Working on criminal intelligence information that hard to pin down Mexican bandits were hiding in the rugged mountains on the Texas side of the river, the posse poked around in the area for awhile, and then made camp for the night. The next morning, leaving their pack-mules hobbled at an out of the way water hole, the stalwarts began their search anew. About seven miles from the international line, once again near Pilares, Joe Sitter and Texas Ranger Eugene Hulen separated themselves from the other posse members, Charlie Craighead, Sug Cummings, and Jack Trollinger. The pair began working their way toward a scratchy observation point atop a chipped rock and cacti cluttered mountain. They never made it to the top—they were bushwhacked! The three remaining lawmen, hearing the booming gunfire rushed to aid their comrades, but five times were driven back by rifle fire.[2] Sadly, all too soon realizing they were of little or no good to Sitter and Hulen, the remaining trio, who by now had lost their horses, hoofed it back to the previous night's campsite, caught up their pack-mules, and sorely rode bareback five miles to the Bill McGee Ranch.[3] From there a dispatch was straight away sent to the Joe Pool ranch, six miles away, and from that point the distressed prayer for help went out via a sometimes reliable rural ranch telephone.[4] At the other end, an eleven man posse from Marfa, Presidio County, turned the hand-cranks, climbed into open-air automobiles and rushed toward the Pool ranch where fresh horses were impatiently standing hitched to a corral fence.[5]

By mid-afternoon next day, May 25, 1915, the grotesquely twisted bodies of Joe Sitter and Eugene Hulen were at last located. Skilled reconstruction of the appalling crime-scene revealed the dead lawmen had sought an improved position after the initial onslaught, and from the new battlefield it was apparent that Hulen had been killed early on. Joe Sitter lay surrounded by sixty spent cartridge cases, and the condition of his body was described by Inspector R. M. Wadsworth:

> He was in a very bad condition…I was right there. I helped to put him on a pack-mule myself. He was lying on his back in a sort of cramped position; looked like he died in great agony, his knees drawed up, cramped up, his hands and fingers drawed up over his face; you could see where his flesh had been knocked off his knuckles by rocks; his left eye in his head had been caved in. The rock was lying a little bit to one side; I judge it weighted about 20 pounds. He had eleven bullet holes in his body.[6]

According to several accounts, the pack-mule which Joe Sitter's mutilated body was strapped to, while on the return trip back to the McGee ranch became sick and vomited.[7] West Texas lawmen working along the U. S./Mexico border were outraged by the killing of Sitter! Aside from the expedient political clamor and cries for better protection along the deathly perilous line, it's a surefire bet resolute ranchers and obstinate officers had already made up their own minds regarding Mexican renegades and revolutionaries.

And that sentiment was toughened three weeks later on June 8th, when a gang of Mexican bandits killed Texas Ranger Robert Lee Burdett near Fabens, on the Rio Grande just a little south of El Paso, slightly to the west of Dave Allison's territory at Sierra Blanca.[8] Reports vary as to what happened to Burdett's killers, some few suggesting that the revolutionist, Pancho Villa, had the murderers executed by a hastily fashioned firing squad while jubilant Texas Rangers looked on.[9] Other accounts mention that Luz Gandera and Isidoro Cadena were arrested by El Paso County deputy sheriffs and charged with the ranger's homicide and were being held at the local jailhouse.[10] Border country lawmen were fast becoming downright expendable, or so it looked to badge-wearing brothers. The southwest border region, as a whole, seemed awash with bandits, rebels, and too, still hiding somewhere, that ever obscure fugitive, "Pascualito."

Pascual Orozco, Jr., since his escape, had first been spotted here—then there—headed this way—going that way—but none, not one, of the investigative leads were panning out for overtaxed Justice Department agents at El Paso, who were steadily working to cut his cunning track and make an apprehension. Pascual Orozco, Jr. had a lot of friends at *Pass of the North.*[11]

Some of the central figures in the chase and killing of Pascual Orozco, Jr. and his platoon of dubious revolutionaries. (Standing L. to R.) George Love, Lizzie Love, Tom D. Love, Wert Love, Bob Love. (Sitting), Dick Love, Fanny Love, Leonard Love, and J. R. "Rowdy" Love. Sierra Blanca, Texas. Courtesy, Bill Love, Sierra Blanca, Texas.

Unquestionably too, Dave Allison, through the news media or by other sources, had been thoroughly posted on Victoriano Huerta's immediate bond revocation and subsequent arrest, an action taken just as soon as it was learned Pascual Orozco, Jr. had skipped—illicitly jumping his bail.[12] After one international arms smuggler had nimbly absconded, United States Government authorities were in not the slightest mood to take any more chances! With Huerta dejectedly peeking out from behind cold-steel jailhouse bars, his revolutionary schemes shattered, the spotlight focused back in the direction of Pascual Orozco, Jr.—trouble is though, nobody could find him. He was everywhere and nowhere, fittingly characterized by Meed as a "phantom of the borderlands."[13] "Pascualito" had vanished!

One of the several Orozco storytellers pulls no punches: "During the remainder of July and in August, 1915, Orozco and a few loyal followers operated along the border trying to gather an army, but with little success. To support themselves they raided ranches on both sides of the border."[14] Orozco's full-length biographer, however, tells it differently: "Throughout July and August, Orozco was reported in and around El Paso, but he always managed to keep at least one step ahead of the federal agents."[15] Orozco's sister, questioned by U. S. investigators, in all candor probably told the gospel truth when she reportedly advised them with heartfelt tears in her eyes, "We simply do not know his whereabouts."[16]

Whether Orozco was hiding in an urban underground setting, being secretly spirited around from one cordial adobe home to another, never sleeping in the same bed twice, or, was in fact, out in the brush supporting himself by raiding ranches made no difference to area peace officers—or cowmen. In the eyes of the law he was a wanted criminal; if he raided a ranch he was a bandit; if he stole a beef he was a "Goddamn cow-thief."

During the waning days of a scorching August, Dave Allison, in the company of U. S. Mounted Custom Inspectors Herff A. Carnes and J. D. White, with packhorses, were making a "scout" southeast of Sierra Blanca. Inspector White's horse, somehow entangled in a odd section of barb-wire, received a nasty disabling fetlock cut. White's packhorse, operating sans iron horseshoes on the rocky broken ground became tender-footed, and White, almost reduced to being afoot, was forced to return to Sierra Blanca.[17]

Herff Carnes, himself a former Texas Ranger under the notable Captain John Hughes, was originally from Fairview, Wilson County, Texas. After an eight year stint with the Rangers, Carnes had signed on with the U. S. Mounted Customs Service and was posted at Sierra Blanca.[18] And, like Dave Allison, Carnes had decided on making law enforcement his lifework. As the two persistent lawmen proceeded with their scout, little did they know it but a hell-to-pop story was unfolding behind them. They had a few hours yet, though, before a thrilling fast-paced Western episode overran them too.

Hudspeth County, Texas, rancher Mart Tidwell. West-face of Eagle Mountains in background. Dick Love's camp house, and the starting point for the chase after Orozco is visible over Tidwell's left shoulder. Author's photo.

By and large there are two renditions of the opening scene in the next act of the Pascual Orozco, Jr. production. The reader can take his or her pick. One story has it that Orozco was desperate to meet with Mexican Revolutionary leader General Eduardo Salinas at Bosque Bonito. Orozco, with three companions, saddles, and packs, boarded an eastbound train at El Paso and journeyed to Etholen, a water-tank stopping spot just four miles west of far-flung Sierra Blanca. Orozco and pals detrained and were met by a confederate, Miguel Terrazas, who had come up from the River to meet the train, supply the group with brand-new rifles, stolen horses, and lead them to the Salinas base camp.[19] Others, however, insistently report a seemingly more logical version, which alleges Orozco and his small party rode out of El Paso undetected on horseback and headed east into the Big Bend country, again ostensibly for the purpose of eventually hooking up with Salinas, and in that vast and lonesome country while trying to reestablish contact with the General "roamed the area for several days until they ran low on supplies."[20] Under such woeful conditions, with empty stomachs and jaded horses, they simply re-supplied, butchering calves and stealing untended ranch horses turned out to graze.[21] Foraging or Thieving?

Argument aside, all agree, that on August 29, 1915, the last act curtain was drawn back and the scene revealed five actors on the stage; the fugitive Pascual Orozco, Jr.; Huerta's former private secretary, Jose F. Delgado; ex-Chief of Customs Guards for Juarez, Christoforo Caballero; Andreas Sandoval, a leading member in the Orozco/Huerta revolutionary movement; and Big Bend country guide, Miguel Terrazas.[22] The five, when the scene opened were taking a breather, standing around smoking and talking, watering stolen horses at what was generally known as the New Well windmill, just above the camp house situated on a little knoll overlooking Red Light Draw at Dick Love's ranch south of Sierra Blanca.[23]

Pascual Orozco, left, about the time of his conquest of Juarez, 1911. Courtesy El Paso Library.

A young cowboy, Joe Thompson, who was working on the Dick Love ranch, espied saddled horses at the New Well windmill and set off to make inquiry. One can only imagine the expression on his youthful face when all at once he was confronted by five sombreros, all heavily weighted with cartridge belts and criss-crossed bandoleers, and each of the camp-weary Mexican strangers held a new Marlin lever-action .30-.30 rifle. Rapidly recognizing Thompson's tender years, and the fact that he was a solitary horseman, the Orozco quintet promptly made known a desire to change their diet from jerked beef to some victuals more substantial. Joe Thompson too, speedily recognized the precarious predicament he had just ridden into, and trying not to telegraph trepidation invited the grubby crowd to noonday dinner at the ranch house.[24]

Two of the strangers, Caballero and Terrazas by some accounts, in other versions Orozco and *someone*, eagerly accompanied Joe Thompson to ranch headquarters.[25] At the house, the trio was met by seventy-two year old August Fransal, a former stagecoach driver and ex-Texas Ranger, but now a camp-cook at the Dick Love ranch.[26] When ordered to prepare food, the crafty August Fransal didn't have to be told twice, he knew what Mexican bandits looked like—and two were standing right in his kitchen—three more lounging around up at New Well. While he started poking around, stoking the fire and fumbling with cast-iron skillets and Dutch ovens, "Orozco curtly instructed Joe to shoe his horse."[27] Joe complied! While waiting for Fransal to fix the meal, Orozco inquired as to the direction of Indian Hot Springs, a comment unquestionably suggesting that his party had indeed suffered "misconnection" with other revolutionary rebels.[28] Once called to dinner the intruders went into the kitchen still cradling their rifles and uneasily began to consume the noonday meal, all the while cat-eyed on the watch.[29] From their side of the coin it's a good thing they were on guard as halfway through dinner one of the *guests* anxiously blurted out, "There comes three men in an automobile. Let's go."[30] Hurriedly the interlopers rushed to their *borrowed* horses and raced to rejoin their three cohorts at the windmill. In a heartbeat the five were racing east at breakneck speed, across the flats, straight for the jagged heights of the picturesque Eagle Mountains in the distance.[31]

Meanwhile back at the ranch. Dick Love, El Paso County Deputy Sheriff W. H. Schrock and cowboy Tom Bell arrive via a steaming and sputtering Ford, completely unawares of impending trouble or the presence of menacing Mexican banditos. Hurriedly brought up to snuff, everyone jumped into action, saddling horses and grabbing Winchesters. It took them about fifteen minutes to gather up, saddle up, and get going.[32]

According to one source, Pete Wetzel and J. P. English were also near the ranch, and joined in the mad-dash pursuit at this time.[33] Knowing they were in fact riding stolen cow-ponies, and full-well knowledgeable as to what the predictable punishment would be if caught red-handed, the Mexicans didn't think twice about sparing horseflesh—it was a do or die race. By just a scant quarter of a mile lead the pursued beat the posse to the mountain foothills, where they speedily scrambled out of saddles which had loosened atop the backs of sweat dripping horses. Clambering for cover at the Black Hills Mine, one held reins of the heaving horses, although it no doubt wasn't necessary, others, and we don't know just who, started scratching out an improvised breastwork of stone, while the remaining duo opened fire on the hard-charging posse in efforts designed to check their forward movement, firing somewhere between fifteen and twenty shots. It worked![34]

After catching their breath, with the posse stopped just out of effective rifle range, the Mexicans palavered about their next move. Two hours later they decamped, headed north along the western edge of the Eagles, the posse respectfully maintaining surveillance, but at safe interval. At the entrance to Frenchman's Canyon the Mexicans turned east into the mountains.[35] Now certain of the escape route, Dick Love raced back to the ranch house. Thankfully he was one of the few in the region to have a rural telephone and he immediately sounded the alarm.[36] As darkness began to overtake the posse in Frenchman's Canyon, up above Frenchman's Well, the decision was made for the short go to abandon the trail—riding into an ambush made absolutely no sense at all, nor did slipping off a narrow mountain trail in the dark, an escape route the *El Paso Morning Times* aptly portrayed as a "perilous path."[37]

Late that afternoon and into the night, Dick Love figuratively burned up telephone line spreading the alarm, recruiting help, and mapping out what was hoped would be an effectual dragnet. By the time Dave Allison and Herff Carnes, who were utterly unaware of what had thus far transpired, arrived at the Tom Yarbo ranch on the east side of the Eagles, the owner had already received a telephone message from Dick Love. The pair of worn out lawman, when brought up to date, wisely opted to rest their personal mounts and pack-animals, eat a home cooked supper, get a decent night's sleep, and strike out at first light in an earnest effort to cut the five bandit's trail. Neither Allison or Carnes, nor anyone else, had the slightest inkling Orozco was in the party scurrying east through the Eagles.[38]

By the time the sun started rising, Dave Allison and Herff Carnes were already up, packed, and in the saddle heading for a gap on the eastern face of the Eagles, the most logical corridor for escaping horse thieves to transverse, and these owl-hoots were sure to be horse thieves, after all, hadn't they taken well-aimed pot shots at honest ranchers?[39]

Just about a mile east of "Yarbo's upper ranch" at 8:00 A. M., Dave Allison and Herff Carnes struck the trail they had been looking for, five horses traveling east, headed toward the imposing High-Lonesome

Mountain in the Van Horn Range.[40] Rushing back to the upper ranch, and a telephone, Allison and Carnes notified others of their discovery, requesting that Dick Love's posse be notified that they were "in hot pursuit" and then they sensibly described their "horses and pack outfit to avoid any conflict between other scouts."[41]

A box canyon just south of High-Lonesome Mountain, Culberson County, Texas. This is the type of topography Pascual Orozco, Jr. chose to make his last gunplay. Author's photo.

Meanwhile, again back at the ranch, the Dick Love ranch, reinforcements arrived. Making up part of the freshly outfitted posse were three of Dick's brothers, George, Bob, Rowdy, and two of his nephews, Prince and B. N., sons of another brother, Tom Love.[42] Joining up with the posse from the previous day, the heavily armed platoon of energetic fighters charged forth back into the bowels of Frenchman's Canyon, where they promptly picked up the trail discarded the night before. From the ranch, Dick Love, who had remained behind to man the telephone and coordinate communications, called Sierra Blanca and had an urgent message telegraphed to the new Culberson County Sheriff, John A. Morine, at Van Horn:

> Look out for five Mexicans in Eagle Mountains, well armed, are going your way. R. C. Love.[43]

Today a tongue-in-cheek decrepit sign hangs in an antiquated historic Van Horn building, "This town is so healthy we had to shoot a man to start a cemetery."[44] There is a smidgen of truth to the claim, and it's how John A. Morine got to be sheriff. It seems the first Culberson County Sheriff, forty-four year old J. H. Feely, was interjecting himself between two ridiculously overwrought disputants, Culberson County Judge J. Y. Canon and O. J. Hammit, who were foolishly engaged in a rather riotous political argument. Near the train station the Judge was blasting away at Hammit with a .30-.30 Winchester. Hammit, armed with a double barreled shotgun, too, was lettin' it rip. Sadly, Sheriff Feely was killed by a bullet from the Judge's incompetently handled rifle. Hammit was punctured through the right testicle and groin, and the Judge himself was wounded in the hand. Judge Canon and Hammit were arrested, and at the next Culberson County Commissioner's Meeting, cowboy John A. Morine was appointed Sheriff and Tax Collector.[45]

Upon receipt of the telegram from Dick Love, the relatively inexperienced Sheriff Morine dutifully summoned his deputy, A. B. Medley, and informally deputized Joel Fenley, but before he could get out of town he was updated, "I received a phone message from Dave Allison, Constable at Sierra Blanca, El Paso County, Texas from D. Taylor's ranch that a Customs Officer, H. A. Carnes was on the trail and that the Mexicans had passed about three quarters of a mile South of Taylor's ranch…"[46] Allison had requested that the sheriff come quick in an automobile, and that fresh horses would be saddled and waiting for him and his deputies.[47] Dave Allison after making the hurried call from the Taylor ranch, caught back up with Carnes who was sticking with the sign cutting task, making sure not to loose the bandit's trail. Near the Green River Draw, Allison and Carnes discovered the smoldering ashes of a breakfast campfire and determined they were no more than two hours behind the desperadoes.[48] Dave Allison and Herff Carnes, confident now they had provided Love's posse and Sheriff Morine's posse sufficient directions to pick up a convincingly discernible trail, and full-well cognizant they were well within easy striking distance of the renegades, sat down and waited.[49] It was a short wait—about an hour—they were joined by both the Sierra Blanca posse and the smaller Culberson County posse.[50]

After mutual consultation, it was rightly decided, as was often done in comparable circumstances, that someone needed to be in charge. Clearly the most experienced man hunter in the group was fifty-four year old W. D. "Dave" Allison. Herff Carnes, Allison's partner on this particular enforcement outing speaks out, and his words in this regard are not ambiguous, "Mr. Allison took charge of both posses…"[51] Sustaining assertions that Dave Allison truly had a legitimate reputation throughout the Southwest, and was in fact the natural choice for chief of the combined posses, can be extrapolated from the remarks of Lt. George S. Patton, Jr., who was not there at the exact instant, but was very soon to be posted at Sierra Blanca. Patton who personally knew Dave Allison wrote, "He was a very quiet looking old man with a sweet face and white hair…He is the most noted gunman here in Texas…"[52] Posse boss Dave Allison gave the order to mount up.

As they were directed, Fenley and Sheriff Morine, having the freshest horses took the lead. At what was then called Stephens Tank the posse came upon Bertie Bristow and Hardy Merchon, two of D. Taylor's cowboys watering their horses. Bristow and Merchon "described the lay of the land to the posse," making the lawmen aware that if the Mexicans rode between two particular hills south of High-Lonesome Mountain and entered a steep rocky canyon, there was not a way out—only the way they rode in.[53] The self-assured posse vigilantly followed the trail heading straight for the towering High-Lonesome. Thinking they had turned back pursuit the evening before on the other side of the Eagle Mountains at the Black Hills Mine, Orozco and his bunch, looking for a secluded spot to "take a siesta and wait out the heat of the day," unwittingly trapped themselves in the blind box canyon.[54] The miscalculation was monumental!

Realizing they had the Mexicans right were they wanted them, Dave Allison hastily issued instructions, dividing his posse into two fast-hitting squadrons. Sheriff Morine and seven men were to "swing around the right hand side of the canyon, take the high ground and then charge."[55] Dave Allison, Herff Carnes and the rest of the men would attack from the left hand side of the canyon, and the Mexicans would effectively be caught in a deathly wicked and inescapably withering cross-fire.[56] Everyone of the posse men knew the graphically chilling and gruesome story of what had happened to U. S. Mounted Customs Inspector Joseph Sitter and Texas Ranger Eugene Hulen just a few months earlier, and of the dreadful fate of Texas Ranger Robert L. Burdett shortly thereafter.

Supplementary bleeding-heart instructions weren't necessary at all. It was unmistakably understood by everybody in the posse, all the Mexican bandits in Chihuahua combined weren't worth spit—take no chances!

These men they were chasing, well, after all they themselves had already opened the ball by shooting the very first shots from their hastily fortified breastwork on the western slope of the Eagles—just yesterday!

Sheriff Morine stated, "The place the Mexicans were in was hidden from our view in a rincon at the head of a very rough rocky canon and after acting upon a plan to surround them I was to take the right hand swing and appear above them and the other part of the posse to swing to the left but before arriving at my position the Mexicans evidently suspicioned something for they immediately grabbed their arms and fired on the left hand party as soon as they made their appearance. We all closed in about the same time and after a fusillade of shots all the Mexicans were killed."[57]

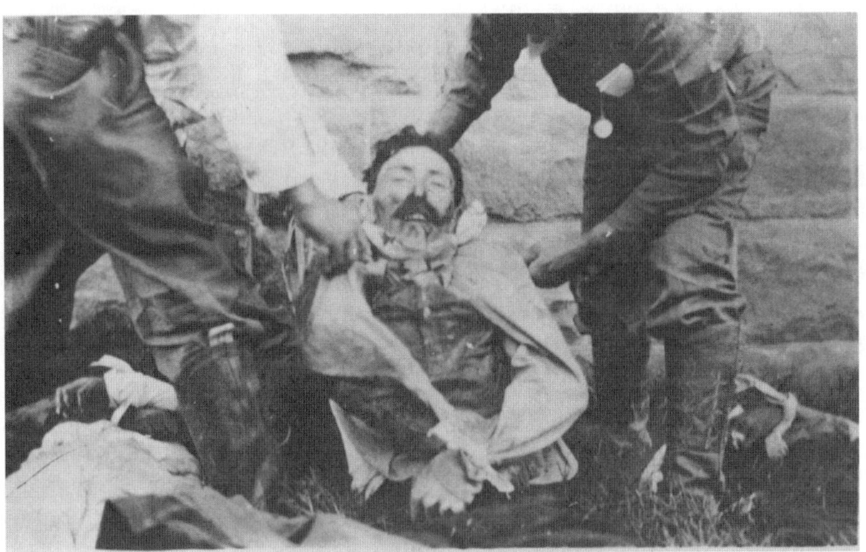

The body of Pascual Orozco after the shootout with the Dave Allison posse. Library of Congress.

U. S. Mounted Customs Inspector Carnes in his official report said, "Mr. Allison took charge of both posses, directing Sheriff Morine and seven men to charge around the mountain and cut them off from escape. The rest of us, with Mr. Allison in lead, charged down the mountain until we were within close firing range. We all dismounted and began firing. The Mexicans having first fired at us as we charged off the mountain. Mr. Allison and several others commanded them to halt, but instead, they returned fire. They were so taken by surprise that their fire was unsteady, and for that reason none of our posse were injured."[58]

Culberson County Deputy Sheriff A. B. Medley simply reported, "When we overtook them they at once gave battle and we also made fight in which all of the Mexicans were killed, five in number."[59]

El Paso County Deputy Sheriff W. H. Schrock of the shooting, related, "There our posse surrounded them and they made fight and fought until they were all dead, hiding behind rocks and shooting with rifles. They were all armed with practically new 30-30 Marlin Rifles, they also had one and perhaps more pistols. After the battle we found in their possession about 1000 rounds of 30-30 cartridges…"[60]

Endeavors designed to reenact the scene, shot by shot, who fell first and just who did what, at this late date, falls into the category of an unqualified exercise in futility, although a few journalists have made an unimpressive stab in that direction. From the theoretical viewpoint it is not unreasonable in the least to offer conjecture that in this particular case *La Ley de Fuga*, the law of the fugitive, which in the sheerest simple form means "no prisoners," was a border country convention, unwritten yet plainly understood by both the Mexicans and Texans on the 30th day of August, 1915, in that High-Lonesome Mountain country.[61] Pascual Orozco, Jr. and his little gang of partisan rebels, or as others chose to see them, "Goddamn horse-thieves," full-well knew if they were caught there could be no expectation of too much mercy, most especially after having delivered the opening salvo the day before at the Black Hills Mine. The lawmen too, were mindful that this was a thoroughly dangerous bunch of Mexicans they had been chasing, *hombres* that would kill you if given the opening. The brigands would deserve whatever medicine they got, wouldn't they? Practically speaking it is not too difficult at all, in the general sense, to figure out what actually happened in that out-of-the-way Culberson County canyon. When lawmen and ranchers came charging down over the ridges from two different directions, "Pascualito" and his followers had no option but to continue with efforts at escape. Official testimony emphasizes the Mexicans fired at the posse men, and undoubtedly it must be acknowledged that no one now knows just who fired at whom, or how many shots were fired that day. Pascual Orozco, Jr. was, however, not the only player with few options at hand. At the time, in Texas, it was legally acceptable, legitimately justifiable, and openly expected that lawmen were duty bound to shoot escaping criminals in their tracks.

One writer, who has conjured up a rather convoluted conspiracy theory surrounding Orozco's death, must be heard from during the telling of a truthful version of Dave Allison's riveting story. The detractor, in part penned:

> The Mexican rebels, having found shelter, were holding their own until Morine's group charged down the right-hand hill and caught them in a cross fire. Further resistance was futile and they threw up their hands and surrendered.
>
> The battle only lasted a few minutes and after the firing stopped, the posse members worked their way to the bottom of the canyon and confronted the Mexicans. Handcuffs were placed on the five and the camp was then inspected for stolen property. Two of the horses taken from Joe Marshall at Etholene were identified and a third horse carried Bob Love's brand.
>
> Because the Mexicans had been caught with stolen horses, La Ley Fuga demanded that they should die. There was no disagreement among the posse as to what must be done, and several of their number stepped forward to administer the golpe de gracia or death blow. They drew their revolvers and went along the line of Mexicans, shooting them at close range, and watching their bodies fall.[62]

Sadly, but not unexpectedly, the writer offers *no* documentary evidence to this uncorroborated allegation, or others. Systematic executions there were not. In fact, the truth of the matter can easily be found by just a partial review of Culberson County Sheriff John Morine's official statement. "We all closed in about the same time and after a *fusillade* of shots all the Mexicans were killed."[63] Once the first shot rang out it turned into an alarming instance of out-and-out commotion, confusion, and chaos! It was simply a case of who had the upper hand; the bandits were taken by surprise; the lawmen got the drop and were shooting from above.

Upon closer inspection on the ground it was determined the deceased, as previously noted, were each armed with new Marlin .30-30 rifles, and two had revolvers, a Smith and Wesson .44 Special and a Colt's revolving pistol, .45 caliber. Collectively there were between 1,000 and 1,500 rounds of ammunition seized from the dead Mexicans.[64] Additionally, the horse-shoeing hammer belonging to Dick Love, the one used by Joe Thompson to shoe the horse Orozco had been ridding, was found among the Mexican's trappings.[65] And the horses? They were positively identified as being stolen.[66]

Even before this rattling string of events, Pascual Orozco, Jr. was a fugitive from United State's justice, and as such, had attempted to alter his appearance somewhat by dying his light reddish brown mustache black. The black dye was found on his person. "There were also coded messages and reports of American troop movements along the border stuffed in his saddlebags."[67] Soon it gradually began to dawn on exhausted posse men that they may have very well in fact killed some pretty extraordinary "Goddamn horse-thieves." Herff Carnes mentioned to Dave Allison that he thought they had actually killed Pascual Orozco, Jr. After examining the body Dave thought so too, but none were really positive.[68]

Sheriff Morine, from the D. Taylor, ranch telephoned Culberson County Attorney A. L. Green and Justice of the Peace T. R. Owen, appraising them of the tragic affair and deaths of the unidentified Mexicans, requesting they at once come to the ranch by automobile, then to be escorted by horseback or wagon to the mountainous box canyon so they could began the preliminary investigation for a legally mandated inquest.[69]

On the morning of August 31, 1915, in the company of County Attorney Green, and "the entire party of officers and ranchmen who took part in trailing up and killing…," T. R. Owen began his inquiry, examining the bodies "lying where they fell in battle that was fought the evening of the 30th of Aug." After gathering up some personal effects of the deceased, for identification purposes, Justice of the Peace Owen ordered the bodies removed to Van Horn, the Culberson County seat.[70] Ranch owner, D. Taylor carried the bodies in a wagon to his headquarters, and from there the remains were transported to Van Horn via Culberson County Judge Green's automobile.[71]

Careful to resolve any legal questions arising over his jurisdiction to make a final ruling as to the cause of deaths, Owen officially recorded, "..I also took the testimony of Geo. G. Kirtley who is working a Mica Mine about two miles from where the fight occurred in order to ascertain definitely whether this killing took place in El Paso or Culberson County."[72] As to the concrete site of the shootout, Kirtley testified, "It was in Culberson County, Texas, about one mile east of the El Paso and Culberson County line."[73]

Once more a conspiratorial spin is irrationally woven into the patchwork blanket one writer has chosen to ineptly throw over the fascinating story. Absent any documentation or citation to sources he somehow concludes:

> None of the men present knew just where the Culberson-El Paso County line lay or on what side of it the battle had taken place. They did realize the possibility of a trial, however, due to the prominence of Orozco, and because of the heavy Mexican population at El Paso that would be sympathetic to him, it would be in the posse's best interest for a trial not to be held there. It was agreed, then, to place the location of the incident in Culberson County, even if the location had to be moved to a different site.[74]

Apparently based solely on speculation and innuendo, the writer charges the reader with accepting the illogical. For this conspiracy to exist the number of co-conspirators are legion. First off, the subject of this biography, William Davis Allison must tell a bald faced lie; followed by untruths uttered from the lips and typewriter of U. S. Mounted Customs Patrol Inspector Herff Carnes; then Culberson County Sheriff John A. Morine, and his deputy, A. B. Medley must commit perjury, and then swear their pal Joel Fenley to unconditional secrecy; the deputy from El Paso County, W. H. Schrock, under oath, also must out and out lie at the coroner's inquest; the Love brothers, Dick, George, Bob, and Rowdy, plus the two nephews, B. N. and Prince, must then make a blood-brother vow to never tell the truth; of course another posse man, Pete Wetzel, would be forced to forevermore conceal the real facts; as would cowboys Bertie Bristow and Hardy Merchon who gave valuable intelligence to the posse men; D. Taylor who recovered the bodies would also have to fib; as would George Kirtley the man who helped Taylor with the distasteful job, and the man who testified under oath the incident indeed happened in Culberson County; and a whole bunch of others would have to keep the actual truth to themselves; not to mention the documents falsely prepared by the Justice of the Peace, T. R. Owen; the conspiratorial participation of Culberson County Judge, A. L. Green; and the whole fabrication legally blessed by 34th Judicial District of Texas Judge, Dan M. Jackson. Each and every one, to the last man, would have to keep deathly quiet or lie about the entire affair—and lie to their wives—for the rest of their lives!

Fallacious conspiracy theories aside, unquestionably rumors were flying about the possibility of the posse having killed Pascual Orozco, Jr. No one knew for sure. It was a story quickly picked up by the news media.[75] Several people were rushed from El Paso to Van Horn to identify the bodies and either confirm or squash the rampant rumors. John Russell who had known Orozco for the past three years was one.[76] Another was U. S. Mounted Customs Inspector Louis Holzman.[77] And yet another asked to make an identification of the remains was a reporter for the *El Paso Morning Times*.[78]

With official identification made, Justice of the Peace T. R. Owen ruled, "…I find that the said Pascual Orozco, Jose F. Delgado, Christoforo Caballero, Andreas Sandoval and Miguel Tarrazas came to their death in Culberson County, Texas, on the 30th, day of August 1915, by gun shots fired by officers and citizens of El Paso and Culberson Counties."[79]

The Mexican's bodies, after being laid out for public display at the Van Horn depot, were then put on a train and shipped west to relatives in El Paso.[80] There were was no riotous outburst of inflamed indignation from the Hispanic population at El Paso, but the Mayor and the Police Chief had feared there very will might have been.[81] Mourners, yes, by the thousands, but behaving with dignity and respect. Clearly, though, in the Anglo community there were apprehensive premonitions, at least according to a report in the *El Paso Morning Times*, "The killing of the Orozco band is expected to bring about reprisals in this section by sympathizers of Orozco. All ranchmen of this district have armed to protect themselves, and the question of asking Governor Ferguson for protection was discussed this afternoon. It is likely that this will be done."[82]

Pascual Orozco, Jr. was temporarily interred in the Concordia Cemetery at El Paso on September 3, 1915. Although Catholic Priests performed services for the other four fallen members of the Orozco group, a Methodist clergyman eulogized before Pascual's Mexican flag-draped coffin. Later, after receiving permission from an old enemy, Pancho Villa, Orozco's remains were removed to Chihuahua, Mexico.[83]

Pascual Orozco, Jr. may have been lain to rest, but the aftermath of his death was far from over, especially for Dave Allison and his fellow posse men. The theories explaining or justifying the next turn in West Texas events abound, some are legally and logically sound, others border on the ridiculous. To cut to the chase, many Mexicans and Mexican-Americans could not bring themselves to terms with the maddening fact Pascual Orozco, Jr., their seemingly superhuman revolutionary champion had been imprudently caught off guard. Surely no posse of *gringos* were a match for "Pascualito!" They all knew Orozco was a superb shooter, why weren't some of the posse men killed too? The Mexican newspaper, *La Justica* was proclaiming his untimely death a murder—surely they knew of what they printed—didn't they?[84] Wasn't it true Orozco had been killed for the bulging money-belt he wore? Weren't the posse men really unscrupulous gun runners? Didn't Pancho Villa secretly have a hand in the killing of Pascual?

And unwittingly, adding volatile fuel to the fiery questions directly affecting Dave Allison and his fellow West Texas posse men, were the various United States government sponsored investigations into Mexican and American relations along the troublesome border, and the emphatically pro-active probes by Senators, especially like New Mexico's Albert Bacon Fall, who was actively involved in pointing out sordid examples of Mexican violence directed toward Americans residing deep in the belly of the Southwest, or even further south across the international line. Just the year before (1914), in a stinging speech before his Senate colleagues, politician Fall had directed their attention to a colossal investigative report detailing "...attacks upon American citizens, of assaults upon innocent women and children...American citizens...in the Republic of Mexico..." and he scolded, "I defy, ...the production of one scintilla of proof that anything whatsoever has been done by this Government or by any of its officials...to show one single instance in which anything more than merely a formal protest has been made,...in which reparation has been sought or obtained."[85] How could Americans register legitimate complaints, and then turn a deaf ear to those Mexican friends and neighbors south of the border when they proffered grievances? Were treacherous and heartless criminals always Mexicans? Wasn't Pascual Orozco, Jr. gunned down north of the border.?[86] Didn't that massacre take place on American soil? And, in the end, indeed it was "likely that the United States was embarrassed about the manner in which Orozco met his death..."[87]

The fermenting disgruntlement over the persnickety problem wouldn't simply fade away. There was, however, a solution to the whole squalid mess, at least to the part about how Orozco met his maker. Truthfully, it probably will never be known, not for sure, just whose hands deftly pulled the strings. *Maybe* it was posse men themselves, in a rather dicey legal maneuver based on perceived Fifth Amendment interpretations about double jeopardy, who cleverly manipulated the Criminal Justice System. *Possibly* it was just the birthing of political correctness and an effort to mollify Orozco's many foreign friends and supporters. *Perhaps* the United States Government herself brought face-saving back-room pressure to bear in an act of international diplomacy.[88] *Perchance* it was purely partisan politics. Regardless of why it happened, indeed, it happened! During the October 1895, term of District Court, Dave Allison and the other posse men were indicted for Murder by a Culberson County Grand Jury.[89] Incontrovertibly, the indictment was a case of either CYA (cover your ass) or governmental scapegoating. The outcome would be dead-shot predictable though—no lawmen, or gringo ranchers, would get convicted by an Anglo jury at Van Horn, Texas, in 1915, for killing some Mexican horse-thieves.

Clearly, whatever it was that was going on—it wasn't District Court business as usual, not when the following news blurb in an edition of the *El Paso Herald* is factored into the equation, "This case will probably be tried this week here and the record of all proceedings will be forwarded to the State Department at Washington."[90]

Van Horn, Texas. During the transitional frontier period. Courtesy, Culberson County Historical Museum. Van Horn, Texas.

One writer, telling his version of a folkloric story, claims shortly after the battle down in the High-Lonesome country, the posse men, at a local

Van Horn café, and in a buoyant and lively mood, treated one of their brethren to a satirical serving of brains and eggs for breakfast, honorarium for "killing the most Mexicans".[91] Admitting that "it is necessary to resort as much to legend as fact" in identifying who actually pulled the triggers and killed anyone, the scribe continues scribbling his tale, naming three persons actually credited with doing the killing.[92] Evaluating the anecdote through the application of historic logic gives rise to an overriding question. If, indeed, standing in the spotlight of public scrutiny there was a jovial hand-shaking and back-slapping celebration in a crowded Van Horn restaurant, with three of the posse men taking adulatory bows because they were in fact responsible for killing the five Mexicans, why was there any need to indict the other posse men? The tale appears to be fanciful fiction, low order dime-novel material.

On October 8, 1915, William Davis "Dave" Allison, accompanied by U. S. Mounted Customs Inspector Herff A. Carnes, and the other nine posse men voluntarily turned themselves in to a Culberson County Deputy Sheriff, J. R. Whitten.[93]

On that same day before State of Texas, 34th Judicial District Judge Dan M. Jackson, the defendants entered pleas of "not guilty" to the charge of murder, having herd the indictment read in open court.[94] After hearing evidence, which everyone was pretty well already familiar with, the Judge made his instructions to the jury, which in part read:

> If from the evidence you believe the defendants killed the said Pascual Orozco, Christoforo Caballero, Andreas Sandoval, Jose F. Delgado and Miguel Terrazas, but further believe that at the time of so doing the deceased had made an attack on them, which from the manner and character of it and the relative strength of the parties and the defendant's knowledge of the character and disposition of the deceased, if any, caused them to have a reasonable expectation or fear of death or serious bodily injury and that acting under such reasonable expectation or fear, the defendants killed the deceased, then you should acquit them; and if the deceased was armed at the time they were killed and were making such attack on defendants, and if the weapons used by them and the manner of their use were such as were reasonably calculated to produce death or serious bodily harm, then

> the law presumes the deceased intended to murder or to inflict serious bodily injury upon the defendants.
>
> You are instructed that the theft of cattle, the theft of a horse, an assault with intent to murder are felonies within this State.[95]

Not surprisingly, to anyone, the jury quickly returned its verdict, "We the jury in the above entitled and number cause find the defendants not guilty."[96]

Judge Dan Jackson firmly decreed, "It is therefore considered, ordered and adjudged by the Court that the defendants and each of them are not guilty of murder, and they each of them go hence without delay and be dismissed."[97]

Of the West Texas posse, one prominent writer of blistering Southwest escapades penned they "were men with reputations for honesty and truthfulness."[98] And of conspiracies? Recognizing the nature of mortal men, he rightfully acknowledged, "there were too many men in the posse for any secrets to be kept for long."[99] The saga of Pascual Orozco, Jr., at last came to an end, but William Davis "Dave" Allison was not through scouring about in that thoroughly beguiling Sierra Blanca country.

ENDNOTES
Chapter 8. "We all dismounted and commenced firing"

[1] *El Paso Herald*, May 25, 1915. The date of this event is indeed significant in telling the Dave Allison's story, and rightfully so, an explanation is in order. In his account of the event, **Webb** reports a date of May 24, 1916, which for whatever reason, maybe even a typesetting mistake, is off by one year. From the broad overview of historical border happenings, an error of relative insignificance, but for a few of those actually on the ground at the time, Allison included, the timing was critical. A partial quote from the May 25, 1915 newspaper is appropriate, "A posse left Valentine early today for a point six miles from the Mexican border, where it is feared, two Americans were captured or killed in a battle Monday night between Mexicans and Texas river guards and rangers. A ranger named Bates and Joe Sitters, a river guard, were missing when the Americans telephoned for help after they had been forced to retreat and their horses had been captured…" **Cox** places the event in 1915, as does **Means**.
[2] **Cox**, P. 141. And see, **Webb**, P. 498. Also see, **Means**, P. 161. All three accounts are in general agreement.
[3] Ibid., P. 142.
[4] *El Paso Herald*, May 25, 1915.
[5] **Cox**, P. 142. And see, **Webb**, P. 498, "A posse of eleven men, among them Inspector R. M. Wadsworth, left Marfa and reached the Pool Ranch that night, where horses were waiting for an all-night ride to the McGee Ranch."
[6] **Webb**, P. 499. Quoting from the testimony of R. M. Wadsworth to United States Senator Albert Bacon Fall.
[7] Ibid.
[8] **Cox**, P. 127. And see, *El Paso Herald*, June, 6, 9, & 11, 1915. "Mexicans entered Fabens Thursday night from the vicinity of Fort Hancock started to terrorize the settlement again as was Monday night when Texas ranger Lee Burdett was shot and killed." Also see, *El Paso Morning Times*, June 8 & 9, 1915. Robert Lee Burdett was born in Travis County, Texas in 1882. He enlisted in the Texas Rangers, for the first time, on October 6, 1911 at Austin. He re-upped for a second hitch with the Texas Rangers, Company B, on February 15, 1915. Four months later he was gunned down in West Texas. His body was returned to Austin for burial. Courtesy, Texas Ranger Hall of Fame and Museum. Waco.
[9] Ibid.
[10] *El Paso Herald*, June 14, 1915.
[11] **Meyer**, P. 130. "Although many reports of Orozco's whereabouts were received by various government agencies, none of them led to his capture."
[12] **Christiansen**, P. 118.
[13] **Meed**, P. 47.
[14] **Christiansen**, P. 118.
[15] **Meyer**, P. 131.
[16] **Blanco**, P. 15.
[17] **Carnes**, *Report to Collector of Customs*, September 1, 1915.
[18] **Gilliland**, Maude T., *Wilson County Texas Rangers, 1837-1977*. P. 47-48. Herff A. Carnes was born at Fairview, Wilson County, Texas on May 23, 1879. He signed on with the Texas Rangers, February 13, 1903, serving under Captain

John Hughes in Company D. In 1911 Carnes joined the U. S. Mounted Customs Service where he served for twenty-one years. On December 1, 1932, in a vicious shootout with liquor smugglers near Ysleta, Texas, Carnes was wounded. On December 3, 1932, fifty-three year old Herff Carnes died at an El Paso hospital as a result of the bullet wounds.

[19] **Bolling**, P. 33.

[20] **Meed**, P. 49. A story in the *El Paso Morning Times*, September 1, 1915, seems to support the author's version making reference to a "misconnection" between Orozco and Salinas.

[21] Ibid.

[22] Ibid., P. 47.

[23] **Meyer**, P. 131. And see, statement of W. H. **Schrock**, for the *Culberson County Inquest* in the matter of the deaths of Pascual Orozco Jr., Jose F. Delgado, Christoforo Caballero, Andreas Sandoval and Miguel Terrazas. Courtesy, Linda **McDonald**, Culberson County District-County Clerk, Van Horn, Texas. Hereafter cited as *Culberson County Inquest.* And see, **Shipman**, Mrs. O. L., *Taming the Big Bend, A History of the Extreme Western Portion of Texas From Fort Clark to El Paso*. P. 146.

[24] *Culberson County Inquest*, Statement of W. H. **Schrock**.

[25] W. H. **Schrock** at the *Culberson County Inquest* stated that one of the men that accompanied Thompson to the ranch house was wearing "black leggings" and the other was wearing a "Kaki suit and tan boots." **Bolling** identifies the two as Caballero and Terrazas. P. 34. **Meed** only identifies one, Pascual Orozco Jr., P. 49. Orozco's biographer, Michael **Meyer**, concurs with **Meed**. P. 131.

[26] **Means**, P. 164. And see, **Bolling**, P. 34. Also see, **Meed**, P. 49.

[27] **Meed**, P. 49. Naturally, since **Bolling** does not put Orozco at the scene, he could not have been the person ordering the horse to be shod. **Bolling** seems to be in error on this account. **Carnes** in his *Report to the Collector of Customs* says, "Only two (one of whom later proved to be Orozco) accompanied this cowboy to the lower ranch, the other three remaining in camp at the upper well."

[28] *El Paso Morning Times*, September 1, 1915.

[29] *Culberson County Inquest*, Statement of W. H. **Schrock**.

[30] **Carnes**, *Report to the Collector of Customs*. Again, **Bolling** is in conflict with contemporary documents and places the men approaching the ranch house on horseback rather than in an automobile, "Presently, one of them glanced out an east window and saw three riders approaching from that direction…" P. 35. **Meed**, P. 50, relying on the primary source material, but with a pleasant journalistic touch says, "About halfway through the meal, Orozco, fork poised for a bite, paused. He thought he heard an automobile. His acute hearing had not deceived him, for seconds later an auto holding three men chugged into view."

[31] *Culberson County Inquest*, Statement of W. H. **Schrock**, who says, "…we could see them going east towards the Eagle Mountains, and they were 'Beating them on the tail too.'"

[32] Ibid. **Carnes**, *Report to Collector of Customs* identifies the three men arriving by automobile as Dick Love, Bill Schrock and Tom Bell. **Bolling** cites, the three automobile passengers as Schrock, Tom Beall, and Foote Boykin's killer, H. L. Roberson. P. 37. According to **Means**, P. 145., "Bill Norton said Roberson didn't go;" No primary source document places Roberson at the scene.

[33] **Bolling**, P. 36.

[34] Ibid., P. 37. And see, **Meed**, P. 51. The comment about the breastworks comes from an interview with Bill **Love** at Sierra Blanca, Texas, the grandson of B. N. Love, who states the formation, after all these years, is still intact and easily observable. Comments about the 15-20 shots comes from the testimony of W. H. **Schrock** as part of the *Culberson County Inquest.*
[35] *Culberson County Inquest*, Statement of W. H. **Schrock**.
[36] **Bolling**, P. 38. And see, *Culberson County Inquest*, Statement of Culberson County Sheriff John A. **Morine**. Also see, **Meed**, P. 51. "By late afternoon rural telephone lines were ringing off their hooks across West Texas."
[37] **Meed**, P. 52. Also see, *El Paso Morning Times*, September 1, 1915.
[38] **Carnes**, *Report to the Collector of Customs.*
[39] Ibid.
[40] Ibid.
[41] Ibid. Curiously, **Bolling** states, "Early on the morning of the same day, customs officer Herff Carnes, Constable Dave Allison, and rancher J. M. Mellard, drove out from Sierra Blanca to the D. Taylor ranch at the head of Green River Draw, in an effort to intercept the Mexicans when they came out from the Eagle Mountains." P. 43. This assertion is in contradiction with primary source materials.
[42] **Bolling**, P. 39.
[43] *Culberson County Inquest*, Statement of Culberson County Sheriff John A. **Morine**.
[44] Sign hanging in Culberson County Historical Museum, Van Horn, Texas.
[45] *Van Horn Advocate*, February 9, 1914.
[46] *Culberson County Inquest*, Statement of Culberson County Sheriff John A. **Morine**.
[47] **Carnes**, *Report to Collector of Customs.*
[48] Ibid. And see, **Meed**, P. 53.
[49] Ibid.
[50] Ibid., And see, **Meed**, P. 53. Also see, *Culberson County Inquest*, Statement of A. B. **Medley**, "John Morine asked me if I would go with him to catch some desperadoes that were coming this way. I went with him in an automobile to the Taylor Ranch were we got horses and took up the trail with the Sierra Blanca boys."
[51] **Carnes**, *Report to Collector of Customs.* Also see, **Meed**, P. 54. "After a brief council-of-war, David (sic) Allison, the range detective took command of the two posses." And see, *Fort Worth Star-Telegram*, July 29, 1923. "Mexicans raids, by the way largely entered into the evidence of these trials, due to the fact that Allison when a Ranger, led the posse which killed Orozco, noted Mexican bandit leader."
[52] **Blumenson**, P. 298.
[53] **Bolling**, P. 45. Also, refer to March 2001 interview with Marvin **Garlick.** Mr. **Garlick** reported that while he was yet a young man, and while Bertie Bristow was an old man, that Bristow told him the story about giving information to the posse and telling them about a box canyon south of High-Lonesome Mountain in the Van Horn Mountains, Culberson County, Texas.
[54] Ibid.
[55] **Meed**, P. 54. And see, *Culberson County Inquest*, Statement of Sheriff John A. **Morine**.
[56] Ibid.

---

[57] *Culberson County Inquest*, Statement of Sheriff John A. **Morine**. Also see, *El Paso Morning Times*, August 31,1915, "In a fight with a posse of deputy sheriffs and United States customs guards from Sierra Blanca, five Mexican bandits from the Orozco band which has been camped near Bosquito Bonito on the Mexican side were killed in the Green River Canyon, twenty-five miles east of Sierra Blanca, this afternoon."

[58] **Carnes**, *Report to Collector of Customs*.

[59] *Culberson County Inquest*, Statement of A. B. **Medley**.

[60] *Culberson County Inquest*, Statement of W. H. **Schrock**.

[61] For a brief, but easily understandable explanation of *the La Fuga*, see **Meed**, P. 48, who approaches the subject with journalistic truism and evenhandedness.

[62] **Bolling**, P. 46-47.

[63] *Culberson County Inquest*, Statement of Sheriff John A. **Morine**. And see, S*t. Louis Post-Dispatch*, July 22, 1923. "…The Mexicans believing they had eluded the posse, camped in a box canyon, their horses unsaddled and hobbled. Their pursuers advanced, dismounted, climbed the rugged side of High Lonesome Mountain, and gained a ridge behind the camp. They poured down a volley, killing all the Mexicans save Gen. Orozco and one other man. These two tried to gain the shelter of a small draw. Both were killed, Allison firing the shots that ended the career of the Mexican adventurer. Four bullet wounds were found in Gen. Orozco's body."

[64] Ibid. And see, **Meed**, P. 55.

[65] **Carnes**, *Report to Collector of Customs*.

[66] Ibid. And see, *Culberson County Inquest*, Statement of John A. **Morine**..

[67] **Meed**, P. 55.

[68] Ibid, P. 34. And see, **Carnes**, *Report to Collector of Customs*.

[69] *Culberson County Inquest*, Statement of Justice of the Peace, T. R. **Owen**.

[70] Ibid.

[71] Ibid.

[72] Ibid. Justice of the Peace **Owen** knew that George **Kirtley** had lived at the mine several years, recently had the site surveyed and "knew within a very short distance were the County line ran."

[73] *Culberson County Inquest*, Statement of George G. **Kirtley**.

[74] **Bolling**, P. 48. To accept this conspiracy theory the reader must also allow as reality, that the plot to lie about the actual location of where the battle occurred was formulated before there was even legitimate conformation one of the deceased was, in fact, Pascual Orozco Jr., an identification which was not positively made until the next day at Van Horn, Texas.

[75] *El Paso Morning Times*, August 31, and September 1, 1915.

[76] *Culberson County Inquest*, Statement of John **Russell**.

[77] **Carnes**, *Report to Collector of Customs*.

[78] Ibid. And see, **Thompson**, Cecilia, *History of Marfa and Presidio County, Texas, 1535-1946. Volume Two, 1901-1946*. P. 118. "General Pasquel (sic) Orozco was identified as one of the victims."

[79] *Culberson County Inquest*. Ruling.

[80] **Meed**, P. 56.

[81] Ibid. According to the author the entire El Paso Police force was mobilized.

[82] *El Paso Morning Times*, September 1, 1915.

[83] **Meyer**, P. 133. And see, **Meed**, P. 56. Also see, *El Paso Morning Times*, September 3, 1915, which printed the following telegram from Pancho Villa to

Orozco's widow, "I have always considered Orozco as an enemy of the faction I sustain and of the democratic cause of the Mexican people but having died all cause of animosity is removed and his family is hereby authorized to bury his body in whatever place they desire in the national territory." Also see, **Metz (II)**, P. 219., "Orozco was later declared a hero to the revolution, and his body returned to Mexican soil."

84 **Meed**, P. 56.

85 **Owen**, Gordon R., *The Two Alberts, Fountain and Fall.* P. 388.

86 Ibid., P. 386-397.

87 **Meyer**, P. 133, n. 93.

88 **Meed**, P. 56. The author offers but two possibilities for the indictments, "Whether to protect them against legal claims or to assuage the outraged cries of the friends of Pascual Orozco and his companions…"

89 Copy of *Indictment* charging John A Morine; Joel Fenley; A. B. Medley; Dave Allison; George Love; Bob Love; Prince Love; Pete Wetzel; H. A. Carnes; Will Schrock; and B. N. Love with Murder. And see, *Culberson County Grand Jury Docket Book.* Courtesy, Linda **McDonald**, County-District Clerk, Culberson County, Van Horn, Texas.

90 *El Paso Herald*, October 7, 1915.

91 **Bolling**, P. 50.

92 Ibid., P. 51. And see the author's comments on P. 49, "There were three members of the posse that had interests across the Rio Grande in Chihuahua, who traveled and lived there at times, and who would be vulnerable to retaliation by Mexican citizens. It was agreed that their names would be withheld as having taken part in the posse. These were Tom Beall, J. M. (J. W.) Mellard, and H. L Roberson." The faulty allegation that Roberson was part of the posse has previously been addressed in an endnote, and no contemporary evidence of any type places him at the scene of the killings. Historically speaking, speculative innuendo must give way to contrary primary source documents when they are available, as they are in this case. Additionally, a review of the Culberson County *Indictment* does reveal that J. W. Mellard was one of the posse men indicted for murder, and examination of the *Capias Warrant and Sheriff's Return* indicates he was also arrested for murder on October 8, 1915 in Van Horn at the courthouse, by Culberson County Deputy Sheriff J. R. Whitten, but *allegedly* his name "fell through the cracks and was inadvertently added to the list of those indicted, but charges were dismissed before trial time." **Bolling**, P. 60. Indeed the cases against Mellard, (along with Rowdy Love and Joe English) were dismissed. Regardless, the fact he was indicted and arrested, both documents of public record, dispels conspiratorial insinuation that the posse men were secretly trying to protect him from "retaliation by Mexican citizens." Additionally, at the time he was arrested, he was in the company of the other posse members. Certainly not an action indicative of someone who was desirous of simply fading into the background, incognito. Additionally, illustrative of just how rumor, innuendo, and outhouse gossip about the affair was literally blowing in the wind can be found in the remarks of George Patton Jr., who erroneously wrote to his wife, "He (Allison) alone killed all the Orasco (sic) outfit, five of them about a month ago…He shot Orasco (sic) and his four men each in the head at sixty yards," a hell-of-a story, to be sure, but one certainly diametrically at odds with primary source materials.

---

[93] *Capias Warrant and Sheriff's Return.* Courtesy Linda **McDonald**, County-District Clerk, Culberson County, Van Horn, Texas.
[94] *Judgment, Case No. 35., The State of Texas vs. John A. Morine et als.*, signed "Dan. M. Jackson," Judge: 34th Judicial District. Courtesy Linda **McDonald**, County-District Clerk, Culberson County, Van Horn, Texas.
Van Horn, Texas.
[95] *Instructions to the Jury, Case No. 35., The State of Texas vs. John A Morine et als.* Courtesy Linda **McDonald**, County-District Clerk, Culberson County, Van Horn, Texas.
[96] Verdict Form, signed, "J. E. Bean, Foreman." Courtesy Linda **McDonald**, County-District Clerk, Culberson County, Van Horn, Texas.
[97] *Judgment, Case No. 35, The State of Texas vs. John A Morine et als* Courtesy, Linda **McDonald,** County-District Clerk, Culberson County, Van Horn, Texas..
[98] **Meed**, P. 57.
[99] Ibid.

9

"always shoot the horse of an escaping man"

When Pancho Villa's insurgent forces, on March 9, 1916, zipped across the international line at Columbus, New Mexico, killing American soldiers and civilians, needless to say the politically wobbly zone along the Mexican border instantaneously ignited into a frightful state of heightened military alert.[1] The conflagration of rumors raged. One of which was thought to be absolutely true. Mexican Revolutionary forces of *someone* were poised to attack Fabens, Texas, which lay vulnerably exposed on Rio Grande River banks, just south of El Paso.[2] United States military forces already deployed along the international line, in quick-time made ready, explicitly mobilizing, and once again the talents of that old veteran of Southwest border-country adventures, William Davis Allison were requested. A contemporary colleague recalled, "He acted as a Civilian Scout for the Troops along the Texas border during the Mexican Revolution."[3] An assignment which can be somewhat confirmed from the pen of Dave Allison himself, in letters written to his wife Lena and daughter Hazel. Herein is part of what he wrote to Lena:

> *...Now I will do the best to explain my position and conduct. I was in El Paso, Wednesday night, to Friday Morning the 24th* (April, 1916), *when on the train I learned John Gardner was on same train bound for Fabens, where it was officially supposed the Mexicans intending doing as was done at Columbus. So I hunted up Mr. Gardner, and he only had a few moments to explain before our arrival at Fabens; but when the train reached Ft. Hancock, he had wired me to ship my horses and mule and come at once. Then upon my arrival here I found the Government had spotted* (arranged) *a car for my horses and in fact the soldiers already had them fed and were*

prepared to load—So I got all my contraptions ready, viz—Bed—Grip—Saddle and Pack Saddle and loaded into the car with the horses. Knowing nothing except going to Fabens to help protect that place...

Saturday the army officers, Major Langhorne the rangers under Ira Frinley, Mr. Gardner and myself consulted all day, and were to make a certain scout, starting that night and to continue four or five days and did start but were overtaken and Mr. Gardner and I turned back to Fabens. Then Major Langhorne with two troops of Cavalry left early Sunday morning for Ft. Bliss, leaving an auto, with instructions to bring Gardner and myself on in...went directly to Ft. Bliss, where I met Major L., Capt. Rhea and Mr. G. Everything was in a rush and hubbub, no explanation, no nothing. So about noon Mr. G. and I went to his home for dinner. There pretty soon came an auto, with General Bell, Maj. L., and another officer, picked up G. and myself, pulled out through Ysleta, and on to Fabens, where they let me drop and picked up another Capt. I do not know where they went nor when they returned. I then caught the first train returned to El Paso. Next morning going to Bliss to see Capt. Rhea, he was still in the dark. I then returned to Fabens, and the rangers and myself have scouted both ways from Ysleta to Ft. Hancock and return...Your loving and affectionate husband.[4]

To his daughter Hazel, Dave Allison, in part, penned:

My reason to going to Fabens was simply to protect it or any other place from such another attack as Columbus, N. Mex. The Government wanted my services only temporarily. I have been scouting both ways, from Fabens to Ysleta and Ft. Hancock. The Government shipped my horse & outfit and I brought them back overland, starting Sunday and arriving here last night. I have made mama a detailed report...Your loving daddy.[5]

Regretfully, further details highlighting Dave Allison's scouting duties for the military during this time period range from skimpy to nonexistent. After a diligent and time consuming search into the matter, National Archives and Records Administration personnel disappointedly elucidated, "Records relating to the civilians hired during this operation are fragmentary."[6] Clearly it is known Dave Allison temporarily scouted for the U. S. Army along the Mexican border. For exactly how long, and just what his specific assignments were, or what he expressly did, remain an unfortunate mystery.

Dave Allison, left, while scouting the Texas Big Bend country for the United States Army, 1916. Other scout unidentified. Courtesy, Pat Treadwell, Tahoka, Texas.

While Dave Allison's exact movements cannot be convincingly documented, clearly it can be determined though, at least for the short while, he decided to remain at Sierra Blanca. One author suggests he "continued working as a gunman for the Love Brothers until about 1917, and then returned to work for the Cattle Raisers Association as a range inspector..."[7] The statement is more than half right, for indeed Dave Allison remained in the employee of area cattlemen, and for sure, the Love brothers were a part of that crowd, but Dave Allison was not on their private payroll as an exclusive "gunman," not the way he had been for Colonel Bill Greene down in old Mexico.[8] And, E. B. "Berk" Spiller, Secretary for the Texas and Southwestern Cattle Raisers Association did write a letter to the Texas Governor, advising the State's chief executive of Allison's appointment as an Inspector stationed at Sierra Blanca, requesting Dave be once more issued an official commission as a Special Texas Ranger.[9] The Governor responded on April 13, 1917, and once again Dave Allison was commissioned a Special Texas Ranger, but his salary was to be paid from Association funds.[10] On January 22, 1918, Dave Allison's official standing as a Special Ranger was updated.[11]

H. L. Roberson, the killer of Foot Boykin and Walt Sitter at Sierra Blanca, also was commissioned a Special Ranger by the State of Texas, and like Dave Allison, he was actually employed as an Inspector with the Association. Unlike William Davis Allison, however, Roberson relocated himself from the mountains and deserts of that Sierra Blanca country, moved northeast, and took up residence in Dickens County, Texas.[12] Later, on assignment, he spent a great deal of time around Magdalena, New Mexico, which resulted in his productively breaking up a troublesome gang of wrongdoing brand-burning cowboys.[13] And, yet still later, but commandingly maintaining employment with the Association, Roberson settled at thriving Midland, Dave Allison's old stomping grounds.[14] The two doughty range detectives were soon to have a great deal more in common.

At fifty-seven years of age William Davis Allison was still on the job—carrying a badge and chasing after "Goddamn cow-thieves." And according to several accounts he was gettin' em' too!

In a letter to his wife, Lt. George S. Patton, Jr. wrote that Dave Allison "...kills several Mexicans each month."[15] Indisputably the remarks are a first-class exaggeration on the one hand, yet still suggestive of the reputation Allison held with the future "Blood and Guts" General and, indeed, the rousing comments are indicative of Dave's no nonsense standing which was well-known across the whole desert Southwest. While the search for verifiable facts to be used in counting notch-stick numbers lumbers on, it is worthy of note that Patton and Allison must have had some intriguing and instructive BS sessions while visiting at Sierra Blanca or while hunting together for deer in the jagged mountains or while trying to jump migrating wildfowl from Rio Grande River puddles and rivulets.[16] On recounting one of his narrow escapes during the Mexican Revolutionary period, Patton later mentions, "I started back, when I saw a man on a horse come right in front of me, I started to shoot at him but remembered that Dave Allison had always said to shoot at the horse of an escaping man and I did so and broke the horse's hip, he fell on his rider."[17] Like U. S. Mounted Customs Inspector Herff Carnes had done before him, George S. Patton, Jr. too was learning a thing or two about six-shooter reality from that "quiet looking old man with a sweet face and white hair."[18]

A vigorous secondary chronicler of West Texas lore and Big Bend area stories simply remarks, "...Dave Allison shot a Mexican or two on the border near Sierra Blanca."[19] The ardent author is forced into reporting rumor and campfire chitchat; the statement could well be true. Unreported killings and unsolved murders along the Rio Grande to some border liners were cases of humdrum normalcy—nothing much out of the ordinary.

On the topic of Dave Allison's killings along the tumultuous border, one writer wrote that, W. T. "Bill" Norton and Pete Bingo, "from a vantage point atop Cerro Alto, a hill on the Kurt White ranch, watched Dave Allison and John Daniel kill two Mexicans across the river."[20] Unfortunately, the story starts and stops in that one sentence.

Another such anecdote involving Dave Allison makes a terrific tale. When but a mere child, Baylus "Little Prince" Love tagged along with his father, B. N. "Judge" Love, uncle Dick Love, and other family members on a cattle gathering trip along the borderline, near Bosque Bonita. As night fell the family-set camped out at the Rio Grande's sandy river bank, a blanket of stars overhead, the enveloping warmth of a flickering fire closer at hand. "Little Prince" Love was eagerly taking it all in—the sights, the smells, the noises, and the campfire cowboy yarns. Pint sized boys could have scads of fun, and at the same time grow up pretty fast in that undomesticated country south of Sierra Blanca. Sometimes boys just needed to be with the men.

As the group piddled and poked at burning coals, causing spewing sparks to declare war on bedrolls and flannel shirts, a Mexican vaquero riding a thoroughly used up horse ambled into the scene. Although they didn't know or recognize him, the Love brothers warmly invited the stranger to partake from the pots of stout boiling coffee, bubbling red beans, and cuts of hot, slab-sided bacon. "Little Prince" Love scooted over nearer his father, and eagerly the observably famished visitor, grabbing a plate, hunkered on his heels in cow-camp fashion. Suspiciously though, as he forked the pintos and pork, he, too, uneasily scanned the surroundings. "Little Prince" thought every thing looked okay, yet something seemed out of kilter. Suddenly the jittery Mexican vaquero jerked his head in the direction of the picketed horses, and just as quickly, although quietly, he set the tin plate by the fire, and without a word walked off into the dark.

"Little Prince" Love didn't hear the noise as quickly as his elders, but soon, he too identified the obvious—iron horseshoes clinking against river rock. A minute later, maybe less, old white-haired Dave Allison rode forward from the gloomy abyss of creepy shadows. He too, like the Mexican, was riding a good horse, but one that at least for the day had been hard-pressed and overworked. As soon as they recognized him, Dave Allison too, was offered the hand of cordiality. He stepped down, squatted by the fire and nonchalantly built a plate. Almost before he took the first bite, Dave Allison's eyes fell on the dish set by the fire—curiously, it wasn't empty. Even "Little Prince" could see the workings of Dave Allison's mind—counting campers and counting plates. Whether or not someone gave him the wink and nod, "Little Prince" never knew, but Dave Allison too set his plate close to the fire and disappeared into night's sinister snare. In a moment, the unmistakable sound of two disquieting gunshots reverberated through camp and across the river's never-ending meandering. Timelessly the ancient river flowed—keeping secrets to herself. Dave Allison moved back into the glimmering firelight and simply said, "He's gone!"

"Little Prince" Love never knew the whole story. There were yet some things little boys weren't privy to. He did remember, though, that night his daddy and Dave Allison traded horses—for keeps—and Dave rode away on the freshly recruited mount. And, not too long after Dave Allison departed—during the middle of the night—"Judge" Love hastily gathered his gear and scooted "Little Prince" Love back to Sierra Blanca. Later, on occasions "Little Prince" would see detective Dave Allison with his new horse as he ambled into or out of town. For sure, "Little Prince" Love couldn't testify to the exact fate of the missing Mexican vaquero, although he was convinced in his own little mind as to what had happened, but for certain, the horse his daddy got from Dave Allison—well, it became his favorite.[21]

During the third quarter of 1919, for whatever reason, at his own request or at the Association's behest, William Davis Allison left the Sierra Blanca country and took up a position at Post, Texas, a then booming community pleasantly located just below the caprock rim on the High Plains of cattle-country Texas. Adding to his already impressive string of law enforcement credentials, William Davis Allison, on September 15, 1919, was commissioned a Garza County Deputy by Sheriff Will Gravy.[22]

Founded in 1907, by the entrepreneurial cereal manufacturer and all around business genius, Charles W. Post, the community was budding forth as a principal illustration of just how much impact thoughtful irrigation and sound management theories could transform unfruitful and desolate West Texas ranchland into decidedly productive farmland.[23] By the time Dave Allison had arrived in thriving Post, the townsmen justifiably boasted about the elegantly furnished thirty room Algerita Hotel, the school system, the bank, churches, and a newspaper, but probably most proudly about the concrete reservoir 300 feet above the town.[24] C. W. Post, at a cost of $650,000 built Postex Cotton Mills in 1911, and it became the first plant in the United States "that received its cotton straight from the fields and turned out finished sheets and pillow cases…"[25] In fairness it's doubtful range detective W. D. "Dave" Allison gave much of a darn about bedcovers and cotton production niceties. He was a cow-country man and, despite the pleasantness of Post, most of the county was still defined by "rough, broken land, with playas, gullies, canyons, and Brazos River forks…"[26] And besides, Dave Allison's job demanded his movement throughout the whole region, an assigned territory "larger than many European principalities," not just confinement within Garza County boundary lines.[27]

An outing in the broken Garza County country. C. W. Post, breakfast cereal entrepreneur and founder of Post, Texas, standing far left. Courtesy, Garza County Historical Museum. Post, Texas.

Had he been there in Post, which he wasn't, Dave Allison no doubt would have marveled at the "rain battles" in which thousands of pounds of dynamite were set off, some even from the tails of kites, but all prayerfully designed to produce "measurable moisture by creating air turbulence when rain clouds were in the sky…"[28] The city of Post literally shook from the "cannonading," and no doubt Association Inspector Dave Allison would have disgustedly mumbled under his breath, "damn farmers!" Dave Allison would have had cow-work to do.

Two views of Post, Texas during the transitional period. Top, Algerita Hotel. Bottom, street scene. Away from town it was still wild and woolly. Courtesy, Garza County Historical Museum. Post, Texas

On one occasion, learning from an informant some cattle were going to be shipped in the "dead of night," which undeniably is not the normal mode of conducting legitimate cow-business, Dave Allison sent word to someone he unconditionally trusted, a youthful cowman, one who had started out as a line-camp cowboy, but whom was now independently burning his own lawful brand, Carl Rains. Dave Allison requested Rains meet him after dark at the cow pens two and a half miles north of Post. As the prescribed time grew closer, Rains buckled on his six-shooter, saddled up, and set off on the friendless ride to meet up with Allison. At the corrals, Dave Allison, whether he actually had the authority to do so or not, deputized Carl Rains and gave him a dented metal flashlight. The two lawmen then began checking the brands of the cattle captured for the clandestine midnight train ride to either the Fort Worth or Kansas City stockyards. The cattle belonged to a highly prominent Garza County cowman—well most of em'.[29]

Charging from the darkness rode the cowman. Dismounting he gruffly demanded to know what-in-the-heck was going on, and why anyone in the whole world could have the unmitigated gall to be inspecting his herd. On the ground Carl Rains made mental note as to just how shrewdly Dave Allison maneuvered, always keeping his gun on the side opposite the belligerently ranting and raving rancher, and using only his left hand to maintain a grip on his flashlight. The right hand—he always kept free. The hollered words became more heated and vile expletives were exchanged as Carl Rains uneasily looked on. The air became thick and seemed to be churning with cuss words and belligerent threats. Dave Allison was no fist fighter. If the confrontation was going to build-up into a hell-in-a-hand-basket mêlée it would be settled with barking six-shooters, not bare bloody knuckles. There wasn't too much light that night, but amid all the mooing and bellowing in that odorous cow-lot, and after intently staring and glaring into Dave Allison's eyes, the irate rancher without lingering turned his wrath on his own hired-help, sorely castigating them for getting his neighbor's steers intermixed with his own. Carl Rains breathed easier! Allison and Rains proceeded to sort the herd, turning out those cattle not belonging to the loud-mouthed cowman. As an Association man Dave Allison had done his rightful duty. Carl Rains admiringly looked on with respectful envy, toying himself with the idea of one day becoming a lawman. The rancher? Well, he just angrily stewed, forevermore, hating William Davis Allison for uncovering his *mistake* and messing up his pocketbook.[30]

In that Garza County country it was customary for Dave Allison while out snooping around, checking brands and trying to ferret out a few red-handed "Goddamn cow-thieves," to swap horses with cooperative and honest ranchers. When Dave's horse played out he would just slip it in to a friendly neighbor's corral, borrow one of their ranch horses and unobtrusively be gone. Sometimes for just one day—sometimes for several. It didn't matter. While away, he could always depend on his horse being exceptionally well cared for. Consequently, at area ranches Dave Allison soon developed a few favorite cow-ponies he much preferred to ride.[31]

One of those steeds belonged to the John W. James ranch. "Meddler" was a white gelding and one of Dave Allison's favorites. Because of his color, however, he was easy to spot at a distance and almost everyone knew Dave Allison would ride him at the drop of a hat. Therefore every owl-hoot in the county was alert; if off toward the horizon they spotted a rider on a white horse it very well just might be Dave Allison. Resourcefulness is but one attribute of an effective and tested investigator. On occasion, when borrowing ole "Meddler," Dave Allison would apply a little dab of black dye here and there, to some extent disguising the horse's overall appearance, at least from far-off examination. By the time the deception could be detected on a nearer approach, well, by then it was just too darn late.[32]

From the purely emotional outlook, Dave Allison, at times led a lonely life. During his tenure down in that Sierra Blanca country Dave lived by himself, dedicating his efforts to doing what he did best, investigating and chasing down cold-hearted criminals. Lena, his cherished wife, remained in Roswell taking care of her aging mother. When he moved to Post, Allison once again "batched," but when he had the chance, which wasn't as frequently as he wished, he traveled by automobile across the New Mexico line and spent several days with Lena before returning to duty in Texas.[33] Thankfully one such visit can be thoroughly documented, and truly, from the historic standpoint the visit is noteworthy.

That W. D. "Dave" Allison was personally allied with well-known Western personalities is factual: he had been a Texas Ranger Sergeant under the renowned Captain John Hughes; while he was an Arizona Ranger he attained the rank of Lieutenant, working for Thomas Rynning; Bill Greene, the Arizona and Mexico mining mogul knew him well; in that Sierra Blanca country he had taught an awe-struck Lt. George S. Patton Jr. a thing or two; during his range detective days he developed a friendship with the controversial reformed outlaw, Joe Horner, alias Frank Canton, who became Adjutant General for the state of Oklahoma;[34] and in a photograph made at Austin, Texas on June 23, 1920, clearly he is associating with a cadre of notable Texas lawmen, one of whom was the famous Texas Ranger, Frank A. Hamer. At the time the cited photo was snapped, W. D. "Dave" Allison was, too, a much heralded Southwestern lawmen.

Carl Rains, authentic Garza County cowboy, and later sheriff. About the time this photograph was made he was "deputized" by Dave Allison for a midnight cow-thieving investigation. Courtesy, Penny Rains, Garza County, Texas.

Penny Rains, widow of Carl Rains. She still actively ranches and was one of the author's delightful historical informants. Author's photo.

After his trip to Austin, Dave Allison returned to duty in West Texas, but by the closing week of September, 1920, in the company of a fellow Texas and Southwestern Cattle Raisers Association Inspector, R. C. Hopping, he had "worked the range," inspecting herds in the eastern part of Lea County, New Mexico.[35] Characteristically, Dave Allison was filtering rumors. There was some pretty fancy cow-stealing going on over around that remote Texas/New Mexico line.

During the Christmas season of 1920, Dave Allison made the lonesome trek to Roswell to see Lena and to visit with old friends. One of his many noteworthy friends, Charles A. Siringo, also happened to be in town. Formerly a cowboy, Pinkerton Detective, and by then a celebrated

Western author, Siringo and Dave Allison mulled over old times and chatted about mutual friends. Siringo who had written the book *A Lone Star Cowboy*, also had published 2000 copies of a forty-two page booklet containing his selection of a few favorite cowboy camp-songs[36]. The pamphlet sized volume was entitled, *The Song Companion of A Lone Star Cowboy*, and on New Years day he gifted Dave Allison with an autographed copy. The inscription read:

> *To Mr. Dave Allison—a cowboy of the old school—this little volume is presented as a New Years gift, with compliments of the author. Chas. A. Siringo. Roswell, N. Mex, Jan. 1st, 1921.* [37]

A hats-on photo of determined lawmen. Dave Allison, front and center. Austin, TX, June 23, 1920. Courtesy, Pat Treadwell, Tahoka, Texas.

After the holiday period Dave Allison returned to Post and resumed routine duties as an Association Inspector. To a career lawman, even today, most days of hard work and nights of lost sleep blend together into a cauldron of mundane repetitiveness and misunderstood monotony. To the uninitiated and uninformed, making an arrest is pretty exciting and heady stuff. However, to a truly experienced and older lawman, investigator, or man hunter, once the new wears off, the work just seems to go on day after day, nothing much to get excited about—most of the time. Such seems the case for Dave Allison's 1921 year. One report at the Texas and Southwestern Cattle Raisers Association archives reveals Dave Allison seized 31 head of stolen cattle.[38] From the historical standpoint, Dave Allison, during 1921, was sailing on reasonably calm waters. The storm, however, was on the horizon and it was brewing.

Dave Allison on duty as a Texas and Southwestern Cattle Raisers Association Inspector in the vicinity of Post, Texas. Note, one rifle in scabbard and another across saddle. Courtesy, Pat Treadwell, Tahoka, Texas.

On the pleasantly temperate summer morning of June 14, 1922, Dave Allison received information that one Milton Paul Good was in the process of moving cross-country a sizable herd of cattle branded "L F" on one side, a herd large enough to attract suspicion if for no other reason than because of who was trail-bossing the outfit. A personal inspection was called for.[39]

Milt Good had been born near Tularosa in what was then Lincoln County, New Mexico on March 17, 1889, but had moved with his family to Texas at an early age. And quite a family he had. His father Isham J.

Good had been depicted by a well-known Texas Ranger Captain as a "notorious cow thief."[40] His uncle, John Good had a deserved man killer reputation and, in fact, his cousin, Walter Good was one of those killed during a New Mexico feud involving the always controversial cattleman, Oliver Lee.[41] After reaching maturity Milt Good cowboyed on various West Texas ranches, eventually establishing his very own "Rail H" brand. However, after the drought of 1917, Milt Good sold the ranch at a staggering loss and commenced "tradin' cattle." A conquering and astute businessman, apparently Milt Good was not, but to take up the financial slack he turned to rodeo, and in 1920, at Shreveport, Louisiana, he was crowned the World's Champion Steer Roper. After the win he triumphantly returned to the level plains of West Texas cow-country, settled in the vicinity of Brownfield, rode loose herd over his eight children, and continued roping steers—*sometimes* his own.[42]

Realizing that a sizable task undeniably lay before him, if he earnestly intended on locating and personally inspecting Milt Good's, or *someone else's* cattle, Allison promptly telephoned Horace L. Roberson and requested a helping hand.[43] While he waited, Dave began reviewing rumors and mentally adding up those "two and two makes four" clues. As a detective, Dave was no slouch. At this stage in his colorful life he was by now well-seasoned in the ways of and cattle-country crooks. Allison sent the following wire:

> American Trust & Savings Bank.
> El Paso, Texas
>
> G. B. Armstrong of Roswell N. Mex—has cattle in Chaves and Lea Counties branded L on left shoulder and F on left hip. Does your bank hold mortgages covering those cattle, and will you prosecute those illegally handling or disposing of them in Texas. Answer explicitly.
>
> W. D. Allison, Inspector[44]

Dave Allison rightly wanted clarification, because the L F brand, depending which side of the cow creature it was burned into, could indicate two separate claims of ownership. If on the right side of cattle, it meant the animal belonged to the Littlefield Cattle Company of Texas; on the other side, however, G. B. Armstrong, owner of the Four Lakes ranch in New Mexico would have a legitimate demand.[45]

West Texas cowboy and lawman, W. M. "Bob" Beverly. He kept Dave Allison from fighting Milton Paul Good on the courthouse steps at Midland. Courtesy, Haley Memorial Library and History Center. Midland, Texas.

After receiving affirmative answers concerning prosecutions, conducting several personal interviews, and examining cattle mortgage records, on the night of June 19th, Allison was joined by Association Inspector H. L. Roberson, up from his post at Midland. The pair met at Lamesa, Texas. On the next morning they set out in a clattering Ford automobile to try and locate a slow moving herd in the vastness of West Texas ranch country. Actually finding the herd was an investigative challenge within itself. At one ranch the lawmen learned the herd had two days previously past by. At a local Post Office, the lawmen were appraised that a sluggishly moving cow-herd had passed by Cedar Lake—heading south. Continuing with their probing inquiries, Dave Allison and H. L. Roberson determined the herd had been watered on the sprawling

Higginbotham range. The Association detectives, at last, had the location of the sought after cattle pinpointed.[46]

The next morning, June 21st, after having spent the night at the Sulfur Camp on the Slaughter ranch with employees Frank Jones and E. S. Cornelius, Dave Allison and H. L. Roberson borrowed saddle horses and rode out to inspect the herd. Eating dinner with the cowboys at the wagon, Dave Allison asked Milt Good what he was going to do with the herd that night. After telling him he was going to take the beeves to a small pasture to the east, Allison told Good that he wanted to question him about ownership of the cattle. Good, Allen Holder, Pete Kyle, and the two Association Inspectors rode off from the herd about three hundred yards, dismounted and began their confab.[47]

During the conference, Milt Good, when initially questioned claimed ownership of the entire herd, less five cows owned by his brother-in-law, Kyle. Allen Holder was just working for wages.[48] Dave Allison continued the questioning:

> I then asked Milt Good where, when and from whom he got those 'L F' cows. He said that he got them in New Mexico, about two years ago, from G. B. Armstrong of the Four Lakes ranch. I asked him how much he paid for them, and he said he had rather not tell. I asked him how he paid for them, and he said he didn't know. I asked him if he bought those cattle on a credit, and he said he didn't know. I asked him what he did with the 1921 calf crop, and he said he cut them out from the cows at the J. J. Lane pasture, drove them to Brownfield and shipped them to market. I asked him what he did with that money that he got for those calves, he said he spent it.
>
> I asked him if he paid any part of that money to G. B. Armstrong, and he said 'no'. I then asked him from whom he had gotten the six head of young bulls with the figure '7' on the left hip. He answered 'from Doc Windham on a credit, and that he was to pay $65.00 apiece for them.
>
> I then asked him how he came in possession of several unmarked and unbranded cows, and he said he had traded for them. I asked him if he had any bills of sale or written instruments and he said that he did not have.

> I then asked him how many saddle horse he had in his remuda belonging to Ray Brownfield, and he said he had nine. I then asked him, 'didn't you have thirteen?' He said, 'yes, but I traded off four to Allen Holder for that black horse', which Holder was then holding.'[49]

Understanding the illicit implications derived from Good's interrogation, Dave Allison and H. L. Roberson began to cut the young bulls branded with the figure "7" from the herd for a closer inspection. Good himself told what happened next: "I asked them not to do that. Roberson had on two six-shooters and Allison had on one, and there was a .30-.30 Winchester there. Allison cussed me and said if I didn't get out of the way he would shoot me."[50] For just a split-second Good mused, and surely it flashed through his mind, for as one contemporary print journalist unequivocally pointed out, *fearless* Dave Allison had a solid "reputation for coolness in emergencies, and he was not an officer to be resisted by men who cared to keep their hides intact."[51] Bowled over, no doubt for his own culpable stupidity, Milt Good stepped aside.

Conclusively, Milt Good realized there wasn't a way out of his slimy self-imposed "Goddamn cow-thief" predicament, and he disgustedly blurted out, "Oh well, if they are you fellows cattle, just take them."[52]

And they did! Not for themselves, but over the course of the next several days the herd seized from Milt Good was sorted, and regional ranchers, many quite prominent, proved ownership and took individual possession of their stolen livestock. Most of the stolen cattle belonged to the Littlefield Cattle Company and were released to ranch manager, J. P. White.[53] Cowmen were euphoric. Everyone that is, but Milt Good, Pete Kyle, and Allen Holder. News of the confiscation traveled the cow-country grapevine like a scorching West Texas prairie fire. Not unexpectedly partisan, but nevertheless printing an unqualified truth, the very next edition of *The Cattleman*, under the caption "**Five Hundred and Sixteen Head of Stolen Cattle Recovered**" eloquently praised their revered inspector's accomplishment:

> Fiction records many instances of wholesale cattle theft, but very few cases have been actually encountered which would rival a deal brought to light by the activities of Inspectors W. D. Allison and H. L. Roberson of the Texas & Southwestern Cattle Raisers' Association...As a result

complaints charging theft of cattle have been filed against Milt P. Good, Pete Kyle, and Allen Holder in Hockly, Lynn and Terry Counties. Trials in these cases will come up some time this fall or winter...Too much cannot be said of the good work done by Inspectors Allison and Roberson in this matter. Even at present market values many thousands of dollars were saved to the collective owners...[54]

Milton Paul "Milt" Good, cowboy, World Champion Steer Roper, suspected West Texas cow-thief, twice convicted killer, and a failed prison escapee. Courtesy, Panhandle-Plains Historical Museum. Canyon, Texas.

Salty old-timers too can take pleasure in victory. Dave Allison and H. L. Roberson, at least for the short go, were real heroes!

Milton Paul Good, after the indictments, however, would not have characterized the Association men as cow-camp champions. He was mad! In telling stories based on fact there isn't too much room for speculative commentary as to what would have, could have, or should have happened. On the courthouse steps in Midland, Milt Good and Dave Allison came face to face with each other, each with their hand on their six-shooters, but were separated by Bob Beverly who "...stood between them, one in each hand and held them apart...," and warned them, "Neither one of you men will kill me and I won't let you kill each other."[55] Hopefully, the men bought Bob Beverly a beer.

William Davis Allison was on a roll, at least he thought so. In the Spring he had filed as a candidate for Garza County Sheriff in the Democratic Primary and his recent investigation in the Good case surely couldn't hurt his political chances.[56] A cursory going over of Allison's personal *Brand and Expense Book* reveals he was campaigning throughout the county, expending funds on printing, postage stamps, vehicle operating expenses, and according to the entries, he was passing out a not inconsiderable amount of cigars, candy, and gum.[57] When the votes were tallied the Association Inspector came out on top: Allison, 418; Will Gravy 311; J. W. Stotts, 309; C. W. Word, 101.[58] Unfortunately for Dave though, his triumph was not of ample margin to preclude an August 26th runoff election and, in the end, when other candidates numbers were redistributed William Davis Allison came out second best.[59] At sixty-two years of age, Dave knew it had been his last political race, but yet, he too knew for sure, his cow-county career wasn't over.

Making the deliberate political decision to run against his incumbent boss—and then loosing—cost him the Garza County deputyship. A dilemma quickly remedied by his appointment as a Deputy United States Marshal, which in itself is indication of Dave Allison's broadly based favorable reputation, and also, once again highlights liberal influence the Texas and Southwestern Cattle Raisers Association had over Lone Star State law enforcement affairs.[60] Dave Allison was obliged to maintain official peace officer status; there were still plenty of "Goddamn cow-thieves" out West Texas way!

And one of them was that guy Hillary Loftis, but for years now he had simply been known as Tom Ross. Tom's 5000 acre ranch straddled the State Line 25 miles west of Seminole, Texas, part of it in Lea County, New Mexico, the other in Gaines County, Texas.[61] He got his mail at

Knowles, New Mexico.[62] For a living he "began to traffic and trade in livestock, but continued his old habit of ignoring such trifles as titles, bills of sale or brands."[63]

If William Davis Allison was *fearless*, so was Tom Ross. If Horace L. Roberson could be dangerously mean, so could Tom Ross. Allison and Roberson worked on one side of the legality line, Tom Ross on the other and; if truth be known, he didn't fear man, nor beast—nor the law. And not unlike so many of the outlaw profession, Tom Ross was a charmer, charismatic, and according to one writer, he had "a certain Robin Hood appeal."[64] Smiling or not, he wasn't someone to monkey with. According to several neighbors, Tom Ross had sworn that no Association man would ever set foot on his ranch—and live to tell about it.[65]

Among his other character traits, Tom Ross was adaptable. Living on the *transitional frontier* he shelved his old single-action six-shooters and replaced them with modern .45 caliber automatic pistols, saying he "preferred it to a six-shooter because it is quicker and doesn't jam." Furthermore, Ross declared he favored the automatic because "it was to the old six-shooter what lightening was to the wind."[66] Reportedly, he was consistently capable of shooting a pheasant or prairie chicken on the fly, rarely if ever missing.[67] The steadfastly committed chronicler of cow-country tales, J. Frank Dobie, said Ross could "...ride a horse at full speed along a fence, hitting every post center."[68] Whether the portrayal of his marksmanship is unerringly accurate or not, Tom Ross had the dead-bang reputation, among other things, of being one of the best pistol shots in West Texas.

One of those other "things" Ross had a reputation for was mentioned by southeastern New Mexico lawmen Dee Harkey, "I liked Tom personally, but it seemed he was just not happy unless he was fixing some way to rob someone. He started to stealing cattle."[69] Maybe it's best to go straight to the horse's mouth, Tom Ross himself said, "I was born to steal, and don't know any other way."[70]

Mary Whatley Clarke, while a young school teacher out in that Western cow-country, knew Tom Ross personally. Impressed with her youthful charm and indisputable concern for her pupils, one day Ross offered her a buggy ride from the one-room schoolhouse to her aunt's residence, where she was staying. On the trip Tom Ross mentioned that he was just going to "brand some calves" for her and that in a few years she would have a herd of her own. As the amiable but not necessarily naïve schoolmarm, who was acquainted with Tom's wide-loop repute, later penned, "He never did, thank goodness."[71]

It seems quite likely the petite educator had not been attuned to all of the rumors wafting back and forth across that Texas/New Mexico line, if she had, perhaps she would have even forgone stepping up and planting her bustle on the wagon-seat beside Tom Ross. Men had disappeared in the vicinity of the Tom Ross ranch—without trace. He was the prime suspect of course, as far as the gossip went, but no evidence had ever been developed to perfect a prosecutable case. One time on his ranch the corpse of a Hispanic cowhand was found burned to a grotesque crisp, and only through dental work was the deceased positively identified.[72] An instance of *transitional* forensic work to be sure, but still, in the final analysis, an unsolved mystery. There was even another rumor circulating that Association man H. L. Roberson was gathering evidence revolving around the death of a Mexican bootlegger, and that he was pretty darn close to having the case made—against Tom Ross.[73] Tom Ross had plenty of cow-country friends, and they too heard the whispered rumors, but discreetly they abstained from giving them any credit, at least within earshot. One well-seasoned Association investigator later remarked, "I'll never forget how frightened the folks were of Tom Ross, they were afraid to tell me anything for fear Ross would have them killed. Several witnesses shook as if they had palsy when talking with me, and closed up like a book."[74]

He too had his enemies, mainly "those who suspected him of being more or less of a cow stealer," but most of them prudently gave the Ross ranch the "go-by."[75] And, as one contemporary journalist pithily penned, Tom Ross "had a superior capacity for loving and for hating."[76]

Maybe in rousing annals of the American West there were tougher people and rougher places—sometime and somewhere—but in 1922, on the *transitional frontier* in that corner of Texas that butts up against New Mexico, with Dave Allison, H. L. Roberson, and Tom Ross all prowling around, it was just a matter of time before a ferocious explosion would send shock waves rippling through Llano Estacado grasslands, and across the nation—and it wouldn't necessitate a Stuart Lake or a Walter Noble Burns to make it real.

During the earlier investigation into the dubious activities of Milt Good, which technically was Dave Allison's case, fellow Association Inspector Horace L. Roberson had lent a helping hand. The situation now reversed, with Roberson attempting to make a rock-solid criminal case on the scheming Tom Ross, supported by able assistance from W. D. "Dave" Allison.[77] Without a shred of doubt they made a "formidable detective team."[78]

The pair of lawmen systematically began their investigation, conducting intensive interviews and pocketing cow-county clues as they developed them. Their sleuthing, however, was no secret. According to a respected scholar who looked in on the matter, "…Roberson made several intemperate remarks to Ross's fellow cattlemen, not the least of which was that he knew Ross was leading a gang of cattle thieves from his ranch and that he would either jail him or kill him, as the need arose."[79] To what degree reported rhetoric is actually verbatim, of course, is inconsequential. Whether or not Roberson actually remarked that he was "going to get him and put him in the penitentiary as a cow thief," or that "if he wanted to shoot it out to come down the street with his pistol in his hand," Tom Ross supposed he had said it.[80] Tom Ross was not happy!

Tom Ross himself alleged that Roberson had approached a boy who worked for him, Roy "Alkali" Adams, and had attempted to dissuade him from continued employment at the Ross ranch, encouraging him to "flip" and become "State's Evidence," and afterward Roberson would then "favor him in every way."[81] Bert Weir ran to Ross with allegations that Roberson had remarked it made no difference to him if Ross was indeed "awful quick with a gun."[82] In addition it is alleged that Walter McGonigil, one of Milt Good's rodeo roping pals, told Ross that Roberson was going to make his West Texas reputation by getting him "one way or the other."[83] Tom Ross may have buffaloed some of the surrounding cowmen, but definitely not Roberson or Allison. On one occasion, at Lovington, New Mexico, Dave Allison openly declared that Tom Ross was the "instigator and the brains" of all the cattle stealing in the area. When told that he and Roberson were going to "stir up a lot of trouble," Allison allegedly remarked: "That won't amount to a thing in the world, Roberson will kill him."[84]

Infuriating Tom Ross, more than anything else, was his knowledge that Roberson (and probably Allison) had visited his ranch on November 11, 1922, while he had been confined in a Lubbock hospital as a result of agonizing gallstone surgery.[85] He pathetically whined that Roberson had inspected and "choused" his cattle around while he was indisposed at Lubbock, and the Association men had, without his authorization, driven off three cows in his absence.[86] Perhaps H. L. Roberson and Dave Allison went to the Ross ranch knowing Tom was under the weather at Lubbock, not necessarily an unwise stratagem while on a thorny fact-finding job, or perhaps they went to the ranch not having the slightest inkling as to his whereabouts—and not giving a damn! Either way, one could walk to the pay-window knowing Association Inspectors Roberson and Allison didn't steal those cows—confiscated, yes.

As a result of investigation at the Ross ranch, coupled with ancillary incriminating proofs, and after positive identification of a few head of legitimately branded cattle standing in the wrong pen, or otherwise, a case of beeves sporting blotched brands standing in Tom's pen, the two Association sleuths were successful in building an air-tight criminal case of sufficient merit to be accepted by the prosecuting attorney for presentation to a local Grand Jury. During the November term of District Court, 1922, charges of cattle theft were filed against Tom Ross at Lovington, the county seat of Lea County, New Mexico, for stealing cattle rightfully belonging on the M. Wilhoit ranch. Tom Ross was indicted.[87] Likewise, over in the Lone Star State, as an effect of their problematic perseverance, Texas and Southwestern Cattle Raisers Association Inspectors Dave Allison and Horace L. Roberson, charted an inescapable date for their pal, Tom Ross—with a Gaines County Grand Jury.[88]

ENDNOTES
Chapter 9. "Always shoot the horse of an escaping man."

[1] Ibid, P. 109. And see, **Blumenson**, P. 317-375. Also see, *Chasing Villa—The Last Campaign of the U. S. Cavalry*, by Colonel Frank **Tompkins**. Also see, **Ritter**, Al, "Captain Fox's Colt," *HANDGUNS*, February 1997. P. 46.
[2] *Letter* of William Davis Allison, Sierra Blanca, Texas, to Lena Allison, Roswell, New Mexico, April 4, 1916. Courtesy **Treadwell**.
[3] Typescript, remarks of former Arizona Ranger Sergeant Arthur A. Hopkins. Courtesy Bill **O'Neal**, Panola College, Carthage, Texas.
[4] *Letter* of William Davis Allison to Lena Allison, April 4, 1916. Courtesy, **Treadwell**.
[5] *Letter* of William Davis Allison to Hazel Allison, April 4, 1916. Courtesy, **Treadwell**.
[6] Correspondence to the author from Michael E. **Pilgrim**, Old Military and Civil Records, Textual Archives Service Division, National Archives and Records Administration, Washington, D. C., November 9, 2000. Mr. Pilgrim had searches made trying to locate information relating to Dave Allison's civilian employment as a military scout, which included; Record Group 94, Records of the Adjutant General's Office; RG 92, Records of the Office of Quartermaster General; RG 395, Records of U. S. Army Overseas Operations and Commands, 1898-1942 (which includes records relating to the Punitive Expedition to Mexico, 1916-1917), and no record could be found.
[7] **Bolling**, P. 67.
[8] Interview with Bill **Love**, Sierra Blanca, Texas March 14, 2001.
[9] *Letter*, E. B. Spiller, Secretary, Texas and Southwestern Cattle Raisers Association, Fort Worth, Texas to James E. Ferguson, Governor, Austin, Texas, April 11, 1917. Courtesy Texas State Library and Archive Commission, Austin.
[10] Ibid. And see, *Enlistment, Oath of Service, and Description Ranger Force*, dated January 19, 1918, which also reflects Allison's April 1917 Special Ranger Enlistment. Courtesy Texas State Library and Archives Commission, Austin.
[11] *Warrant of Authority and Descriptive List*, W. D. Allison, January 11, 1918. Courtesy, Texas Ranger Museum and Hall of Fame. Waco. And see, *Report of Executive Committee, Report of Inspections Work, 1919*. Texas and Southwestern Cattle Raisers Association. Courtesy, Texas and Southwestern Cattle Raisers Association, Library and Archives, Fort Worth.
[12] *Enlistment, Oath of Service, and Description, Ranger Force*. H. L. Roberson, dated May 8, 1916. Courtesy, Texas State Library and Archives Commission, Austin. And see, *Executive Committee, Report of Inspection Work-1921*. "Inspector—H. L. Roberson; Location—Magdalena, N. M.; No. Caught—39. Courtesy, Texas and Southwestern Cattle Raisers Museum, Library and Archives. Fort Worth.
[13] *The Cattleman*, May, 1923. P. 15.
[14] **Perkins**, Doug and **Ward**, Nancy. *Brave Men & Cold Steel—A History of Range Detectives and Their Peacemakers*. P. 22-23. Hereafter cited as **Perkins & Ward**.
[15] **Blumenson**, P. 298.
[16] Ibid. Whether Allison and Patton actually engaged in a hunt together is undetermined, however, the future World War II General did write in a letter to

his wife, "He (Allison) seemed much taken with me and is going hunting with me."
[17] Ibid., P. 333.
[18] Ibid., P. 298.
[19] **Means**, P. 74.
[20] **Bolling**, as quoted in **Means**, P. 159.
[21] Interview with Bill **Love,** the son of Baylus Prince Love, at Sierra Blanca, Texas on March 14, 2001. After telling the story to the author, one which he had heard many times from his father, Bill Love was asked, "haven't you told this story to other writers or historians, I have never seen it in print before?" **Love**, with typical West Texas stoicism simply replied, "No, nobody ever asked me." Implausible at it may seem, no journalists have ever questioned Bill **Love**, a descendant of B. N. "Judge" Love who actually rode in the posse chasing Pascual Orozco, Jr., captained by W. D. "Dave" Allison.
[22] *County Clerk Certification* of appointment for W. D. Allison as Deputy Sheriff, dated September 15, 1919, and re-appointment dated December 4, 1920, signed Ira Weakley, Garza County Clerk, Post, Texas. Courtesy, Texas State Library and Archives Commission, Austin.
[23] *Post City, Texas—Reflections by Garza County Historical Museum*, written by **Cornish**, Jim. Hereafter cited as **Cornish**. Courtesy, Linda **Puckett**, Director, Garza Historic Museum, Post, Garza County, Texas.
[24] Ibid.
[25] Ibid. Products produced at the Postex Mill were manufactured under the trade name GARZA, from the name of the county. And see, *The New Handbook of Texas*, Volume V, P. 290.
[26] **Kingston**, P. 204.
[27] *The Cattleman*, October, 1923. Volume IX, No. 5. P. 9.
[28] **Cornish**, n. p. n.
[29] Interview with Penny **Rains**, and her granddaughter, Ryn **Rains**, at their Garza County ranch, August 15, 2000. Penny, originally from Josephine, Collin County, Texas, at an early age moved to West Texas. At Post she was courted by Carl Rains, a local cowboy, later becoming a rancher himself. Also, Carl Rains served as Garza County Sheriff. The couple were married in 1925 at Post, Texas.
[30] Ibid. Penny **Rains**, although she furnished the author with the name of the belligerent misappropriating rancher, she asked that it not be used in Allison's biography— his descendants still live in Garza County. Her wishes are honored.
[31] Ibid. When asked the obvious question, "Penny how come Dave Allison was riding horses from ranch to ranch, weren't their automobiles at the time?" Smartly she replied to the author's inquiry. "Yes, at the time there were plenty of autos in town, but between ranches there weren't many roads." It was, after all, still a *transitional frontier*.
[32] Ibid.
[33] **Perkins & Ward**. P. 22. Although it was indeed difficult for Lena and Dave Allison at the time, their long separations, from the historic standpoint have produced valuable primary source materials in the form of letters written by W. D. "Dave" Allison.
[34] **DeArment**, Robert K., *Alias Frank Canton*. P. 303. "Canton had known Allison and Roberson well…"
[35] *Lovington Leader*, October 1, 1920.
[36] **Pingenot**, Ben E., *SIRINGO*. P. 94.

[37] Autographed copy of *The Song Companion of A Lone Star Cowboy*, courtesy **Treadwell**.
[38] *Report of Executive Committee*, 1921. Texas and Southwest Cattle Raisers Association. Courtesy, Texas and Southwest Cattle Raisers Museum, Library and Archives. Fort Worth.
[39] *Affidavit* of W. D. Allison for *The State of Texas vs. Milt P. Good, et al.* Courtesy, **Treadwell**. This is the affidavit Dave Allison prepared for the testimony he was to present to the Grand Jury. Hereafter cited as **Allison**—*Affidavit*. Also see, W. D. Allison's *Brand and Expense Book*. Courtesy, Texas and Southwest Cattle Raisers Association Museum, Library and Archives. Fort Worth. Hereafter cited as *Brand and Expense Book*.
[40] **DeArment**, P. 16. C. L. **Sonnichsen** in *Tularosa—Last of the Frontier West*, characterized Milt Good's daddy, Isham. "John and his brother Isham had been close to trouble some time. In the lonesome limestone hills west of Austin they were well, if not favorably, known. There they held their own with the rough characters who haunted the cedar brakes and periodically blasted each other into eternity." P. 18.
[41] Ibid. Walter Good was killed and his body left in New Mexico's White Sands, allegedly as payback for the death of Oliver Lee's close friend, George McDonald.
[42] **Good**, Milt. *Twelve Years In A Texas Prison*. P. 8-10. Hereafter cited as **Good**. And see, Texas Prison Interview, Milt Good, aka E. Kyle, Inmate No. 97300. Courtesy, Texas State Library and Archives Commission. Austin.
[43] *Brand and Expense Book*. Entry, June 15, 1922. "Phone to H. L. Roberson at Midland—$1.00."
[44] *Telegram* to American Trust & Savings Bank, June 17, 1922, from W. D. Allison. Courtesy, Texas and Southwestern Cattle Raisers Association Museum, Library and Archives. Fort Worth.
[45] *The Cattleman*, July 1922, Volume 9, No. 2, P. 15.
[46] **Allison**—*Affidavit* And see, *The New Handbook of Texas*, Volume III, P. 45. "Cedar Lake in northeastern Gaines County is the largest slat lake on the Texas plains."
[47] Ibid.
[48] Ibid.
[49] Ibid. Also see, *Brand and Expense Book*, "Recovered 13 Head of Saddle Horses leased to Milt Good."
[50] *The Abilene Reporter*, September 19, 1923.
[51] *The St. Louis Post-Dispatch*, July 22, 1923.
[52] **Allison**—*Affidavit*.
[53] Ibid.
[54] *The Cattleman*, July 1922, Volume 9, No. 2. P. 15.
[55] **DeArment**, P. 16. And see, Typescript, Bob Beverly to J. Evetts **Haley**, March 24, 1945. Courtesy, Nita Stewart Haley Memorial Library and J. Evetts Haley History Center. Midland.
[56] *Tabulated Statement of Garza County Democratic Primaries*, July 22, 1922. Garza County District Clerk, Post, Texas. Courtesy, Garza Historic Museum, Post, Texas. Hereafter cited as *Tabulated Election Returns*.
[57] *Brand and Expense Book*. "Cigars and gum—$5.20." "Cigars and candy—$2.90."
[58] *Tabulated Election Returns*.

---

[59] Garza Historic Museum, Post, Texas.

[60] Dayton Moses, Attorney, Texas and Southwestern Cattle Raisers Association, Fort Worth, to Mrs. W. D. Allison, Roswell, April 5, 1923. "I wish you would send me Dave's commission as Deputy United States Marshal, so that I can put it in my file, as we will want to show that he was a peace officer, and entitled to carry a six-shooter at the time of his death." Courtesy, **Treadwell**. Also see, *St. Louis Post-Dispatch*, July 29, 1923. And see, *The Abilene Reporter*, September 12, 1923. "W. D. Allison had been a cattle inspector off and on for 30 years. At the time of his death he was also a United States deputy marshal." Also see, *The Seminole Sentinel*, April 5, 1923. "Dave Allison was formerly sheriff of Midland County, but for the Cattle Raiser's Association, and at the time of his death also held a commission as Deputy United States Marshall…"

[61] **Clarke (II)**, P. 62. And see, *St. Louis Post Dispatch*, July 29, 1923. Gaines County on the southern High Plains of West Texas, butting up against the New Mexico boundary line, was until modern times truly frontier territory, Comanche country, and reportedly the birth place of Quanah Parker. "The United States census reported only eight people in the county in 1880." *The New Handbook* of *Texas*. Volume III, P. 45.

[62] Ibid.

[63] **Sterling**, P. 379.

[64] **Clarke**, P. 146.

[65] **Fenton (II)**, P. 90.

[66] *St. Louis Post-Dispatch,* July 15, and July 29, 1923.

[67] Ibid.

[68] **Dobie**, J. Frank. *COW PEOPLE.* P. 247. Hereafter cited as **Dobie**.

[69] **Harkey**, P. 208.

[70] **DeArment**, P. 15.

[71] **Clarke (II)**, P. 60.

[72] *Lubbock Avalanche-Journal*, September 25, 1949.

[73] **DeArment**, P. 16.

[74] **Clarke**, P. 147. The belligerent reputation of Tom Ross was such, that at least on one occasion, a person falsely assumed his name just to scare another party. "This man really was not Hill Loftos (sic), but he told Ed that was his name, because he knew of Loftos' (sic) bad reputation as a fighter, and he wanted Ed to be afraid of him." See, **Sullivan**, W. J. L. "Twelve Years In The Saddle For Law And Order on the Frontiers of Texas." *Old West*. Spring, 1967. P. 86.

[75] *St. Louis Post-Dispatch*, July 29, 1923.

[76] Ibid. Of Ross, the reporter went on to write, "Highly hospitable to those he liked, it was a dangerous business for anybody against whom Ross had a grudge or a grouch to happen along in his vicinity."

[77] **Perkins & Ward**. P. 25.

[78] Ibid., P. 23.

[79] **Fenton (II)**, P. 91.

[80] **Clarke**, P. 145-146.

[81] *The Semi-Weekly Farm News*, April 17, 1923.

[82] Ibid.

[83] Ibid.

[84] *The Abilene Reporter*, September 13, 1923.

---

[85] *The Abilene Reporter*, September 12, 1923. **Pettey** reports that Roberson was accompanied by Gaines County Sheriff Cleve Cobb (his term was to expire on December 31, 1922) and does not mention Allison. P. 138.

[86] *The Semi-Weekly Farm News*, April 17, 1923.

[87] *267 Southwestern Reporter, Good v. State* (No. 8608), P. 508. "…Moreover, from the bill as qualified and the evidence in the case we understand that the cattle involved in the indictment belonged to Mrs. Wilhoit, and involved cattle taken both in Gaines County (which borders on New Mexico) and in New Mexico..." And see, *The Cattleman*, October, 1923. Volume IX, No. 5., P. 10.

[88] Ibid. And see, *The State of Texas vs. Tom Ross*. Indictment. No. 54. Theft of Cattle. Gaines County, Texas. Courtesy, Virginia **Stewart**, District Clerk, Gaines County, Seminole, Texas.

10

"I jerked the gun and pushed off the safety"

Unquestionably satisfied that investigative resolve, at long last, was going to pay major dividends in a sometimes overwhelming struggle to police the pastures, Association men Dave Allison and Horace Roberson returned to their respective cattle ranges and once more resumed normal duties. The cases against Milt Good, they both knew, were dead-on-the-money, and as for Tom Ross, well, he was already suffering the New Mexico cattle theft indictment, and on April 2, 1923, evidence of his thievery in the Lone Star case was to be presented at Seminole, Texas, for a Gaines County Grand Jury to think about. One way or the other, it seemed like Tom Ross too, was penitentiary bound.

Gaines Hotel, Seminole, Texas. The scene of the murderous crime. Courtesy, Heritage Center Museum, Seminole, Texas.

Decades of first-rate experience weren't wasted. Dave Allison knew to take advantage of the impermanent lull pertaining to his law enforcement tasks, and quickly scooted over to Roswell for a agreeable rendezvous with Lena. Interestingly, by examining his monthly expense report, it can be determined that besides gas and oil for the Ford, Dave Allison bought a cardboard box of .45 caliber cartridges for $2.50 and paid $1.00 for a felt-covered gallon canteen.[1] By the 23rd of March (1923), Dave Allison was lazily working his way back toward his bachelor-type quarters at Post. After managing stops at Portales, New Mexico, and Bovina, Littlefield, Lubbock, and Slaton, Texas, the Association man rolled into Post on the evening of the 27th.[2]

Next morning at the post office, Dave Allison picked up his mail. One of the several letters addressed to him was from Texas and Southwestern Cattle Raisers Association Secretary, E. B. "Berk" Spiller, who unequivocally directed Dave to "attend Seminole court without fail."[3] Most assuredly fellow Association detective H. L. Roberson received equivalent marching orders. In an enlightening letter to his wife, Allison acknowledged he would soon be traveling to Seminole, but would write her another letter before departing on the trip.[4]

Down Midland way, H. L. Roberson, cross-deputized as a Midland County deputy, too, was amicably fiddling around with customary constabulary duties, nothing out of the ordinary or spine-tingling. From appearances, if one didn't know better, Roberson with his snap-brim hat slightly cocked to the side, might have been mistaken for a smartly dressed businessman or merchant, at least when he was right there in town. And that was exactly where he was living, not camped out at some stinky cow-camp windmill or secluded on an off the beaten track West Texas ranch. Although late in life, Roberson, just two years earlier had married Miss Martha Plummer, a highly qualified professional nurse and hospital administrator from San Antonio.[5] The couple lived in Midland, next door to Porter and Julia Rankin. Julia was the daughter of one of Dave Allison's most fervent friends and staunchest supporters, "Lish" Estes, and the mother of Nancy (McKinley). In a much simpler time, when Nancy was just a wee sprout, she fondly remembers her prized possession was a bright red coat with gold buttons. Pleasantly she recalls, every school day morning she walked in front of the Roberson's house. Often were the times when Horace L. Roberson, that ham-fisted and fearsome looking Association man, would be standing on his front porch gingerly sipping from a steaming cup of hot tea, and he always could be counted on to teasingly remark, "I can't go to work till my little redbird passes by."

Nancy just blushed, but from with inside she thought the pleasant comment delightfully funny.[6]

Hill Loftis, aka Tom Ross, aka Charlie Gannon, convicted murderer, Texas prison inmate, escapee, and wily fugitive. Courtesy, Haley Memorial Library and History Center. Midland, Texas.

To the north of Midland, however, nothing was hilarious to Tom Ross and Milt Good, not anymore. Each day that passed brought them that much closer to trials, and as they both knew, that damn April 2nd meeting with the Gaines County Grand Jury was still on tap. While Dave Allison and Horace Roberson nonchalantly went about everyday business, Ross and Good each at their own respective ranch headquarters, agonized—gloomily! Eavesdropping over the party line might have blistered an ear.

As the weekend approached, on Friday, March 30th, Milt Good sauntered down an agreeably broad Brownfield street and into Albert Enderson's mercantile store. For the purchase price of one dollar the suspected cow-thief and indicted steer roper bought fifteen ".45 automatic cartridges."[7] Just enough it seems to stuff one in the firearm's chamber and have two fully loaded magazines, one in the pistol and one in a pant's pocket.

On Saturday, March 31st, Milton Paul Good, seemingly conceding to churning internal pressure, went to the local Santa Fe Railroad depot at Brownfield. At the train station, ticket agent Ella Detro quite naturally asked Good his intended destination and he hastily responded "just as far that way as possible" pointing in a southerly direction. Ms. Detro said jokingly, "I'll just book you through to Seminole then," although the terminus extended only as far south as Seagraves. Milt Good replied, "that will suit me fine, that is where I'm going, and I'm rearing to get there." Why she said it we will never know, but Mrs. Detro then remarked, "You must be going there to whip someone," and Milt Good countered, "yes, or get whipped, maybe." And again, she quipped, "Well, just going down there looking for trouble then? Good answered, "Well, I do not know but that I am."[8]

At Seagraves, Milt Good may not have seen the local banker, Jim Williams, but the financier saw him step off the train, and later watched him riding around town with Tom Ross. Also, Williams made mental note that during the day he observed Milt Good huddled with his pal Walter McGonigal and Tom Ross's man, Roy "Alkali" Adams. Still later he looked on as Good and Ross drove out of town in Tom's Ford.[9]

So they say, Tom Ross's wife, Trixie, fixed dinner, and after the meal they all "went to a pasture five miles southwest to help gather up some cows." After gathering the cattle, and returning home, Tom Ross put his rifle and shotgun into the Ford convertible. He, by his own words, was never without at least one pistol, usually a .45 automatic, and the majority of the time sported two. Trixie and Tom exchanged a brief farewell, and he and Milt Good headed for Seminole.[10] Saturday darkness finally overtook the solemn travelers about two-thirds of the way to Seminole, and lacking crystal-clear clarification to the contrary, it is generally thought the pair camped out for the night, although the distance to their final destination was short.[11] Listening in on their late-night conversation is historically speculative—it is not, however, difficult to imagine.

While Tom Ross and Milt Good were making plans and starting on their sneaky trip to Seminole, Dave Allison too was making preparations. In Post, at Mrs. Floyds', knowing his items would be ready because she had promised him a Saturday delivery even if she had to "dry them by the stove," he picked up two suits which she had cleaned and pressed for

$3.50, an "old every day suit" for the trip and a "blue suit" for proper courtroom attire. With gasoline in the auto, $35.00 cash in his pocket, and his reliable Colt six-shooter cleaned and oiled, Dave Allison only had time to kill until his early Sunday morning departure. At the boarding house Dave sat down and penned another letter to Lena. Out of the blue, so to speak, Dave Allison felt a pessimistic premonition and wrote, "*Now for your information and guidance in case of any misfortune to me...*" and then he appraised his wife how much money the Association owed him—salary and expenses—and he called her attention to where his five $1000 insurance polices were located. After making sure he didn't receive any news update from Roswell on the two o'clock afternoon train, Dave, in part, wrote:

> *The mail had nothing from you so I suppose nothing more will be heard, unless extraordinary, until after Seminole Court. It is uncertain the time to be spent there...I will know by Monday night, and will then write fully: If the sign is right I will go on from there to Roswell. Now don't fret...*[12]

At Midland, the Robersons too were making ready for the trip to Seminole and the scheduled meeting of the Gaines County Grand Jury. Horace L. had lots to tell about that "Goddamn cow-thief" Tom Ross. On this trip, Martha was going to accompany her husband, something she frequently did when he traveled the local area. And besides, the next day was Sunday, Easter Sunday, and there was positively no reason for her to sit home alone while her beloved husband was simply going to Seminole for court. It would be a nice outing, and perhaps they would even stop along the way on a remote stretch of dusty country road and plink at some rusty tomato cans or pop bottles. H. L. was in the process of teaching her to shoot a handgun, and she was taking enthusiastic pleasure in the lessons. Martha was making a surprisingly apt pupil.[13]

From a historical viewpoint it's equitable to presume Milt Good and Tom Ross weren't playing practical jokes on each other, even though, as it popped up from the eastern horizon, the morning sun was cracking first light over a brand new April Fool's Day. And equally, it's reasonable to proffer the pair didn't kneel before the Cross or pitch silver coins in the offering plate that Easter Sunday morning. Factually, even though Tom Ross and Milt Good had but a little way to go that day, they lolly-gagged. It wouldn't do for them to get to Seminole—too soon!

William Davis Allison, although a headache had been bothering him all day, finally reached Seminole about five o'clock in the afternoon, and promptly went to the Gaines Hotel. Whether he had telephoned ahead to reserve one of the eleven rooms, we cannot be sure, but for certain, the proprietor, Mrs. Jim Averett, welcomed him with a cordial smile and West Texas hospitality. At Seminole, since its wood-frame construction in 1907, the landmark Gaines Hotel had been a "center of activity" for area cowmen.[14] After hanging up the blue suit in his upstairs room, Dave Allison took a seat in the hotel lobby, resting, waiting, and conversing with sixty-nine year-old lawyer, Judge N. R. Morgan, who boarded at the hotel.[15]

Around six o'clock in the evening H. L. and Martha Roberson marched up the three outside steps, walked through the little lobby to the front desk, and registered their name in the guest book. Dave and H. L. affably shook hands, always thankful over the years, that the other's journey had proved free from unexpected hardship or hazard. The Robersons, Dave Allison, Judge Morgan, District Attorney Gordon B. McGuire, and most likely several others, had a pleasant supper prepared by Ms. Averett. After the meal, regrettably, Allison's nagging headache failed to abate, and graciously Judge Morgan, accompanied by another visitor, Will Cunningham, walked over to the local drugstore and procured a package of headache powder for Dave.[16]

Sometime thereabouts as darkness began to close in, and there is no exactness, cow-stealing suspects Tom Ross and Milton Good smartly slipped into sleepy Seminole, unannounced, unnoticed, and underestimated.

District Court sessions and Grand Jury meetings had always been big doings in scattered Western communities, and even on the 1923 *transitional frontier* the local legal proceedings were the talk of the town and categorically worthy of especial interest. Accordingly the modest lobby at the Gaines Hotel seemingly began to bulge as first one person and then another, most of them actually scheduled with business before next day's court, entered, pulled up a chair, lit a cigar, and caught up on the latest news or simply shot the breeze with friends and colleagues.

Pushing the room to near overflowing capacity, were of course, Association men, Dave Allison and H. L. Roberson. Adding to the conglomeration were the three lawyers, Morgan, McGuire, and George E. Lockhart, of Tahoka, who was, in point of fact, there to act as counsel for Tom Ross the next morning. Also in attendance was an unarmed Gaines County Sheriff, Frank L. Britton, who had stopped by after changing his mind about going to Church. Rounding out the assemblage were "substantial local citizens" Bill Birdwell, a Gaines County farmer, and William "Billy" Williams, who, as a newsman wittingly remarked, "were not Judges even by brevet."[17]

Martha Roberson, as the cramped quarters filled with tobacco smoke and quite probably the pungent scent of bourbon vapors escaping from pint flasks, politely excused herself from the fun and retired to her upstairs room and a good book. George Lockhart who had arrived after the others, courteously asked Ms. Averett to serve him a late supper. Good-naturedly she complied. While he was in the kitchen eating, Charley Richards, a well-known Seminole citizen, a good friend of Tom Ross, and more intriguing, a co-defendant under indictment with Ross in the New Mexico case for stealing Wilhoit cattle, came to the hotel and inquired if Lockhart was there. Learning that he was in the kitchen eating supper, Richards "sat down near the door," waited, and when Lockhart finished his meal, the two went outside for a confab. Afterwards, Lockhart returned to the hotel lobby by himself and perceptibly repositioned his chair.[18]

Dave Allison, the headache still an annoying and throbbing nuisance, sat with elbows on a table, his down turned head supported by aged and weathered hands. Five feet away, H. L. Roberson sat at the other end of the table, his cane-bottom chair precariously tilted back against the wall.[19] General conversation swirled about them during that eight o'clock hour. Out the corner of his eye, Sheriff Britton caught a glimpse of blue steel. About an eighteen inch section sinisterly poked into the tiny lobby, between the outside door and doorjamb. Straight away a deafening roar ripped congeniality and conversation from the room, as the charge of buckshot tore across the tiny space and sledge hammered into Horace Roberson's head, smashing it into a wall-hanging calendar behind him. He continued to sit in the chair, upright, frozen in time—dead! *Fearless* Dave Allison abruptly looked up, knowing something "extraordinary" was at hand, but he never even heard the second shot. The pellets punched through his "everyday suit," into his heart, and instantaneously slammed him to the hardwood floor—dead![20]

As would be expected, the remaining actors in the drama "broke" like a covey of quail, simultaneously flushing from the cramped blood-splattered room at breakneck speed, except for old Judge Morgan, who set motionless in his chair even though a stray bullet zinged between his arm and his body.[21] As others scampered out, Milt Good, shotgun in one hand and a pistol in the other, brazenly charged into the room.[22] Tom Ross, always cocksure, right behind. Standing in front of the mangled Roberson,

Tom Ross, "aimed at the head, at the neck, at the heart, and at the hip."[23] He milked his .45 automatic pistol dry. Turning to Milt Good, Ross infuriatingly admonished him to "do your duty," and the champion steer roper likewise emptied his self-loading .45 into the already lifeless Dave Allison lying before him.[24] Tom Ross and Milt Good, their murderous mission accomplished, hurriedly rushed back to the convertible parked at the curb.

Dave Allison's modern-day counterpart, Dean Bohannon, Field Inspector, (Special Texas Ranger) Texas and Southwestern Cattle Raisers Association, Lubbock, Texas. Bohannon, who currently works the same West Texas geographical territory as did Allison, examines a bullet hole in a Gaines Hotel wall-board made during the horrific shotgun and automatic pistol bullet mêlée, which caused the untimely deaths of William D. "Dave" Allison and Horace L. Roberson. Author's photo.

Upstairs, Martha Roberson, already attired in her nightgown, was jolted out of bed by the crashing crescendo below. Barefooted, and grabbing a kimono on the fly, Martha, horrified at what she might find, raced to the stairway landing, paused a split-second, and then dashed into the hotel lobby. In disbelief she at once saw her husband sitting upright, the gaping hole in his left temple, blood dripping from the calendar behind his head. Racing toward Horace's side, she unconsciously stepped over Dave Allison's cataleptic form. A graduate nurse by profession, straight away she could tell medical help for her husband was hopeless. Her next move, it came natural, she reached for her husband's revolver. Placing her hand on the weapon she instantly determined the handle was broken, a result of the destructive gunshot blasts—it was useless. Knowing he had a "back up," a small automatic tucked in his waistband, she "jerked the gun and pushed off the safety."[25] Rushing to the doorway, she fired twice through the screen door at the Stetson-clad murderers. Just before jumping into the car, Tom Ross heard a ping on his cowboy belt buckle, and instantly winced as the tiny bullet ricocheted, puncturing the fat surrounding his abdomen, but not piercing through to his gut. The second copper-jacketed projectile punched through flesh in Milt Good's arm, and then into the meat casing his hip.[26]

Ross and Good, no doubt in disbelief at having been struck by bullets fired by a woman, promptly leaped into the Ford, and recklessly raced out of Seminole town at high-speed. Inside the Gaines Hotel, Martha quickly focused her attention to the face down figure of Dave Allison, turned him over, but soon realized that he too was dead.[27] Gaines County Sheriff Britton made it back to the crime scene, after having rushed home to get his six-shooter, but by then the murderers had already fled—chugging and sputtering somewhere out there on a dark prairie night. As shocked bystanders began to return, their numbers were steadily reinforced by genuinely concerned citizens and gawking rubber-neckers. It was calculatingly clear that no pursuing posse need be pressed into hurry-up service. Everyone, to the last man, knew who was responsible for the callous killings, and it would simply be a routine legal matter to file complaints and obtain warrants when the sun came up. Besides, after the brutality of what had just transpired, bumping into Tom Ross and Milt Good on some dark and desolate dirt road, well, maybe things really could wait till morning light.

Predictably, Tom Ross and Milt Good's first stop was at the residence of none other than Charley Richards, Ross's alleged copartner in the New Mexico cattle theft case. Purportedly, from the Richard's house, Tom Ross telephoned Gaines County Sheriff Britton's residence, but the busy lawman, not unsurprisingly, wasn't at home.[28] Realizing their wounds for the moment were not life threatening, but nevertheless painful, the pair too were also glumly aware, without medical attention complicated infection might just do what Allison and Roberson hadn't. Too, they were running hazardously short of gasoline. They next stopped at Soon Birdwell's ranch thirteen miles northwest of Seminole. Birdwell knew Tom Ross, and when the latter asked if he could stay the night, the cowman replied in the affirmative. When Ross and Good came into the house they had three long guns in tow, an automatic shotgun and two .30-.30 Winchesters.[29] After a somber counseling session, Birdwell suggested they go ahead and call the sheriff that night. Ross after mulling his delicate medical and entangled legal situation over, concurred.[30] Ross telephoned Sheriff Britton who was by now back home, and advised him that he and Good were ready to capitulate, but were out of gas, unable to get back to Seminole. Area rancher Forest Sherman was listening in on the party line, and volunteered to provide the requisite taxi service.[31] At the buzzing Birdwell ranch, Sherman, probably thinking the three long guns stacked in the parlor was a sum total for his *prisoner's* armament, loaded the wounded men into his car and delivered Ross and Good to the sheriff who was standing on the Gaines County courthouse steps. Upon surrendering to Britton, both Ross and Good turned over Colt .45 automatics to the first-term lawman, telling him someone from the Birdwell family would bring him the other three guns the next day.[32] Without fanfare, Tom Ross and Milt Good were locked up.

Advancing technology and improved communication services were progressively shrinking the *transitional frontier*. West Texas and eastern New Mexico were being dragged, like it or not, into the roaring twentieth-century. The same night William Davis Allison was viciously gunned down in Gaines County, over in Roswell, Lena was given notice of the killings by telephone. Without waiting for further information or amplification, she "left immediately by automobile for Seminole..."[33]

At the time Tom Ross and Milt Good, suffering their nasty gunshot wounds, turned themselves over to the Texas criminal justice system, it is typically underscored that the prisoners anticipated cow-country cohorts hastily securing and posting their bail-bonds. With epidemic proportion, malicious gossip was being spread that previously the killer's attorney had "advised it might be easier to beat a murder charge than one for stealing cattle," in West Texas.[34] And too, the incontestable fact that on the night of the murders, Panhandle cowboy Charley Richards was at the Gaines Hotel conferring with lawyer Lockhart, and possibly pinpointing the Association men's seating arrangements, was astringently fueling the treacherous speculation and uncorroborated innuendo. Dave Allison and Horace L. Roberson, looking back through the lens of historical hindsight, had clearly undervalued their adversary's penchant for skullduggery and gratuitous violence. Hillary Loftis, aka Tom Ross, and Milton Paul Good miscalculated too! When they heartlessly pulled the triggers on Allison and Roberson, they had done more than simply snuff out the life of two West Texas lawmen—they had vilely spit in the face of the Texas and Southwestern Cattle Raisers Association. Aside from the noticeable issue of unbridled immorality, it was a colossal misstep. Later, even Milt Good bellyached, "I think we made a mistake by surrendering that night, because as soon as our guns were out of our possession, things began to happen. The circumstances clearly entitled us to bail, but we were never granted an opportunity to make it."[35]

To the defendant's befuddled astonishment, on Monday, April 2nd, the very next day after the killing, they were indicted by a Gaines County Grand Jury and the formality of issuing arrest warrants was adhered to.[36] On April 3rd, the trial court judge, on his own initiative granted a *Change of Venue* and moved the high-profile case to Lubbock.[37] A *Writ of Habeas Corpus* hearing was set for April 12, 1923.[38] Things were moving fast—too fast for Ross and Good.

The Association's voice in Texas politics had never before been muted, and without doubt, the act of slaying two of their very own put Fort Worth front-office personnel and the general membership on the warpath. Lone Star judges were elected. Votes, campaign contributions, pluck, and plenty of first-rate political influence the Association had—in spades! Quickly *The Cattleman* thumped out the message and made the Association's position crystal clear:

> Every member of the Association, every stockman, and every red-blooded American citizen should do all in his power to assist in developing the truth in regard to this assassination.
>
> Every member of the Association should redouble his loyalty and assistance to the maintenance of the Cattle Raisers' Association, and every man engaged in the livestock business, who is opposed to cattle stealing and who abhors murder, should immediately join the Association and help us carry on the work to completion, begun by Dave Allison and Horace Roberson, to the end that cow thieves and murders may know and understand there is no place within the limits of this state where they can thrive and ply their vocation, without feeling the heavy hand of the law.[39]

The Texas cow business was Association business, so too were "Goddamn cow-thieves." Tom Ross and Milt Good qualified, and they indisputably needed to feel that mighty hand of stern justice slap them down. Public relations rhetoric, Association monies, and high-powered legal talent without delay were focused on Lubbock and those two thoroughly scurrilous scoundrels.

Meanwhile, during the time Ross and Good had been languishing in the jail house, and while their lawyers were busily engaged tilting with the Criminal Justice system, William Davis Allison's sixty-two year-old body had been respectfully removed to Roswell.

On April 5, 1923, at the Chapel of Roswell Undertaking Co., the once *fearless* William Davis Allison, lay peacefully resting in a beautifully decorated metal casket under an "immense wreath" from the Texas and Southwestern Cattle Raisers Association.[40] As throngs of mourning spectators reverently looked on, a quartet from the First Christian Church sang *Nearer My God to Thee*. Reverend Sidney M. Bedford officiated during the poignant ceremony, which was then followed by another song, *Asleep in Jesus*.[41] Pall Bearers, including Burt Mossman, first Captain of the Arizona Rangers and a renowned Southwestern cattleman, gently loaded Dave's coffin into the hearse. Of the list of Pall Bearers, Roswell educator and a noted historian, Elvis E. Fleming, remarked, "it sounded like a Who's Who of Roswell."[42]

At South Park Cemetery, Jaffa Miller conducted the graveside service. William Davis Allison was buried with full Masonic honors. The *Roswell Daily Record* eulogized, "W. D. Allison was recognized as one of the most efficient officers of the Southwest. He was a deputy U. S. Marshal and had served as a peace officer practically all of his life. He was regarded as one of the best men ever in the employ of the Texas and Southwestern Cattle Raisers Association."[43]

The Association was not about to forget the widows. During their next annual convention, the 48th, Resolution 9 was unanimously accepted, making the ladies honorary Association members, and providing that they be paid a monthly stipend of $50 throughout their lives. Lena Allison and Martha Roberson, in a joint letter of appreciation, expressed their gratitude "for the splendid spirit shown by the members of the Association in making provisions for us."[44] The Association faithfully honored their commitment to widows Allison and Roberson.[45]

The book may have closed on William Davis Allison's colorful life, but taken as a whole, the story did not merely end at Roswell's South Park cemetery with the somber internment of an icon. A comprehensive narration of "the rest of the story" should unmistakably remain the domain of a biographer tackling an all-inclusive narration of the Hillary U. Loftis saga; however, a review is not inappropriate.

Dave Allison's casket, lavishly draped with flowers, at the chapel, Roswell Undertaking Company, Roswell, New Mexico. Courtesy, Pat Treadwell, Tahoka, Texas.

Needless to mention, the murder of two well-known West Texas lawmen made the news—big time! The story was drawing national interest, and the *St. Louis Post-Dispatch* cleverly crafted a three-part series, double paged, with photographs and crime-scene drawings which ran as an added feature in their editions of the Sunday supplement magazine.[46] Other far-away newspapers sent correspondents. Truthfully, the tragic tale was undeniably rich, a journalistic gold mine, for not only was drama of the crime itself attracting attention, the personalities flocking to Lubbock for the upcoming trial were a newspaper writer's delight. All of a sudden, converging on the town were Texas Rangers, grizzled ex-Texas Rangers, Lone Star Sheriffs and their faithful deputies and, of course, a cadre of classically rough-hewn Texas and Southwestern Cattle Raisers Association Inspectors. Their purpose? To serve as witnesses on behalf of their fallen comrades, and too, to assist local authorities with keeping the lid on disorderly behavior at twenty-one identifiable security posts, and everyone entering the courtroom—every one—was to be hand-searched for weapons.[47] Nearly all the peace officers were wearing ornately stitched cowboy boots, most were crowned with an expensive hand-creased broad-brim hat, and every one of them sported a Colt single-action revolver or a cocked and locked .45 automatic, many decorated with deep-cut scroll engravings and bedecked with grips of fancy carved woods—or Mother of Pearl—or Ivory that was once pure white—or even Mexican silver coins. And too, it was no secret, in their hotel rooms or in their separate autos parked around town, in front of a café or down at the county courthouse, there was a virtual arsenal of lever action and automatic rifles, and not just a few sawed-off shotguns.[48] A newspaper correspondent on the scene wryly noted, "All were loaded for bear in case there should happen to be an open season for bear."[49] Readership was hungrily salivating for another romantic true-life Western adventure story, and especially ready to gobble it up were those far-off souls living east of the Pecos River, hence, well-removed from *transitional frontier* familiarity. Effusive journalists were poised to make darn sure they didn't miss out.

Present too were West Texas cattle kings, and as a "Cowtown" reporter for the *Star-Telegram* mentioned, "One heard 200,000 and 300,000 acres pastures discussed with the same nonchalance as two Fort Worth citizens would talk of their lots, 50 by 120 feet."[50] Many prominent businessmen and bankers were also going to make Lubbock home for a spell, one of whom was a staunch friend of Dave Allison from days gone by, W. E. Connell, President of the First National Bank of Fort Worth.[51] Not unsurprisingly of course were the adversarial contingent of high-priced lawyers, who were studiously preparing for a protracted courtroom battle. Lubbock was bursting at the seams, it seems. A reporter for the *Dallas Morning News* offered helpful advice, "…it will be difficult for late arrivals who have not made reservations to obtain rooms. A list of private residences which have spare rooms has been compiled by Curtis Keen, secretary of the Chamber of Commerce, and he already has had some calls for them."[52]

Tom Ross and Milt Good remained in jail, stunned that their *Writ of Habeas Corpus* had been denied by 72nd Judicial District Court Judge, Clark M. Mullican.[53] The confined defendants, each to be tried separately, would stand trial in Lubbock for the murder of Dave Allison. Afterwards, two separate trials for the killing of Inspector H. L. Roberson were to be held at Abilene, Texas.

Roswell Police Commander Richard D. Lucero inspects the Allison family plot and Dave Allison's grave site, South Park Cemetery, Roswell, New Mexico. Author's photo.

Milt Good, left, and Tom Ross at the time of their Lubbock trial for the murders of Texas and Southwestern Cattle Raisers Association Inspectors Dave Allison and Horace L. Roberson. Note, handcuffs barely visible on Tom Ross. Courtesy, Dean Bohannon, Field Inspector, Texas and Southwestern Cattle Raisers Association.

Tactics of the prosecution team were understandably predictable, the evidence overwhelming. Two "Goddamn cow-thieves" were on trial, and, indeed, hadn't they, as *The Cattleman* said, gunned down and . . .

> …sent into eternity the souls of W. D. Allison and H. L. Roberson, two honest, faithful and efficient inspectors of our Association, killed without a moment's warning on Holy Easter Sunday night, in the little hotel at Seminole, where they were waiting to lay before the Grand Jury of Gaines County the next day the testimony against Tom Ross for the unlawful handling of M. Wilhoit's cattle.[54]

The defense team was in a bind from the beginning, mainly because of having acknowledged their clients, "…murdered by discharges from an automatic shotgun and automatic pistols.." the two decedents.[55] Their strategy therefore hinged on an attack aimed at the character and reputations of Dave Allison and H. L. Roberson. Simply stated, the defense attempted to paint a picture of two "hard and dangerous" lawmen out to get the defendants at all cost, and in an act of self-defense, Tom Ross and Milt Good effected, what in today's jargon would be labeled a justifiable "preemptive strike." Kill before being killed. Old allegations about Allison's involvement in the Pascual Orozco killing and Roberson's trials and tribulations linked to the shooting of Foot Boykin at a Sierra Blanca cow-lot were rehashed and retrashed in a barefaced scheme designed to prove the lawmen were downright poison. It would, as everyone well suspected, boil down to nothing more than tit for tat—Roberson and Allison supporters testifying for the prosecution—detractors speaking for the defense. But of course neither Allison nor Roberson was there to defend himself.

At the Lubbock trial for the murderers of their husbands. From left to Right: J. A. Harvick, Mrs. Horace L. Roberson, Mrs. Hazel Cummins (Dave Allison's daughter), Mrs. Dave Allison, E. B. Spiller, Secretary, Texas and Southwestern Cattle Raisers Association, E. T. Davis and A. L. Chester. Courtesy, The Cattleman.

The sheer magnitude of the legal battle shaping up can be quickly extracted from the pages of the *Seminole Sentinel*, "There are about 250 witnesses for both State and Defense…the jury was secured out of a special venire of 125 men…a total of four hundred and sixty eight subpoenas…"[56]

Dayton Moses, General Attorney for the Texas and Southwestern Cattle Raisers Association. Moses played the pivotal role in the prosecution of Milt Good and Tom Ross. Courtesy, The Cattleman.

Taking a break at the Lubbock County Courthouse. District Attorney Gordon B. McGuire, left, and District Judge Clark Millican. Courtesy, Dean Bohannon, Field Inspector, Texas and Southwestern Cattle Raisers Association.

A partial sampling of Sheriffs, Deputies, Texas Rangers, and Texas and Southwestern Cattle Raisers Association Inspectors at Lubbock, Texas for the trial of Tom Ross and Milt Good. (Top Row. Left to Right) J. M. Walker, Midland, Texas; Jack James, Roaring Springs, Texas; J. E. Russell, Matador, Texas; J. C. Russell, Matador, Texas; (Second Row) James Powers, Post, Texas; F. L. Britton, Sheriff Gaines County; N. H. Sweeney, Dalhart, Texas. (Bottom Row) U. L. George, Lubbock, Texas; John C. Keller, Sheriff, Yoakum County; N. M. Koonsman, Texas Ranger, Wichita Falls, Texas; H. L. Johnston, Sheriff, Lubbock County; John Southworth, Dickens, Texas; Samy Rogers, Seymour, Texas; E. T. Davis, Paducah, Texas. (Corner inserts.) Upper left, J. A. Grisby, Sheriff, Floyd County; Upper Right, W. T. St. John, Deputy Sheriff, Taylor County; Lower Left, W. B. Bingham, Sheriff, Stonewall County; Lower Right, John R. Hughes, Ex-Captain, Texas Rangers. So many colorful transitional frontier lawmen grouped together for one happening, the murder trial drew National attention and widespread newspaper coverage. Courtesy, The Cattleman.

Making sure justice would be effectively administered in first-class cow-country fashion, Dayton Moses, Attorney for the Texas and Southwestern Cattle Raisers Association would astutely handle the prosecution, *of course*, in conjunction with state District Attorney Gordon

McGuire, S. C. Rowe of Fort Worth, and J. E. Vickers of Lubbock. On the other side, defense attorneys were W. H. Bledsoe, a Texas State Senator from Lubbock, Perry Spencer of Lubbock, John Howard of Pecos, along with lawyer Lockhart from Tahoka.[57]

A comprehensive legal or historical analysis of trial testimony and courtroom choreography would prove much too voluminous for repeating in this, Dave Allison's biography, although the story in its own right might very well merit a book. The killing of Dave Allison and Horace Roberson, after all, were not "who done it" murders. There was not the slightest question as to who had pulled the triggers; the issue was, would the defendant's elaborate attempt at justification prove convincing? Suffice to say, after the sparring, chicanery, and posturing, the Lubbock juries in each of the two trials returned guilty verdicts against Tom Ross and Milt Good for murdering Dave Allison. Likewise, afterward, at agreeable Abilene, both defendants were convicted of murdering Horace L. Roberson. And still later, the Texas Court of Criminal Appeals affirmed their murder convictions.[58]

Waiting for the verdict on the Lubbock County courthouse square. Courtesy, Dean Bohannon, Field Inspector, Texas and Southwestern Cattle Raisers Association.

Twelve Good Men, the Lubbock Jury in the Tom Ross trial. Courtesy, Dean Bohannon, Field Inspector, Texas and Southwestern Cattle Raisers Association.

Tom Ross and Milt Good were sent to the Texas State Penitentiary at Huntsville, and one would think that is where the story should end—not just yet.[59] On November 29, 1925 the pair, aided by other convicts, "mugged a guard" and escaped.[60] Milt Good offers his brand of justification:

> The main cause for this escape was Tom Ross' dissatisfaction. We had spent so much money and felt sadly mistreated. Not by the prison officials, because up to this time we had been treated as well as we could have expected. If our sentences had been permitted to run concurrently, as we had been promised, I think I could have served my sentence out, but it is doubtful that Tom could have done so. He was fifty-five years of age and under sentence of fifty-five years. Red Whalen was under a ninety-nine year sentence; George Arlington was serving a thirty-five year term; and mine was fifty-one years. It

> seemed hopeless. I planned the escape because of my friendship for Tom.[61]

After successfully managing their flight from Texas, and briefly slinking around in New Mexico, Ross and Good roamed the Northwest, mistrustful of everybody and living the fugitive life, always uncomfortably leery of apprehension.[62] On an anxious and sneaky return trip to the Southwest, Ross and Good decided it best to part company, and did so in pleasant Pushmataha County, Oklahoma, because "too many officers were looking for them together." Shortly thereafter Milton Paul Good managed to get himself caught near Antlers, and quickly was placed back behind the tall red brick ivy-covered walls at Huntsville prison.[63]

Tom Ross roamed around in the North country for awhile and according to a news report in the *Cut Bank Pioneer Press* it was "definitely established" that across the international line in a "Canadian cattle camp" he killed a Chinese cook with a club. On the run once more, he crossed back into the United States and landed a job as cow-camp foreman on the Frye Cattle Company's Rimrock Division, located on the Blackfoot Indian Reservation not far from Browning, Glacier County, Montana.[64] Locals, however, didn't know him as Tom Ross, nor did they know him as Hillary Loftis—for use in Montana he'd lassoed on to the alias of Charles Gannon—but not for too long!

In some sort of fanatical dispute with Ralph Hayward over "details as to management of ranch affairs," Gannon belligerently cried, "I have a gun and I have a notion to kill you; in fact I am going to do so." And he did! Remorselessly shooting Hayward in the left breast, and then, as he staggered from the initial deafening blast, Gannon shot him five more times. Gannon then went into the bunkhouse, placed his coat on his cot, sat down and hurriedly scribbled the following terse note about his latest murder victim:

> This fellow is a new man in the cow business. He may be all right among Dagoes but not among cow punchers. Good bye to the world.[65]

Hillary U. Loftis, aka Tom Ross, aka Charles Gannon, chambered a round, put the .45 pistol to his right ear, pulled the trigger, unceremoniously ending his own life.[66] Upon learning of his demise *The Cattleman* mockingly mentioned, "The Way of the Transgressor Is Hard."[67] Cashing in his chips, Hillary Loftis joined historical company with the toughest of the tough, Dave Allison and H. L. Roberson, who like him, had tirelessly forged a hard-scrabble living on the harsh and hazardous Southwestern *transitional frontier*, but unlike him, they never assumed false names and frantically ran away, hiding from their past.

Milt Good, after a botched escape attempt—trying to worm his way out through an underground tunnel in 1927—was finally pardoned by the Governor, Miriam "Ma" Ferguson, on November 26, 1934.[68] In 1935 he published his autobiography, *Twelve Years in a Texas Prison*, for the express purpose of "a desire for financial reward" and he pitifully opines that his family had been "deprived" of his earning power due to his being imprisoned.[69] Incredibly, Milt Good in writing of the murders simply remarks "…the less that is said about this affair the better it will be for all concerned."[70] That's it! It seems, in the end, he wasn't overly concerned for his family's financial well-being though. On the 1st day of June, 1941, resulting from a charge of Theft Over $50 in Motley County, Texas, Milt Good once again donned inmate clothes in the prison at Huntsville.[71] At the time, he was also facing a serious charge of cattle theft in Levelland, Hockley County, Texas.[72] Milt Good finally ended up in the "free world" at Cotulla, in South Texas. He died the day before Independence Day in 1960, an old man, when his sedan slipped out of gear and brutally crushed him between the bumper and a pasture gate.[73]

The killing of Dave Allison and Horace Roberson, and the subsequent trials of Tom Ross and Milt Good had presented the American public with a last curtain-call, a final glimpse at a real life Western frontier stage, and at an attention-grabbing troupe of bona fide stereotypical Western lawmen—and bad guys. The last act played before a national audience who knew those pistol-packin' peace officers and outlaws who had converged on Lubbock and Abilene were the last of a vanishing breed. That they were a concluding ensemble of stalwart characters who in point of fact had begun their policing careers chasing after crooks as members of a horseback posse, but who now manned roadblocks from behind the hood of a car, was not unnoticed. Perceptive newsmen keenly knew they had been standing at the edge of a quickly closing era, and so, skillfully and shrewdly they wrote of pant legs stuffed into high-top boots, string ties, no nonsense wisdom hidden in leathery wrinkled faces, and of tough as anvil Association men dragging Winchesters through hotel lobbies. They wrote generically of Western Sheriffs and Texas Rangers. And they had written specifically too, making sure not to have missed a word when Captain John "Border Boss" Hughes took the witness stand and incontestably spoke well of his friend Dave Allison, nor did they neglect to report when

Frank Canton's pistol had inadvertently slipped from a hip pocket, and his matter-of-fact reply as a total stranger called it to his attention, "That's all right son, I have another one."[74] They wrote of cowboys, colossal cow ranches and flamboyant cattle kings. They failed not to write about .45 Colt's six-shooters and a few Association men's particular preference for more modern slab-sided automatics. Everything had been real, the people, the places, the things, as well as the sensational reason for being there in the first place. It wouldn't happen again, and they knew it! The reading public knew it too! It was an orgy of Western Americana and everyone had wanted to attend, in the flesh or in fantasy—the next generation, well, it would only be silver screen melodrama and sometimes boring history books for them.

A biographic examination should be an impartial undertaking. Dave Allison's life story is rightfully deserving a historic inspection, and without doubt he earned his spot in the history book. Admittedly, he was not a perfect man. Analytically, although there is not an abundance of quantifiable evidence, there is sufficient material to support the suggestion, that for at least part of his fearless life, Dave Allison was a problematic gambler. Unquestionably Dave Allison resigned as Midland County Sheriff under the darkness of a financial cloud, at least by one report. A well-respected political opponent simply said he gambled some money away, inferring that Dave had dipped into county coffers. When he resigned from sheriff's position County Commissioners offered an official resolution liberally praising his past "efficiency and faithfulness." The misappropriating of county funds were allegations vehemently denied by Lena Allison, as would well be expected, and, in reality, her argument is somewhat shored up with acknowledgment that Dave did, indeed, return to bustling Midland town and, with powerful political support, albeit unsuccessful, run once again for the sheriff's job.

In Arizona, however, there is less ambiguity. Dave Allison's resignation from the Arizona Rangers was not voluntary, a fact supported by archival records, and from the writings of his captain. Whether Dave was spending too much time gambling, neglecting his duties, or was in fact bringing undue and unfavorable attention to himself and the state police force through irate creditors is indeterminate. Generally where there's smoke, there's fire—and clearly Dave Allison's career as an Arizona ranger was barbecued. Truthfully, his forced termination may have served as a "wake up call," for after his Arizona days there seems no longer to be any gambling or undue financial problems in the Allison household.

Quite naturally, spirited debate might well initiate during the course of exploring Dave's relationship with the Texas and Southwestern Cattle Raisers Association. From the outset, early in his teenage life Dave Allison was beguilingly and magnetically drawn to the cattle culture. At Midland when he first buckled on the gun belt of judicial righteousness, Dave Allison made his lifelong career decision and stuck with it. Employment with the Association as range detective, commingling his two major interests, was an ideal solution for professional fulfillment, and it proved to be Dave Allison's forte. From the Association's management viewpoint he was an indisputably efficient and incontestably loyal foot soldier in the unremitting war against "Goddamn cow-thieves." Undoubtedly though, anyone at odds with the Association saw him as too loyal, too partisan, and too beholden.

At Roswell when he was indicted for trying to bribe the District Attorney, as could have well been predicted, the charges stemmed from a cow-country controversy. There was no doubt where Dave Allison's sympathy lay—it wasn't with the Chaves County sheep men. From the witness stand, Dave's defense that he was only trying to *see if* the county prosecutor would accept the proffered money for looking the other way, seems but an unreasonable excuse and damn lame defense. He stuck by his story though. What was a jury supposed to do? Call him an outright liar and send an otherwise good man to the penitentiary? Clearly, whether actually believing him or not, they didn't wish to convict him, and they didn't. Cowmen too knew, as did everyone else, Dave Allison was a devoted husband and doting daddy. Examination of his personal letters to Lena and Hazel makes profusely clear that *fearless* Dave Allison had two affectionate soft spots branded onto his heart. Absent evidence to the contrary—Dave Allison was a family man.

If in order to legitimize Dave Allison as a worthy Southwestern lawman there must be a detailed body-count of dead desperadoes, candidly, a reader must look elsewhere. When future World War II General, George S. Patton Jr., described Dave Allison as "the most noted gunman here in Texas" he wasn't making a self-serving tongue-in-cheek remark, he was telling it like it was. Who could with quantifiable accuracy make a tally-sheet for hush-hush deeds happening along an unfathomable Rio Grande river or out beyond that scrub-oak on a lonesome West Texas cattle range? Who could rightfully jump over that eighteen-inch stone wall surrounding Colonel Bill Green's mansion in Mexico, and rush headlong amidst wild-eyed rioters just to make a count of dead Mexican nationals littering Cananea's cobblestone streets? For sure, Pascual Orozco, Jr. would have classed Dave Allison as a gunman.

If a judgment of historical worth must be made, surely it should be done with evenhandedness. Dave Allison didn't conquer a *transitional frontier*, he was a part of it. He played well his assigned role.

Above all else, Dave Allison was a peace officer. He was not, however, like certain contemporaries concerned with trying to promote himself and puff up specious stories. He didn't have to. William Davis Allison was not a braggadocios man. The chips could fall where they very well may. From behind the badge Dave Allison had lived a rich and rewarding law enforcement life, and to him that was plenty good enough. There weren't too many men roaming the magnificent Southwest who could lay claim to having once been a six-term Lone Star sheriff; a sergeant in the legendary Texas Rangers; a lieutenant in the illustrious Arizona Rangers, top bodyguard and Head of Security for a Mexico mining mogul; Chief of Police for a major New Mexico municipality; wide-ranging West Texas constable; redoubtable United States Deputy Marshal; and an acclaimed Inspector for the influential Texas and Southwestern Cattle Raisers Association. William Davis Allison, as they say, had "been there, done that," but he would let someone else do the writin'.

A legitimate peace officer, whether serving on the emerging and constantly expanding wild and woolly *Western Frontier*, or later, on the equally perilous *Transitional Frontier*, or even today on the *Technological Frontier*, could expect no more gratifying tribute than words uttered in memory of William Davis Allison by a contemporary journalist: "He was respected by all honest men and feared by all law breakers…he was recognized as *fearless…*"[75]

ENDNOTES
Chapter 10. "I jerked the gun and pushed the safety off"

[1] *Inspector's Expense Blank*, March, 1923. Inspector W. D. Allison. Courtesy, Texas and Southwestern Cattle Raisers Association Museum, Library and Archives. Fort Worth.
[2] Ibid. And see, *Roswell Daily Record*, April 4, 1923. "Dave Allison made his home here for a number of years serving as city marshal of this city. He was here only a few days ago visiting members of his family."
[3] *Letter* from W. D. Allison, Post, Texas, to Mrs. W. D. Allison and Mrs. John A. Cummins, Roswell, New Mexico. March 28, 1923. Courtesy, **Treadwell**.
[4] Ibid.
[5] *Lubbock Morning Avalanche*, June 22, 1923. Also see, **DeArment**, P. 14. "...Martha Plummer, a nurse and superintendent of the Lee Surgical Hospital in San Antonio. They settled in Midland." And see, *The Seminole Sentinel*, April 5, 1923. "H. L. Roberson was reared near San Antonio, Texas, and had been a peace officer practically all of his life, serving first on the Ranger force of Texas, later in the service of the Cattle Raisers Association having served in the latter capacity for a number of years, he being one of the veteran officers of this Association. Roberson also held a deputyship under the Sheriff of Midland County."
[6] Interview with Nancy **McKinley** at Midland, Texas, March 11, 2001.
[7] *Abilene Reporter*, September 12, 1923.
[8] *Lubbock Morning Avalanche*, June 22, 1923. Years later Milt Good wrote that he left Brownfield on a Thursday and took the train to Seagraves. "Upon my arrival there I met Tom Ross; and when he learned that I was in the market for steer calves, he insisted on my going to see some of his. After looking At Ross' calves, I saw that they were short ages, and asked him if he had sold the long ages. He answered, 'Yes'; that Nick Alley of Hale Center had bought his long age calves...I stayed Saturday with Tom Ross and we spent the day feeding cattle and looking at a polo pony...Nothing would satisfy Tom but that I spend Saturday night and Sunday with him. People who know Mr. Ross known that he was a man you could not get away from easily. I rode out to his ranch and spent Saturday and Sunday there; and Sunday evening he took me to Seminole where the trouble occurred." **Good**, P. 16-17. His version regarding the day he left Brownfield does not mesh with courtroom testimony. Also see, *267 Southwestern Reporter*, *Good v. State* (No. 8608). P. 507.
[9] Ibid.
[10] *Abilene Reporter*, September 12, 1923.
[11] Ibid.
[12] *Letter* from W. D. Allison, Post, Texas, to Lena Allison, Roswell, New Mexico. March 31, 1923. Dave Allison's salary was $150 per month, plus expenses. Courtesy, **Treadwell**. And, Texas and Southwestern Cattle Raisers Association Museum, Library and Archives, Fort Worth. Also see, **Perkins & Ward**, P. 25-26.
[13] *Lubbock Morning Avalanche*, June 22, 1923. And see, *St. Louis Post-Dispatch*, July 22, 1923. "A skilled marksman himself, he had taught her how to shoot straight."
[14] *Lubbock Avalanche-Journal*, Sept 25, 1949, and *Lubbock Morning Avalanche*, June 22, 1923.

[15] *The Cattleman*, May 1923. P. 12.
[16] *Lubbock Morning Avalanche*, June 22, 1923.
[17] *St. Louis Post-Dispatch*, July 22, 1923.
[18] *Lubbock Morning Avalanche*, June 22, 1923. And see, **Fenton (II),** P. 138. "As a parting shot at the witness, the State had Richards reveal under oath that once he had been indicted in Bosque County, Texas, for theft of cattle. Of course, more recently he had been indicted along with Ross in Lovington for stealing Wilhoit stock."
[19] *Abilene Daily Reporter*, September 11, 1923. And see, **Clarke**, P. 145.
[20] *The Cattleman*, May 1923. P. 12. And see, *The Seminole Sentinel*, April 5, 1923. "…when without warning Tom Ross and Milt Good suddenly appeared in the doorway, and opened fire, both men being instantly killed. Roberson simply falling back in his chair, while Allison's body fell to the floor. It is not known how many shots were fired, but both victims were hit more than one time." Also see, *The Semi-Weekly Farm News*, April 17, 1923. "I (Milt Good) shot one time at Roberson and then at Allison with the shotgun."
[21] **Clarke**, P. 146.
[22] *Abilene Daily Reporter*, September 11, 1923. "The witness (Judge N. R. Morgan) declared that he turned his head and saw Ross and Good in the door. Ross was firing a pistol. Good had a shotgun in one hand and a pistol in the other. Good then stepped over and shot Allison." And see, *St. Louis Post-Dispatch*, July 22, 1923. "Then Milt Good, followed by Tom Ross, entered the room, each holding an automatic pistol in the right hand."
[23] *The Cattleman*, July, 1923. P. 12.
[24] Ibid., May 1923. P. 13. And see, *267 Southwestern Reporter*, *Ross v. State* (No. 8607) P. 500. "…He (Roberson) started to raise up with his hand over this way, and I commenced shooting as quick as I could shoot, I do not know how many times I shot him." And see **Fenton (II)** P. 106. "Dumbfounded, the witnesses stared in shock as in response to Ross's command: 'Milt, do your duty!'"
[25] *Lubbock Morning Avalanche*, June 22, 1923. Lewis **Nordyke** in *Great Roundup—The Story of Texas and Southwestern Cowmen*. P. 246, reports that Roberson was armed with a .45 caliber automatic. "But the handle had been shattered by bullets, and then Mrs. Roberson grabbed a small-caliber pistol which Roberson carried under his belt."
[26] **Clarke**, P. 146. Also see, *St. Louis Post-Dispatch*, July 22, 1923. "She stopped, felt for the six-shooter which she knew Horace Roberson wore in a holster at his left side, found that the handle had been hit by a bullet and broken off. Then she felt for and found, at the right side of the dead man an automatic pistol, a small one, which she knew he carried there. She threw the automatic off safety, turned swiftly, ran to the front door, which had been closed by the retreating gunmen. She jerked the door partly opened. Holding the weapon in her left hand, with her kimono still draped over her right arm, she fire two shots through the screen." **DeArment**, P. 17., identifies the "hideout gun" as a small .25 caliber automatic.
[27] *Lubbock Morning Avalanche*, June 22, 1923.
[28] *Abilene Daily Reporter*, September 19, 1923. As mentioned in the text, much speculation revolved around the Ross/Richards relationship. Many were of the opinion that when Richards entered the hotel on the night of the killings, and asked to see lawyer Lockhart, he was really on an intelligence gathering

assignment for Ross—determining if Allison and Roberson were indeed in the hotel lobby, and just where they were sitting.

[29] In other accounts one of the rifles is described as what would be a Savage, Model 99, .250/3000 caliber.

[30] *Lubbock Morning Avalanche*, June 22, 1923. And see, **Pettey**, P. 134. "They had become frightened by the continued bleeding from their wounds and asked him (Sheriff Britton) to come out and take them into town so that they could surrender and receive medical aid."

[31] Ibid.

[32] *Abilene Daily Reporter*, September, 11, 1923.

[33] *Roswell Daily Record*, April 2, 1923.

[34] **Petty**, P. 14.

[35] **Good**, P. 17.

[36] Indictment, Cause No. 50 and No. 52., Murder. *Tom Ross vs. The State of Texas*. Cause No. 51 and No. 53., Murder. *Milt Good vs. The State of Texas*. And warrants of arrests. Courtesy, Virginia **Stewart**, Gaines County District Clerk, Seminole, Texas.

[37] Order of Change of Venue, April 3, 1923. Courtesy, Virginia **Stewart**, Gaines County District Clerk, Seminole, Texas.

[38] Application for Writ of Habeas Corpus. Courtesy, Virginia **Stewart**, Gains County District Clerk, Seminole, Texas.

[39] *The Cattleman*, May, 1923. P. 13.

[40] Record of Funeral, Allison, William Davis. No. 84. Roswell Undertaking Company, Roswell, New Mexico. Courtesy, **Treadwell**. And see, *Roswell Daily Record*. April 5, 1923.

[41] *Memorial Service Program*, William Davis Allison. April 5, 1923. Roswell, New Mexico. Courtesy, **Treadwell**.

[42] Elvis **Fleming**, Roswell, New Mexico, to the author, July 29, 2000.

[43] *Roswell Daily Record*, April 5, 1923.

[44] Mrs. W. D. Allison and Mrs. H. L. Roberson to the Members of the Texas and Southwestern Cattle Raisers Association. October 18, 1923. Courtesy, Texas and Southwestern Cattle Raisers Association Museum, Library and Archives. Fort Worth.

[45] Texas and Southwestern Cattle Raisers Association Records—Payroll Ledger. Courtesy, Stephanie **Malmarous**, The Center for American History—The University of Texas. Austin.

[46] *St. Louis Post-Dispatch*, July 15, 22, 27, 1923.

[47] Security Post Assignments. Courtesy, Vicky **Jones**, Southwest Collection, Texas Tech University. Lubbock. **Pettey** reports that twelve Texas & Southwest Cattle Raisers Association Inspectors and thirty-eight Sheriffs and deputies were in attendance at the Lubbock trial. P. 139.

[48] St. Louis *Post Dispatch,* 07-15-1923. "They loped in from every point of the compass, two-gunned as to a person, mostly, and some of them had Winchesters rifles or sawed-off shotguns in their Fords."

[49] Ibid. "The Colt's .45 is the favorite of the Sheriff as of the brand inspectors; though some them have adopted the automatic pistol."

[50] *Fort Worth Star-Telegram*, July 29, 1923.

[51] Ibid.

[52] *Dallas Morning News*, June 18, 1923.

---

[53] Order of 72nd Judicial District Court Judge Clark M. Mullican denying release of Tom Ross and Milt Good. Courtesy, Virginia **Stewart**, District Clerk, Gaines County, Seminole, Texas.
[54] *The Cattleman*, October, 1923, Volume IX, No. 5.
[55] Ibid.
[56] *Seminole Sentinel*, April 19 & June 21, 1923. **Pettey** reports, "In all, two hundred and sixty witnesses had been heard, four hundred venire men had been called..." P. 139.
[57] Ibid., April 12, 1923. And see, *The Cattleman*, July 1923. P. 12. Up until the mid-twentieth century the Association "employed a staff attorney to assist with the prosecution of those charged with theft, as well as with other matters." *The New Handbook of Texas*, Volume VI, P. 418.
[58] *267 Southwestern Reporter, Tom Ross v. State* (No. 8607) and *Milt Good v. State* (No. 8608.) P. 499-511.
[59] *Conduct Register Transcription Form* Number 52153 (Milt Good) and Number 52154 (Tom Ross), Texas Department of Corrections. Courtesy, Texas State Library and Archives Commission. Austin.
[60] Ibid.
[61] **Good**, P. 29-43.
[62] Ibid. Also see, **DeArment**, P. 18. "At Tacoma, Whalen and Arlington went their separate ways. Good and Ross continued to Blaine, a small town near Vancouver, British Columbia, where they found work and remained several months."
[63] Ibid. And see, *The Cattleman*, November, 1926, Vol. XIII, No. 6. P. 14. "The reward of $300 offered for his capture following the escape of Milt Good from the state penitentiary at Huntsville on November 29, 1925, has been paid by Governor Miriam A. Ferguson. Check for $300 of the $800 paid to Sheriff N. F. Kirpatrick of Antlers County, Oklahoma, when Good was captured on June 26 of this year, was received by the Texas and southwestern Cattle Raisers Association on October 12..." Dee **Harkey** told the story differently, having Ross fly off into the unknown from a New Mexico landing strip, while Milt Good stayed behind on the ground, and then later, traveling to Oklahoma where he was eventually captured. P. 210.
[64] *Cut Bank Pioneer Press* (Montana), February 8, 1929.
[65] Ibid. And see, **Pettey**, P. 141. According to J. Frank **Dobie** the dispute between Ross and Hayward was because "...it was midwinter—the new manager (Hayward) walked into the bunkhouse where Gannon (Hillary Loftis, aka Tom Ross) and two cowboys loitered. He began by raising hell at their not cutting ice so that cattle could get to water more easily, though there was plenty of running water free of ice...He went too far. Gannon raised and shot five bullets into his heart." P. 249.
[66] *Death Certificates* for Tom Ross, aka Charles Gannon, and for Ralph C. Hayward, February 3, 1929. Glacier County, Montana. Courtesy, Sylvia **Berkram**, Glacier County Clerk & Recorder, and Gail **Davis**, Cut Bank, Montana.
[67] *The Cattleman*, March, 1929, Vol. XV, No. 10. P. 14.
[68] **DeArment**, P. 19. Information referencing a second escape attempt can be found in Conduct Register Transcription Form, No. 5213, (Milt Good) Texas Department of Corrections. "10-13-1927—Escaped from Prison Yard at Huntsville Prison. Recaptured same date." Courtesy, Texas State Library and Archives Commission. Austin. Also see, *The Cattleman*, November, 1927, Vol.

XIV, No. 6. P. 11. "Watchfulness of a guard at the State penitentiary prevented the escape of Milt Good and others on October 13th. A tunnel had been dug under the east wall of the penitentiary."

[69] **Good**, P. 5.

[70] Ibid., P. 16.

[71] Prison Interview, No. 97300. June 6, 1941. Texas Department of Corrections. Courtesy, Texas State Library and Archives Commission. Austin.

[72] Ibid. The prison official preparing the report of interview characterized Milt Good: "The subject presents a picture of a spoiled, middle-aged man who has had quite a bit in his time."

[73] **DeArment**, P. 19.

[74] **DeArment (II)**, P. 303.

[75] *Roswell Daily Record*, April 4 & 5, 1923.

BIBLIOGRAPHY

Non-published sources—manuscripts, official documents, court records, tax rolls, correspondence, census records, interviews, etc. Cited with specificity in chapter endnotes. From the following institutions:

Texas and Southwestern Cattle Raisers Association Museum, Library and Archives. Fort Worth, Texas.
Southwest Collection, Texas Tech University, Lubbock, Texas.
Nita Stewart Haley Memorial Library & J. Evetts Haley History Center, Midland, Texas.
Texas State Library and Archives Commission, Austin, Texas.
Texas Ranger Hall of Fame and Museum, Library and Archives. Waco, Texas.
Panhandle-Plains Historical Museum, Canyon, Texas.
The Center for American History, University of Texas. Austin, Texas.
Midland County Historical Society, Midland, Texas.
Permian Basin Petroleum Museum Library and Hall of Fame, Midland, Texas.
Harold B. Simpson History Complex, Hillsboro, Texas.
Garza County Historic Museum. Post, Texas.
Heritage Center Museum, Seminole, Texas.
Hudspeth County Historical Society, Sierra Blanca, Texas.
Culberson County Historical Museum, Van Horn, Texas.
Historical Center for Southeast New Mexico, Roswell, New Mexico.
Yuma Territorial Prison State Historic Park, Yuma, Arizona.
Arizona Department of Library, Archives and Public Records, Phoenix, Arizona.
Arizona Historical Society, Tucson. Arizona.
National Archives, Washington, D. C.
National Archives, College Park, Maryland.
Albert B. Alkek Library, Southwest Texas State University. San Marcos, Texas.
Wildenthal Memorial Library, Sul Ross University, Alpine, Texas.
Midland County Public Library, Midland, Texas.
Lubbock County Public Library, Lubbock, Texas.
Abilene Public Library, Abilene, Texas.
El Paso Public Library, El Paso, Texas.
McKinney Memorial Public Library, McKinney, Texas.
Gaines County Public Library, Seminole, Texas.
Roswell Public Library, Roswell, New Mexico.
Glacier County Public Library, Cut Bank, Montana.
Culberson County District Clerk, Van Horn, Texas.
Hudspeth County District Clerk, Sierra Blanca, Texas.
Gaines County District Clerk, Seminole, Texas.
Chaves County District Clerk, Roswell, New Mexico.
Glacier County Clerk and Recorder's Office, Cut Bank, Montana.
Midland County Sheriff's Office, Midland, Texas.

Gaines County Sheriff's Office, Seminole, Texas.
Hudspeth County Sheriff's Office, Sierra Blanca, Texas.
Culberson County Sheriff's Office, Van Horn, Texas.
Roswell Police Department, Roswell, New Mexico.
U. S. Border Patrol, Sierra Blanca and Van Horn, Texas.

BOOKS:

Adams, Clarence and Joan. *The Old-Timer's Review—Old-Timer's Stories of Long Ago—A Collection of Stories from the past eight years of Old-Timer's Review.* By the Authors. 1987. Roswell.

Alexander, Bob. *Dangerous Dan Tucker, New Mexico's Deadly Lawman.* High-Lonesome Books. Silver City. 2001.

Bailey, Lynn R. (and **Chaput**, Don) *Cochise County Stalwarts.* Two Volumes. Westernlore Press. Tucson. 2000.

Barnes, Will C. *ARIZONA PLACE NAMES.* University of Arizona Press. 1988. Tucson.

Ball, Larry D. *DESERT LAWMEN, The High Sheriffs of New Mexico and Arizona—1846-1912.* University of New Mexico Press. 1992. Albuquerque.

____*The United States Marshals of New Mexico & Arizona Territories, 1846-1912.* University of New Mexico Press. 1978. Albuquerque.

Benner, Judith Ann. *Sul Ross—Soldier, Statesman, Educator.* Texas A & M University Press. 1983. College Station.

Bennett, James A. *Forts & Forays, A Dragoon in New Mexico, 1850-1856.* University of New Mexico Press. Albuquerque. 1948.

Biggers, *Don Buffalo Guns & Barbed Wire, Two Frontier Accounts by Don Hampton Biggers.* Texas Tech University Press 1991. Lubbock.

Bishop, Lorene. *IN THE LIFE AND LIVES OF BROWN COUNTY PEOPLE—CIVIL WAR VETERANS BIOGRAPHICAL SKETCHES. BOOK TEN.* Brownwood Historical Society. 1993. Brownwood, Texas.

Blumenson, Martin. *The Patton Papers, 1885-1940.* Da Capo Press. New York. 1998.

Bolling, Robert S. *Death Rides The River, Tales of the El Paso Road.* By author, 1993.

Bonney, Cecil. *Looking Over My Shoulder, Seventy-five Years in the Pecos Valley.* Hall-Poorbaugh Press, Inc. Roswell. 1971.

Breakenridge, William M. *Helldorado, Bringing the Law to the Mesquite.* Richard Maxwell **Brown**, editor. R. R. Donnely & Sons Co. Chicago. 1982.

Bruce, Leona. *Banister Was There.* Branch-Smith, Inc. 1968. Fort Worth.

Burrows, Jack. *JOHN RINGO, The Gunfighter Who Never Was.* University of Arizona Press. 1987. Tucson.

Cashion, Ty. *A Texas Frontier, The Clear Fork Country and Fort Griffin, 1849-1887.* University of Oklahoma Press. 1996. Norman.

Chaput, Don. (and **Bailey**, Lynn) *Cochise County Stalwarts.* Two Volumes. Westernlore Press. Tucson. 2000.

______ *The Odyssey of Burt Alvord—Lawman, Train Robber, Fugitive.* Westernlore Press. Tucson. 2000.

Champ, Minnie Pitts. (and **Pitts**, Alice Ellison) *COLLIN COUNTY, TEXAS FAMILIES. VOLUME II.* Landmark Publishing, Inc. 1998. Fort Worth.

Chesley, Hervey E. *Adventuring with the Old-Timers, Trails Traveled—Tales Told.* Nita Stewart Haley Memorial Library. 1979. Midland.
Clarke, Mary Whatley. *A Century Of Cow Business—The First Hundred Years Of The Texas And Southwestern Cattle Raisers Association.* Fort Worth.
Coolidge, Dane. *Fighting Men of the West.* E. P. Dutton and Company. 1932. New York.
Cornish, Jim. *Post City, Texas—Founded 1907.* Garza County Historical Museum. Post, Texas. 1998.
Cox, Mike. *Texas Ranger Tales—Stories That Need Telling.* Republic of Texas Press. Plano, Texas. 1997.
___ *Texas Ranger Tales II*, Republic of Texas Press, Plano, Texas. 1999.
DeArment, Robert K. *Alias Frank Canton.* University of Oklahoma Press. Norman and London. 1996.
________ *George Scarborough—The Life and Death of a Lawman on the Closing Frontier.* University of Oklahoma Press. 1992. Norman and London.
Dobie, J. Frank . *COW PEOPLE.* Little, Brown and Co. Boston. 1964.
Forbis, William H. *The Cowboys.* Time-Life Books. New York. 1973.
Frost, H. Gordon and **Jenkins**, John H. "I'M FRANK HAMER". The Pemberton Press. 1968. Austin and New York.
George, Steve and **Trafzer**, Cliff. *PRISON CENTENNIAL, 1876-1976.* Rio Colorado Press. 1980. Yuma.
Gibbs, William E. *TREASURES OF HISTORY—Historic Buildings In Chaves County, 1870-1935.* Chaves County Historical Society. 1985. Roswell.
Gillett, James B. *Six Years With The Texas Rangers, 1875-1881.* University of Nebraska Press. 1976. Lincoln and London.
Gilliland, Maude T. *WILSON COUNTY TEXAS RANGERS, 1837-1977.* By Author. 1977. Pleasanton, Texas.
_______ *Horsebackers Of The Brush Country—A Story Of The Texas Rangers And Mexican Liquor Smugglers.* By Author. 1968. Pleasanton, Texas.
Good, Milt. *TWELVE YEARS IN A TEXAS PRISON.* Russell Stationery Company. 1935. Amarillo.
Gournay, Luke. *Texas Boundaries—Evolution of the State's Counties.* Texas A & M University Press. 1995. College Station.
Hall, Roy F. and Helen Gibbard. *COLLIN COUNTY—Pioneering In North Texas.* Nortex Press—Bicentennial Publication. 1975. Quanah, Texas.
Haley, J. Evetts. *JEFF MILTON—A Good Man with a Gun.* University of Oklahoma Press. 1948. Norman.
Hanes, Bailey C., *Bill Doolin, Outlaw O. T.* University of Oklahoma. Norman 1968.
Harkey, Dee. *MEAN as HELL, The Life of a New Mexico Lawman.* Ancient City Press. 1989. Santa Fe.
Hill, Frank P. and **Jacobs**, Pat Hill. *GRASSROOTS UPSIDE DOWN—a History of Lynn County, Texas.* Nortex Press. 1986. Austin.
Holden, William Curry. *THE ESPUELA LAND AND CATTLE COMPANY.* Texas State Historical Association. 1970. Austin.
Howell, Jr., H. Grady. *For Dixie Land I'll Take My Stand! A Muster Listing of All Known Mississippi Confederate Soldiers, Sailors and Marines.* Chickasaw Bayou Press. 1998.
Hunter, J. Marvin and **Rose**, Noah H. *The Album of Gunfighters.* By Authors. 1955. Bandera, Texas.

Jacobs, Pat Hill and **Hill**, Frank P. *GRASSROOTS UPSIDE DOWN—A History of Lynn County Texas*. Nortex Press. 1986. Austin.
Jenkins, John H. and **Frost**, H. Gordon. *"I'M FRANK HAMER"*. The Pemberton Press. 1968. Austin and New York.
Johnson, David. *John Ringo*. Barbed Wire Press. Stillwater. 1996.
Julyan, Robert. *THE PLACE NAMES OF NEW MEXICO*. University of New Mexico Press. 1998. Albuquerque.
Kelly, George H. *LEGISLATIVE HISTORY—ARIZONA, 1864-1912*. The Manufacturing Stationers Inc. 1926. Phoenix.
Kerber, Frances. **(consultant)** *The Pioneer History of Midland County, Texas,* 1880-1926. Midland County Historical Society. Midland. 1974.
Kingston, Mike **(editor)** Texas Almanac, 1994-95. Dallas Morning News. Dallas. 1995.
McCallum, Henry D. and Frances T. *THE WIRE THAT FENCED THE WEST*. University of Oklahoma Press. 1965. Norman.
Madison, Virginia. *The Big Bend Country of Texas*. October House Inc. 1955. New York.
Marks, Paula Mitchell. *AND DIE IN THE WEST*. William Marrow and Company. 1989. New York
Marohn, Richard C. *THE LAST GUNFIGHTER, John Wesley Hardin*. The Early West-Creative Publishing. 1995. College Station.
Martin, Jack. *BORDER BOSS, Captain John R. Hughes—Texas Ranger*. State House Press. 1990. Austin.
Means, Joyce E. *Pancho Villa Days at Pilares*. By author. 1994.
Meed, Douglas V., *BLOODY BORDER: Riots, Battles and Adventures Along the Turbulent U. S.—Mexican Borderlands*. Westernlore Press. 1992. Tucson.
____*THEY NEVER SURRENDERED: Bronco Apaches of the Sierra Madres, 1890-1935*. Westernlore Press. 1993. Tucson
Metz, Leon C. *BORDER—The U. S.-Mexican Line*. Mangan Books. 1989. El Paso.
_____*John Wesley Hardin, Dark Angel of Texas*. Mangan Books. 1996. El Paso.
_____*The SHOOTERS*. Mangan Books. 1976. El Paso.
Meyer, Michael C. *Mexican Rebel: Pascual Orozco and the Mexican Revolution 1910-1915*. University of Nebraska Press. 1967. Lincoln and London.
Miller, Rick. *SAM BASS & GANG*. State House Press. 1999. Austin.
Murrah, David J. *C. C. SLAUGHTER—RANCHER, BANKER, BAPTIST*. University of Texas Press. 1881. Austin.
Nordyke, Lewis. *GREAT ROUNDUP*—The Story of Texas and Southwestern Cowmen. William Morrow & Company. 1955. New York.
O'Neal, Bill. *ENCYCLOPEDIA of WESTERN GUNFIGHTERS*. University of Oklahoma Press. 1979. Norman.
______*The ARIZONA RANGERS*. Eakin Press. 1987. Austin.
______*HISTORIC RANCHES of the OLD WEST*. 1997. Eakin Press. Austin.
Paine, Albert Bigelow. *CAPTAIN BILL McDONALD TEXAS RANGER—A Story of Frontier Reform*. State House Press (Facsimile Reproduction). 1986. Austin.
Pearce, T. M. *NEW MEXICO PLACE NAMES*. University of New Mexico Press. 1965. Albuquerque.
Perkins, Clifford Alan. *Border Patrol—With the U. S. Immigration Service On the Mexican Boundary 1910-1954*. Texas Western Press. El Paso. 1978.

Perkins, Doug. *BRAVE MEN & COLD STEEL—A History of Range Detectives and Their Peacemakers.* Texas and Southwestern Cattle Raisers Association. 1984. Fort Worth.
Pingenot, Ben E. *SIRINGO.* Texas A & M Press. College Station. 1989.
Pitts, Alice Ellison. (and **Champ**, Minnie Pitts). *COLLIN COUNTY, TEXAS, FAMILIES. VOLUME II.* Landmark Publishing, Inc. 1998. Fort Worth.
Prassel, Frank Richard. *THE WESTERN PEACE OFFICER, A Legacy of Law and Order.* University of Oklahoma Press. 1972. Norman.
Raht, Carlysle. *THE ROMANCE OF DAVIS MOUNTAINS AND BIG BEND COUNTRY*, The Rathbooks Company (Texana Edition). 1963. Odessa.
Robinson, III, Charles. *The Frontier World of FORT GRIFFIN.* The Arthur Clark Co. 1992. Spokane.
Rose, Noah H. and **Hunter**, J. Marvin. *The Album of Gunfighters.* By Authors. 1955. Bandera, Texas.
Rowland, Dunbar. *MILITARY HISTORY OF MISSISSIPPI, 1803-1898.* Indexed by **Howell, Jr.**, H. Grady. The Reprint Company, Publishers. Spartenburg. 1988.
Rynning, Thomas H. *GUN NOTCHES—A Saga of Frontier Lawman Captain Thomas H. Rynning As Told To Al Cohn and Joe Chisholm.* Frontier Heritage Press. 1971. San Diego.
Sheridan, Thomas E. *ARIZONA—A HISTORY.* University of Arizona. 1996.Tucson.
Shipman, Mrs. O. L. *Taming the Big Bend: A History of the Extreme Western Portion of Texas from Fort Clark to El Paso.* Privately printed. 1926. Marfa, Texas.
Skiles, Jack. *Judge Roy Bean Country.* Texas Tech University Press. 1996. Lubbock.
Sonnichsen, C. L. *TULAROSA—Last of the Frontier West.* University of New Mexico Press. Albuquerque. 1960.
Stambaugh, J. Lee and Lillian J. *A History of Collin County, Texas.* The Texas State Historical Association. 1958. Austin.
Steckmesser, Kent Ladd. *The WESTERN HERO in History and Legend.* University of Oklahoma Press. 1965. Norman and London.
Stephens, Robert W. *MANNING CLEMENTS—Texas Gunfighter.* By Author. 1996. Dallas.
________ *TEXAS RANGER SKETCHES.* Privately Printed. 1972. Dallas.
Sterling, William Warren. *TRAILS AND TRIALS OF A TEXAS RANGER.* University of Oklahoma Press. 1959. Norman.
Sullivan, W. J. L., *Twelve Years in the Saddle with the Texas Rangers.* 2001. University of Nebraska Press. Lincoln. Reprint of 1909 *Twelve Years In The Saddle For Law And Order on the Frontiers of Texas.*
Tanner, Karen H. & John D., *Last of the Old Time Outlaws, The George Musgrave Story.* University of Oklahoma, Norman, 2002
Tefertiller, Casey. *WYATT EARP, The Man Behind The Legend.* John Wiley and Sons, Inc. 1997. New York.
Thompson, Cecilia. *History of Marfa and Presidio County, Texas 1535-1946.* Nortex Press. 1985. Austin.
Tise, Sammy. *Texas County Sheriffs.* By Author. Hallettsville, Texas. 1989.
Thrapp, Dan L. *ENCYCLOPEDIA of Frontier Biography.* Three Volumes. University of Nebraska Press. 1988. Lincoln and London.
Tompkins, Colonel Frank. *CHASING VILLA—The Last Campaign of the U. S. Cavalry. High-Lonesome Books. 1996. Silver City.*

Trachtman, Paul. *THE GUNFIGHTERS.* Time-Life Books. 1974. New York.
Trafzer, Cliff and **George**, Steve. *PRISON CENTENNIAL, 1876-1976.* Rio Colorado Press. 1980 Yuma.
Tyler, Ronnie C. *THE BIG BEND, A History Of The Last Texas Frontier.* National Park Service. 1975. Washington, D. C.
____ **(editor)** *The New Handbook of Texas.* Six Volumes. Texas State Historical Association. 1996. Austin.
Wagoner, Jay J. *Arizona Territory, 1863-1912.* University of Arizona Press. 1970. Tucson.
Walter, John F., *Unit History, Twenty-fourth Mississippi Infantry.* Self-published. 1988. Middle Village, New York.
Ward, Nancy. *BRAVE MEN & COLD STEEL—A History of Range Detectives and Their Peacemakers.* Texas and Southwestern Cattle Raisers Association. 1984. Fort Worth.
Webb, Walter Prescott. *THE TEXAS RANGERS—A Century Of Frontier Defense.* University of Texas Press. 1935. Austin.
Wedin, AnneJo P. *The Magnificent Marathon Basin—A History of Marathon, Texas, its people and events.* Nortex Press. 1989. Austin.
Wilkins, Frederick. *THE LAW COMES TO TEXAS, The Texas Rangers, 1870-1901.* State House Press. 1999. Austin.
Williams, J. W. *THE BIG RANCH COUNTRY.* Nortex Press. 1954. Austin.
Worchester, Don. *The Chisholm Trail—High Road of the Cattle Kingdom.* University of Nebraska Press. Lincoln and London. 1980.
Wylie, Rosa Lee. *History of Van Horn and Culberson County, Texas.* Culberson County Historical Survey Committee. 1973.
Young, Roy B. *COCHISE COUNTY COWBOY WAR—A Cast of Characters.* Young & Sons Enterprises. 1999. Apache, Oklahoma.

PERIODICALS AND JOURNALS:

Alexander, Bob. "Hell Paso," *Quarterly of the National Association for Outlaw and Lawman History, Inc.* Vol. XXVI, No. 2 (April-June 2002)
Ball, Larry D. "Frontier Sheriffs at Work," *The Journal of Arizona History.* No. 27.
Blanco, Serafina Orozco vda de. "MY RECOLLECTIONS OF THE OROZCO FAMILY AND THE MEXICAN REVOLUTION OF 1910," *Password.* Vol. XXV, No. 1. (Spring, 1980).
Boren, Sanford, as told to **Packer**, C. L., "End of the Trail for Red Buck," *Frontier Times.* July 1970.
Brayer, Herbert O. "THE CANANEA INCIDENT," *NEW MEXICO HISTORICAL REVIEW.* Vol. XIII, No. 4, (October, 1938).
Christiansen, Paige W. "Pascual Orozco: Chihuahua Rebel—Episodes in the Mexican Revolution, 1910-1915.," *NEW MEXICO HISTORICAL REVIEW.* XXVI, (April, 1961).
Clarke, Mary Whatley. "Bad Man…Good Man?," *The Cattleman.* Vol. LVIII, No. 7. (December 1971).
Croce, Antonio. "In The Line of Duty," *The Texas Gun Collector*, Fall 1996.
Davis, Chuck & **Ritter**, Al. "Captain Monroe Fox *and the* Incident at Pourvenir," *Oklahoma State Trooper*, Winter 1996.
DeArment, R. K., "Bloody Easter," *OLD WEST*, Vol. 30, No. 3. (Spring 1994)

Edwards, Harold S., "Tribute to Frank S. Wheeler—Arizona Ranger," *Quarterly of the National Association for Outlaw and Lawman History, Inc.* Vol. XIX. No. l. (1995).
Edwards, Harold S. "Burt Alvord, The Train Robbing Constable," Old West, October, 2002
Fenton, James I. "Tom Ross: Ranger Nemesis," *Quarterly of the National Association and Center For Outlaw And Lawman History.* Vol. XIV, No. 2 (Summer 1990).
Haley, J. Evetts., "Cowboy Sheriff," *The SHAMROCK.* Summer 1963.
Jensen, Jody. "Birth of the Arizona Rangers," *Old West.* Spring 1882.
McAlavy, Don. "Henry Hawkins: Last Cowboy Outlaw in Eastern New Mexico," *Quarterly of the National Association For Outlaw and Lawman History.* Vol. XIX, No. 1 (January-March, 1995).
McCool, Grace. "With Grace McCool," Series on Arizona Rangers. *Gateway Times.* April 16 & 23, 1964.
Macklin, William F., "Three Finger-Jack, Labor Leader or Morenci Mine Martyr?," *VALLEY GROWERS MAGAZINE.* Unidentified citation.
Meed, Douglas V., "DAGGERS ON THE GALLOWS, The Revenge of Texas Ranger Captain 'Boss' Hughes," *TRUE WEST.* May 1999.
O'Neal, Bill., "The Cananea Riots of 1906," *Real West.* August 1984..
Park, Joseph F. "The 1903 'Mexican Affair' at Clifton," *The Journal of Arizona History* (Summer 1977).
Pettey, Weston A. "The Seminole Incident and Tom Ross," *West Texas Historical Association Year Book.* 1980.
Ritter, Al. "Captain Fox's Colt," *Handguns.* February 1997.
Ritter, Al & **Davis**, Chuck. "Captain Monroe Fox *and the* Incident at Pourvenir," *Oklahoma State Trooper*, Winter 1996.
_____"Death on the Rio Grande," *Texas Department of Public Safety Officers Association Magazine*, March/April 1996.
Sharp, Patricia. "The Maxwells of Arizona—Trackers and Lawmen," *Frontier Times.* July 1972.
Sonnichsen, C. L., "Col. W. C. Greene and Cobre Grande Copper Company," *The Journal of Arizona History.* (Summer 1971)
Spangenberger, Phil. "Thomas H. Rynning, Adventurer With a Six-Gun," *Guns and Ammo Guide to Guns of the Gunfighters.* (1975)
Spiller, E. B. "Five Hundred and Sixteen Head of Stolen Cattle Recovered," *THE CATTLEMAN*, Vol. 9, No. 2. (July 1922)
______"Cattle Thieves Kill Two Association Inspectors," *THE CATTLEMAN*, Vol. IX, No. 11. (May 1923)
______"Prison Gates Await Slayers of Inspectors Allison and Roberson," *THE CATTLEMAN*, Vol. X, No. 2. (July 1923)
______"Ross and Good Found Guilty of the Murder of Inspector Roberson," *THE CATTLEMAN.* Vol. IX, No. 5. (October 1923)
Steele, Phillip. "The Woman Red Buck Couldn't Scare. *The West.* April 1971.
Sullivan, W. J. L. "Twelve Years In The Saddle For Law and Order on the Frontiers of Texas," *Old West.* Spring 1967.
Traywick, Ben T., "Copper King of Cananea," *Golden West.* November 1970.
Waltrip, Lela & Rufus. "Top Man of the Fearless Thirteen," *TRUE WEST.* November-December. 1970.
Warren, C., "Joe Beckham, The Outlaw Sheriff," *Real West.* August 1983.

Weiler, Linda Stockley. "The Story of Our Old House," *OLD TIMERS' REVIEW.* Vol. IV, No. 4. (Summer 1983).
Winsor, Mulford. "The Arizona Rangers," *Our Sheriff and Police Journal.* Vol. 31, No. 6. (1936)

INTERVIEWS AND CORRESPONDENCE:

Dean Bohannon, Lubbock, Texas
Patricia Bramblett, Sierra Blanca, Texas.
W. W. Crowe III, Van Horn, Texas.
James I. Fenton, Lubbock, Texas.
Elvis E. Fleming, Roswell, New Mexico.
Button Garlick, Van Horn, Texas.
Marvin Garlick, Gazelle, California.
Bill W. Hargis, Van Horn, Texas.
Sarah Hindman, Albia, Iowa.
Bill Love, Sierra Blanca, Texas.
Richard Lucero, Roswell, New Mexico.
Dennis McCown, Austin, Texas
Nancy McKinley, Midland, Texas.
Clayton McKinney, Midland, Texas.
Paula Mitchell Marks, Austin, Texas.
Carol Marlin, Albia, Iowa.
Leon Metz, El Paso, Texas.
Bill O'Neal, Carthage, Texas.
Penny Rains, Post, Texas.
Ryn Rains, Post, Texas.
John Sullivan, Sierra Blanca, Texas.
Pat Treadwell, Tahoka, Texas.
Linda Stockley Weiler, Roswell, New Mexico.

NEWSPAPERS:

Silver City Enterprise
El Paso Herald
El Paso Times
El Paso Daily Times
El Paso Morning Times
Livestock Weekly
Midland Reporter-Telegram
Lubbock Avalanche-Journal
Tombstone Epitaph
Arizona Sentinel
Lovington Leader
Galveston Daily News
Grant County Herald
Seminole Sentinel
Abilene Reporter
Fort Worth Star-Telegram
Dallas Morning News
St. Louis Post-Dispatch
Roswell Daily Record
Cut Bank Pioneer Press
Arizona Daily Star
The Semi-Weekly Farm News
Roswell Morning News & Register
Van Horn Advocate

INDEX

A retired Special Agent with the U. S. Treasury Department, and a former city detective, Bob Alexander is a thirty-five year law enforcement veteran. His practical, no nonsense glimpses at the realities of frontier police work offers a fresh perspective to the reader delving into the goings-on of early day outlaws/lawmen. Mr. Alexander is also the author of two other biographies, *Dangerous Dan Tucker: New Mexico's Deadly Lawman* and *John H. Behan, Sacrificed Sheriff.* His articles profiling often overlooked legitimate frontier characters frequently appear in historical journals. Bob lives near Maypearl, Texas where he continues to avidly pursue his research into the escapades and exploits of Old West personalities.